LORRAINE COHEN received her B.A. from Fairleigh Dickinson University in New Jersey and a Master of Arts degree in Theater from Montclair State College. In addition to teaching in the New Jersey school system, she has served as Assistant Director of New Dimension Theatre's Drama School and as drama reviewer for *Grade Teacher* Magazine. Ms. Cohen has also written articles for Shakespeare and Children.

Edited by
Lorraine Cohen
from Avon Books

MONOLOGUES FOR YOUNG ACTORS
SCENES FOR YOUNG ACTORS

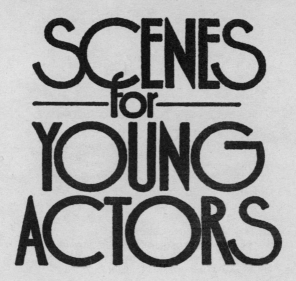

SCENES for YOUNG ACTORS

EDITED BY
LORRAINE COHEN

AVON BOOKS
An Imprint of HarperCollinsPublishers

AVON BOOKS
An Imprint of HarperCollins*Publishers*
10 East 53rd Street
New York, New York 10022-5299

First Avon Books printing: April 1973

Avon Trademark Reg. U.S. Pat. Off. and in Other Countries, Marca
Registrada, Hecho en U.S.A.
HarperCollins® is a trademark of HarperCollins Publishers Inc.

Printed in the U.S.A.

40 39 38 37 36 35 34 33 32

ACKNOWLEDGMENTS

tional performance one week before the play is to be given to
Samuel French, Inc., at 25 West 45th Street, New York, New York
10036, or 7623 Sunset Blvd., Hollywood, California or if in Canada
to Samuel French (Canada) Ltd., 27 Grenville St., Toronto, On-
tario. Copies of this play, in individual paper covered acting edi-
tions, are available from Samuel French, Inc., 25 West 45th Street,
New York, N.Y. or 7623 Sunset Blvd., Hollywood, Cal., or in Canada
Samuel French (Canada) Ltd., 26 Grenville Street, Toronto.

From THE CRUCIBLE by Arthur Miller. Copyright 1952, 1953
by Arthur Miller. Reprinted by permission of The Viking Press, Inc.

From DARK OF THE MOON by Howard Richardson and William
Berney. Copyright 1944 by Howard Dixon Richardson and William
Berney; Copyright 1942, © 1966 by Howard Dixon Richardson. Re-
printed with permission of the Publisher, Theatre Arts Books, New
York.

From FIVE FINGER EXERCISE by Peter Shaffer. © 1958 by
Peter Shaffer. Reprinted by permission of Harcourt Brace Jovano-
vich, Inc. Caution: FIVE FINGER EXERCISE is the sole property
of the author and is protected by copyright. It may not be acted by
professionals or amateurs without permission and the payment of
a royalty. All rights, including professional, amateur, stock, radio
and television broadcasting, motion picture, recitation, lecturing,
public reading, and the rights of translation in foreign languages are
reserved. All inquiries should be addressed to the author's agent,
Harold Freedman, Brandt & Brandt, Dramatic Department, 101
Park Avenue, New York, New York.

From GOLDEN BOY by Clifford Odets. Copyright 1937, renewed
© 1965 by Nora Odets and Walt Whitman Odets. Caution: GOLD-
EN BOY is the sole property of the author and is protected by
copyright. It may not be acted by professionals or amateurs without
permission and the payment of a royalty. All rights, including professional, amateur, stock, radio and television broadcasting, motion
picture, recitation, lecturing, public reading, and the rights of translation in foreign languages are reserved. All inquiries should be addressed to the author's agent, Harold Freedman, Brandt & Brandt,
Dramatic Department, 101 Park Avenue, New York, New York.

From LOOK HOMEWARD, ANGEL, a play by Ketti Frings from
the novel by Thomas Wolfe. Copyright © 1958 by Edward C. Aswell
as Administrator, C.T.A. of the Estate of Thomas Wolfe and/or Fred
W. Wolfe and Ketti Frings. Reprinted by permission.

From THE MEMBER OF THE WEDDING by Carson McCullers.
Copyright 1951 by Carson McCullers. Reprinted by permission of
New Directions Publishing Corporation.

From OH DAD, POOR DAD, MAMMA'S HUNG YOU IN THE
CLOSET AND I'M FEELIN' SO SAD by Arthur Kopit. Copyright as an unpublished work, © 1959 by Arthur L. Kopit. Copyright © 1960 by Arthur L. Kopit. Reprinted by permission of Hill
and Wang, Inc.

From PRIDE AND PREJUDICE by Helen Jerome. Copyright 1934
by Helen Jerome. Reprinted by permission of Doubleday and Company, Inc.

From THE ROPE DANCERS by Morton Wishengrad. © 1958 by
Morton Wishengrad. Reprinted by permission of Crown Publishers,
Inc.

From SAINT JOAN by Bernard Shaw. Copyright by Bernard Shaw.
Reprinted by permission of The Society of Authors, for the Bernard
Shaw Estate.

From SUMMER AND SMOKE by Tennessee Williams. Copyright
1948 by Tennessee Williams. Reprinted by permission of New Directions Publishing Corporation.

From A VIEW FROM THE BRIDGE by Arthur Miller. Copyright © 1955, 1957 by Arthur Miller. Reprinted by permission of The Viking Press, Inc.

From THE WINSLOW BOY by Terence Rattigan. Copyright, 1946, by Terence Rattigan. The scene from THE WINSLOW BOY included in this volume is reprinted by permission of the author and of Dramatists Play Service, Inc. The use of the scene in question must be confined to study and reference. Attention is called in particular to the fact that this scene, being duly copyrighted, may not be publicly read or performed or otherwise used without permission from the author's representative. All inquiries should be addressed to Dramatists Play Service, Inc., 440 Park Avenue South, New York, New York 10016.

From WINTERSET by Maxwell Anderson. Copyright 1935 by Anderson House. Copyright renewed © 1963 by Gilda Oakleaf Anderson. All rights reserved. Reprinted by permission of Anderson House.

From THE CORN IS GREEN, by Emlyn Williams. Copyright 1941 by Emlyn Williams. Reprinted by permission of Random House, Inc.

From DEAD END, by Sidney Kingsley. Copyright 1936 and renewed 1964 by Sidney Kingsley. Reprinted by permission of Random House, Inc.

From A CLEARING IN THE WOODS, by Arthur Laurents. Copyright © 1957 by Arthur Laurents. Reprinted by permission of Random House, Inc.

From THE DIARY OF ANNE FRANK, by Albert Hackett and Frances Goodrich. Copyright 1954, 1956 by Albert Hackett, Frances Goodrich Hackett and Otto Frank. Reprinted by permission of Random House, Inc.

From THE DARK AT THE TOP OF THE STAIRS, by William Inge. Copyright © 1958 by William Inge. Reprinted by permission of Random House, Inc.

Copyright 1953, © 1962 by William Inge. Reprinted from SUMMER BRAVE AND ELEVEN SHORT PLAYS, by William Inge, by permission of Random House, Inc.

From THE CHILDREN'S HOUR, by Lillian Hellman. Copyright 1934 and renewed 1962 by Lillian Hellman. Reprinted by permission of Random House, Inc.

From THE SOUND OF MUSIC, by Howard Lindsay and Russel Crouse. Copyright © 1960 by Richard Rodgers, Oscar Hammerstein II, Howard Lindsay and Russel Crouse. Reprinted by permission of Random House, Inc.

From ANTIGONE, by Jean Anouilh, translated by Lewis Galantiere. Copyright 1949 by Random House, Inc. Reprinted by permission of the publisher.

From TEA AND SYMPATHY, by Robert Anderson. Copyright 1953 by Robert Anderson. Reprinted by permission of Random House, Inc.

From SUMMER BRAVE AND ELEVEN SHORT PLAYS, by William Inge. Copyright © 1962 by William Inge. Reprinted by permission of Random House, Inc.

From WEST SIDE STORY, by Arthur Laurents and Leonard Bernstein. Copyright © 1957 by Leonard Bernstein and Stephen Sondheim. Copyright © 1956, 1958 by Arthur Laurents, Leonard Bernstein, Stephen Sondheim and Jerome Robbins. Reprinted by permission of Random House, Inc.

SCENES FOR YOUNG ACTORS

CONTENTS

from SUMMER AND SMOKE by Tennessee Williams 17
    Alma, John
from THE MEMBER OF THE WEDDING
        by Carson McCullers   23
    Frankie, John Henry
from THE CHILDREN'S HOUR by Lillian Hellman
        Act I, scene 1   27
    Mary, Peggy, Evelyn, Rosalie
        Act II, scene 2   37
    Mary, Rosalie
from THE RAINY AFTERNOON by William Inge   42
    Wilma, Billie Mae, Vic
from DEAD END by Sidney Kingsley
        Act I   53
    Philip, Tommy, Dippy, Angel, T.B., Spit, Milton
        Act III   62
    Tommy, Angel
from ALICE IN WONDERLAND. Adapted for the
        stage by Eva Le Gallienne and Florida
        Friebus from Lewis Carroll's *Alice In
        Wonderland and Through The Looking
        Glass.*   65
    Alice, The Red Queen
from HEIDI by Johanna Spyri adapted from the
        novel by Lorraine Cohen   70
    Heidi, Clara
from MACBETH by William Shakespeare adapted
        by Lorraine Cohen   75
    The Three Witches
from the novel LITTLE WOMEN by Louisa May
        Alcott adapted by Lorraine Cohen   78
    Meg, Jo, Amy, Beth
from STRAWBERRY ICE CREAM SODA by Irwin
        Shaw adapted from the short story by Lor-
        raine Cohen   85
    Eddie, Lawrence

xi

from JANE EYRE by Charlotte Bronte adapted
        from the novel by Lorraine Cohen   89
  Jane, Helen
from THE CRUCIBLE by Arthur Miller   96
  Abigail, Mercy, Mary Warren, Betty
from THE DIARY OF ANNE FRANK by Francis
        Goodrich and Albert Hackett
        Act I, scene 2   100
  Anne, Peter
        Act II, scene 2   103
  Anne, Peter
        Act II, scene 4   108
  Anne, Peter
from THE DARK AT THE TOP OF THE STAIRS
        by William Inge   111
  Reenie, Sonny
from FIVE FINGER EXERCISE by Peter Shaffer   114
  Clive, Pamela, Walter
from THE SOUND OF MUSIC. Book by Howard
        Lindsay and Russell Crouse, Music by
        Richard Rodgers and Lyrics by Oscar
        Hammerstein II   119
  Liese, Rolf
from THE BEAUTIFUL PEOPLE by William Sa-
        royan   122
  Owen, Agnes
from TEA AND SYMPATHY by Robert Anderson   126
  Tom, Al
from EASTER by August Strindberg
        Act I   133
  Benjamin, Eleonora
        Act II   142
  Benjamin, Eleonora
        Act III   147
  Benjamin, Eleonora
from OH DAD, POOR DAD, MAMMA'S HUNG
        YOU IN THE CLOSET AND I'M
        FEELIN' SO SAD by Arthur L. Kopit   150
  Jonathan, Rosalie
from ROMEO AND JULIET by William Shake-
        speare   162
  Romeo, Juliet
from WINTERSET by Maxwell Anderson
        Act I, scene 3   169
  Mio, Carr, Miriamme
        Act I, scene 3   175
  Mio, Miriamme
        Act III   183

Mio, Miriamme, Carr

from WEST SIDE STORY. Book by Arthur Laurents, Music by Leonard Bernstein, Lyrics by Stephen Sondheim, Directed and Choreographed by Jerome Robbins
Act I, scene 2   195
Tony, Riff
Act I, scene 3   200
Maria, Anita, Bernardo, Chino
Act I, scene 5   203
Tony, Maria

from A VIEW FROM THE BRIDGE by Arthur Miller   208
Catherine, Rodolpho

from GOLDEN BOY by Clifford Odets   214
Joe, Lorna

from SUMMER BRAVE by William Inge
Act I   221
Alan, Hal
Act II   228
Madge, Millie

from PRIDE AND PREJUDICE dramatized by Helen Jerome from the novel by Jane Austen
Act I, scene 2   232
Charlotte, Elizabeth
Act II, scene 1   235
Elizabeth, Jane

from LOOK HOMEWARD, ANGEL by Ketti Frings from the novel by Thomas Wolfe
Act 1, scene 2   237
Eugene, Laura
Act II, scene 1   243
Eugene, Laura
Act III   246
Eugene, Laura

from THE CORN IS GREEN by Emlyn Williams   249
Morgan, Bessie

from A CLEARING IN THE WOODS by Arthur Laurents   252
Nora, Hazelmae, The Boy

from ANTIGONE by Jean Anouilh   259
Antigone, Ismene
Antigone, Haemon   265

from DARK OF THE MOON by Howard Richardson and William Berney   270
John, Barbara Allen, Dark Witch, Fair Witch

from THE ROPE DANCERS by Morton Wishen-
          grad, slightly revised by Lorraine Cohen   275
     Margaret, Lizzie
from BAD SEED by Maxwell Anderson   284
     Christine, Rhoda
from THE CORN IS GREEN by Emlyn Williams   290
     Miss Moffat, Morgan
from ANTIGONE by Jean Anouilh   295
     Nurse, Antigone
from THE CHILDREN'S HOUR by Lillian Hellman
          Act II, scene 1   302
     Mary, Mrs. Tilford
          Act I   312
     Karen, Mary
from THE DARK AT THE TOP OF THE STAIRS
          by William Inge   315
     Cora, Reenie
from THE WINSLOW BOY by Terence Rattigan   321
     Sir Robert, Ronnie
from THE WILD DUCK by Henrik Ibsen, revised
          by Lorraine Cohen   331
     Gregers, Hedwig
from THE CHALK GARDEN by Enid Bagnold
          Act I   339
     Miss Madrigal, Laurel
          Act II   344
     Miss Madrigal, Laurel
from SUMMER AND SMOKE by Tennessee Wil-
          liams   349
     Alma, Nell
from THE CORN IS GREEN by Emlyn Williams   354
     Morgan
from SAINT JOAN by Bernard Shaw   356
     Joan •
from BONTCHE SCHWEIG by Arnold Perl   358
     The Defending Angel
from EASTER by August Strindberg adapted by
          Lorraine Cohen   362
     Eleonora
from IPHEGENIA IN AULIS by Euripides, trans-
          lated by Charles R. Walker   366
     Iphegenia
from THE DARK AT THE TOP OF THE STAIRS
          by William Inge   369
     Sammy
from HAMLET by William Shakespeare   371
     Ophelia

CONTENTS

from UNCLE VANYA by Anton Chekhov, adapted
           by Lorraine Cohen   373
      Sonya
Scenes Classified by Number of Characters   379
Index   381

from
SUMMER AND SMOKE
by Tennessee Williams

Part I, Prologue
ALMA, JOHN (as children)

This play, which takes place in a small southern town, revolves around the meetings and partings of Alma and John.
Alma is an extremely proper minister's daughter, who,
burdened with the care of a mentally disturbed mother,
functions as the woman of the house. Her upbringing, her
intense and sensitive nature, and her premature responsibilities have made her spinsterish and uncomfortable with
other young people. Nonetheless she is in love with John, a
dissolute young doctor whom she has known since childhood. Their relationship effects dramatic changes in their
respective philosophies but Fate decrees that they always
cross each other's lives at the wrong time and thus remain
estranged from each other.

The following scene, from the prologue when Alma and
John are children, foreshadows the characterizations and
the mood of the play. It is dusk on a May evening shortly
after the turn of the century. The setting is the fountain
in the park. Alma, as a child of ten, enters. After a few
moments in thought she bends to drink from the fountain.
John enters and shoots a pea shooter at her bent back.
She utters a startled cry and whirls about. John laughs.

John.
  Hi, Preacher's daughter. (*He advances toward her.*) I
  been looking for you.
Alma.
  (*Hopefully*) You have?

17

John.
Was it you that put them handkerchiefs on my desk?
(ALMA *smiles uncertainly*.) Answer up!

Alma.
I put a box of handkerchiefs on your desk.

John.
I figured it was you. What was the idea, Miss Priss?

Alma.
You needed them.

John.
Trying to make a fool of me?

Alma.
Oh, no!

John.
Then what was the idea?

Alma.
You have a bad cold and your nose has been running all week. It spoils your appearance.

John.
You don't have to look at me if you don't like my appearance.

Alma.
I like your appearance.

John.
(*Coming closer*) Is that why you look at me all the time?

Alma.
I—don't!

John.
Oh, yeh, you do. You been keeping your eyes on me all the time. Every time I look around I see them cat eyes of yours looking at me. That was the trouble today when Miss Blanchard asked you where the river Amazon was. She asked you twice and you still didn't answer because you w' lookin' at me. What's the idea? What've'y'got on y' mind anyhow? Answer up!

Alma.
I was only thinking how handsome you'd be if your face wasn't dirty. You know why your face is dirty? Because you don't use a handkerchief and you wipe your nose on the sleeve of that dirty old sweater.

John.
(*Indignantly*) Hah!

Alma.
That's why I put the handkerchiefs on your desk and I wrapped them up so nobody would know what they were.

It isn't my fault that you opened the box in front of everybody!

John.
What did you think I'd do with a strange box on my desk? Just leave it there till it exploded or something? Sure I opened it up. I didn't expect to find no—*handkerchiefs!*—in it . . .

Alma.
(*In a shy trembling voice*) I'm sorry that you were embarrassed. I honestly am awfully sorry that you were embarrassed. Because I wouldn't embarrass you for the world!

John.
Don't flatter yourself that I was embarrassed. I don't embarrass that easy.

Alma.
It was stupid and cruel of those girls to laugh.

John.
Hah!

Alma.
They should all realize that you don't have a mother to take care of such things for you. It was a pleasure to me to be able to do something for you, only I didn't want you to know it was me who did it.

John.
Hee-haw! Ho-Hum! Take 'em back! (*He snatches out the box and thrusts it toward her.*)

Alma.
Please keep them.

John.
What do I want with them? (*She stares at him helplessly. He tosses the box to the ground and goes up to the fountain and drinks. Something in her face mollifies him and he sits down at the base of the fountain with a manner that does not preclude a more friendly relation. The dusk gathers deeper.*)

Alma.
Do you know the name of the angel?

John.
Does she have a name?

Alma.
Yes, I found out she does. It's carved in the base, but it's all worn away so you can't make it out with your eyes.

John.
Then how do you know it?

Alma.
You have to read it with your fingers. I did and it gave me cold shivers! *You* read it and see if it doesn't give *you* cold shivers! Go on! Read it with your fingers!

John.
Why don't you tell me and save me the trouble?

Alma.
I'm not going to tell you.

(JOHN *grins indulgently and turns to the pediment, crouching before it and running his fingers along the worn inscription.*)

John.
E?

Alma.
Yes, E is the first letter!

John.
T?

Alma.
Yes!

John.
E?

Alma.
E!

John.
K?

Alma.
No, no, not K!—R! (*He slowly straightens up.*)

John.
Eternity?

Alma.
Eternity!—Didn't it give you the cold shivers?

John.
Nahh.

Alma.
Well, it did me!

John.
Because you're a preacher's daughter. Eternity. What is eternity?

Alma.
(*In a hushed wondering voice*) It's something that goes on and on when life and death and time and everything else is all through with.

John.
There's no such thing.

Alma.
There is. It's what people's souls live in when they have left their bodies. My name is Alma and Alma is Spanish for soul. Did you know that?

John.
Hee-haw! Ho-hum! Have you ever seen a dead person?

Alma.
No.

John.
I have. They made me go in the room when my mother was dying and she caught hold of my hand and wouldn't let me go—and so I screamed and hit her.

Alma.
Oh, you didn't do that.

John.
(*Somberly*) Uh-huh. She didn't look like my mother. Her face was all ugly and yellow and terrible—bad-smelling! And so I hit her to make her let go of my hand. They told me that I was a devil!

Alma.
You didn't know what you were doing.

John.
My dad is a doctor.

Alma.
I know.

John.
He wants to send me to college to study to be a doctor but I wouldn't be a doctor for the world. And have to go in a room and watch people dying! . . . Jesus!

Alma.
You'll change your mind about that.

John.
Oh, no, I won't. I'd rather *be* a devil, like they called me and go to South America on a boat! . . . Give me one of them handkerchiefs. (*She brings them eagerly and humbly to the fountain. He takes one out and wets it at the fountain and scrubs his face with it.*) Is my face clean enough to suit you now?

Alma.
Yes!—Beautiful!

John.
What!

Alma.
I said "Beautiful"!

John.

Well—let's—kiss each other. (ALMA *turns away.*)

John.

Come on, let's just try it! (*He seizes her shoulders and gives her a quick rough kiss. She stands amazed with one hand cupping the other. The voice of a child in the distance calls "Johnny! Johnny!" He suddenly snatches at her hair-ribbon, jerks it loose and then runs off with a mocking laugh. Hurt and bewildered, ALMA turns back to the stone angel, for comfort. She crouches at the pediment and touches the inscription with her fingers. The scene dims out with music.*)

from
THE MEMBER OF THE WEDDING
by Carson McCullers

Act I
FRANKIE, JOHN HENRY

The play centers around Frankie, a girl of twelve, who, in her restless adolescent way, is trying to find out where she belongs. She feels she has outgrown her small world— her remote father; the black housekeeper, Berenice; and the little boy next door, John Henry. Her brother, who has just returned from the Army, is about to be married. Frankie wants desperately to become a part of this new exciting world and to go away with him and his bride on their honeymoon. As the events in the play unfold, Frankie comes to terms with herself and does a great deal of maturing.

In the following scene she is thinking and feeling her way towards her plan to become a member of the wedding. It is early evening and she and John Henry are in the yard. She is talking to John Henry simply because he is present, but she is really talking to herself. The scene can be played very easily as a monologue for a young girl simply by leaving out John Henry's lines. However, the actor playing John Henry should not underestimate his role. John Henry is a serious boy, wanting to please his only friend but also struggling to understand the world. His death later in the play adds immeasurably to Frankie's new insights.

There is one short deletion from the play. It consists of lines of Frankie's father calling from the house and Frankie's brief response to him. They are marked by asterisks.

Frankie.

(*Looking at the house*) I wonder when that Papa of mine is coming home. He always comes home by dark. I don't want to go into that empty, ugly house by myself.

John H.

Me neither.

Frankie.

(*Standing with outstretched arms, and looking around her*) I think something is wrong. It is too quiet. I have a peculiar warning in my bones. I bet you a hundred dollars it's going to storm.

John H.

I don't want to spend the night with you.

Frankie.

A terrible, terrible dog-day storm. Or maybe even a cyclone.

John H.

Huh.

Frankie.

I bet Jarvis and Janice are now at Winter Hill. I see them just plain as I see you. Plainer. Something is wrong. It is too quiet. (*A clear horn begins to play a blues tune in the distance.*)

John H.

Frankie?

Frankie.

Hush! It sounds like Honey. (*The horn music becomes jazzy and spangling, then the first blues tune is repeated. Suddenly, while still unfinished, the music stops. FRANKIE waits tensely.*) He has stopped to bang the spit out of his horn. In a second he will finish. (*After a wait*) Please, Honey, go on finish!

John H.

(*Softly*) He done quit now.

Frankie.

(*Moving restlessly*) I told Berenice that I was leavin' town for good and she did not believe me. Sometimes I honestly think she is the biggest fool that ever drew breath. You try to impress something on a big fool like that, and it's just like talking to a block of cement. I kept on telling and telling and telling her. I told her I had to leave this town for good because it is inevitable. Inevitable.

* * *

John H.
You want me to get the weekend bag?

Frankie.
Don't bother me, John Henry. I'm thinking. About the wedding. About my brother and the bride. Everything's been so sudden today. I never believed before about the fact that the earth turns at the rate of about a thousand miles a day. I didn't understand why it was that if you jumped up in the air you wouldn't land in Selma or Fairview or somewhere else instead of the same back yard. But now it seems to me I feel the world going around very fast. (*FRANKIE begins turning around in circles with arms outstretched. JOHN HENRY copies her. They both turn.*) I feel it turning and it makes me dizzy.

John H.
I'll stay and spend the night with you.

Frankie.
(*Suddenly stopping her turning*) No. I just now thought of something.

John H.
You just a little while ago was begging me.

Frankie.
I know where I'm going. (*There are sounds of children playing in the distance.*)

John H.
Let's go play with the children, Frankie.

Frankie.
I tell you I know where I'm going. It's like I've known it all my life. Tomorrow I will tell everybody.

John H.
Where?

Frankie.
(*Dreamily*) After the wedding I'm going with them to Winter Hill. I'm going off with them after the wedding.

John H.
You serious?

Frankie.
Shush, just now I realized something. The trouble with me is that for a long time I have been just an "I" person. All other people can say "we." When Berenice says "we" she means her lodge and church and colored people. Soldiers can say "we" and mean the army. All people belong to "we" except me.

John H.
What are you going to do?

Frankie.
Not to belong to a "we" makes you too lonesome. Until this afternoon I didn't have a "we" but now after seeing Janice and Jarvis I suddenly realize something.

John H.
What?

Frankie.
I know that the bride and my brother are the "we" of me. So I'm going with them, and joining with the wedding. This coming Sunday when my brother and the bride leave this town, I'm going with the two of them to Winter Hill. And after that to whatever place that they will ever go. (*There is a pause.*) I love the two of them so much and we belong to be together. I love the two of them so much because they are the *we* of me. (*The curtain falls.*)

from
THE CHILDREN'S HOUR
by Lillian Hellman

Act I, scene 1
MARY, PEGGY, EVELYN, ROSALIE

Lillian Hellman has stated that the theme of THE CHIL-
DREN'S HOUR is good and evil, and that some of the
incidents in the play are from her memories of the "world
of the half-remembered, the half-observed, the half-under-
stood. . . ." The evil is personified by the `child Mary, whose
ability to rouse fear and horror in those with whom she
comes into contact, ultimately destroys the good and the
innocent.

Most of the play takes place at the Wright-Dobie School
for girls, which Karen Wright and Martha Dobie have
struggled to make successful both educationally and fi-
nancially. By the time the play opens, they seem to be
well on their way to achieving their goals, and Karen is
making plans to marry her patient fiancé. There are two
immediate problems, however. One is Martha's parasitic
and foolish aunt Lily Molar, a member of the staff, and
the other is Mary, one of the students. The child is spoiled,
unhappy, and troublesome, and to complicate the situation,
it is her grandmother who has helped sponsor the school
and who wields a great deal of influence and authority.

The following scene takes place in the large room that
serves as both living room and study. Evelyn, Mary and
Peggy are in the room. Miss Wright has just punished
Mary for her behavior. A second after she leaves, Mary
springs up, throws a cushion from the sofa at the door.

Evelyn.
  (*Closing door*) Don't do that. She'll hear you. (PEGGY
picks up cushion, puts it back on sofa.)

27

Mary.
Who cares if she does? And she can hear that, too. (*Takes a small China kitchen ornament, a kitten, from table and throws it on the floor. EVELYN and PEGGY gasp, and MARY's bravado disappears for a moment. She rises.*)

Evelyn.
(*Frightened*) Now what are you going to do?

Peggy.
(*Stooping down to pick up the pieces, EVELYN helps her.*) You'll get the devil now. Dr. Cardin gave it to Miss Wright. It was a lover's gift. There's nothing like a lover's gift. (*They put pieces on the desk. PEGGY sits in chair R. of the desk, EVELYN gets some scotch tape from lower shelf of the stage L. bookcase, comes to upstage of desk. Together they try to fix the kitten.*)

Mary.
Oh, leave it alone. She'll never know we did it.

Peggy.
We didn't do it. *You* did it.

Mary.
And what will you do if I say *we* did do it? (*Laughs. Sits on sofa and balances cushion on her head*) Never mind, I'll think of something else. The wind could've knocked it over.

Evelyn.
Yeh. She's going to believe that one!

Mary.
Oh, stop worrying about it. I'll get out of it. (*Puts pillow down*)

Evelyn.
Did you really have a pain?

Mary.
I fainted, didn't I?

Peggy.
I wish I could faint. Is it hard? I've never even worn glasses, or braces, and I've got my own tonsils.

Mary.
A lot it'll get you to faint.

Evelyn.
What did Miss Wright do to you when the class left?

Mary.
Told me I couldn't go to the boat-races.

Evelyn.
(*Sits on R. down side of chair upstage of desk.*) Gosh. . . .

Peggy.
But we'll tell you everything that happens and we'll give you all the souvenirs and things.

Mary.
I won't let you go if I can't go. But I'll find some way to go. What was she talking about when she moved you? What were *you* doing?

Peggy.
We came down to see what was happening to you, but the doors were closed and we could hear Miss Dobie and Mortar having an awful row. Then Miss Dobie opens the door and there we were.

Mary.
And a lot of crawling and crying you both did too, I bet.

Evelyn.
We were sort of sorry about listening. I guess it wasn't—

Mary.
Ah, you're always sorry about everything. What were they saying?

Peggy.
What was who saying?

Mary.
Dobie and Mortar, silly.

Peggy.
(*Evasively*) Just talking, I guess.

Evelyn.
Fighting.

Mary.
About what?

Evelyn.
Well, they were talking about Mortar going away to England and—

Peggy.
(*To* EVELYN) You know, it really wasn't very nice to've listened, and I think maybe it's worse to tell.

Mary.
(*Rises, crosses upstage between sofa and desk to* R. *of* EVELYN.) You do, do you? You just don't tell me and see what happens. (PEGGY *sighs*.)

Evelyn.
Mortar got awful sore at that and said they just wanted to get rid of her, and then they started talking about Dr. Cardin.

Mary.
What about him?

Peggy.
We'd better get started moving; Miss Wright will be
back first thing we know.

Mary.
(*Fiercely*) Shut up! (*Pokes* EVELYN) Go on, Evelyn.

Evelyn.
They're going to be married. The two of them.

Mary.
(*Crosses* R. *to above* R. *end of sofa*) Everybody knows
that.

Peggy.
But everybody doesn't know that Miss Dobie doesn't want
them to get married. How do you like that? (*The* C. *door
opens and* ROSALIE WELLS *sticks her head in.*)

Rosalie.
I have a class soon. If you're going to move things—

Mary.
Close that door, you idiot. (ROSALIE *closes door, stands
near it*) What do you want?

Rosalie.
(*Crosses to* MARY) I'm trying to tell you. If you're
going to move your things—not that I want you in with
me, the devil knows—you'd better start right now. Miss
Wright's coming in a minute.

Mary.
(*Sits back of sofa*) Who cares if she is?

Rosalie.
I'm just telling you for your own good, the devil knows.

Peggy.
(*Starts to get up*) We're coming.

Mary.
No. Let Rosalie move our things.

Rosalie.
You crazy? (*Voice mounts*)

Peggy.
(*Rises, crosses* L. *below desk. Nervously*) It's all right.
Evelyn and I'll get your things. Come on, Evelyn.

Mary.
Trying to get out of telling me, huh? Well, you won't
get out of it that way. Sit down and stop being such
a sissy. (PEGGY *crosses* U.L. *of desk, sits on* L. *arm of
chair upstage of desk.*) Rosalie, tell you what, you go

on up and move my things and don't say a word about our being down here.

Rosalie.
And who was your French maid yesterday, Mary Tilford? And who will wait upon you in the insane asylum?

Mary.
(*Laughing*) You'll do for today. (*Picks cushion up from sofa, hits* ROSALIE *with it.* ROSALIE *backs away.*) Now go on, Rosalie, and fix our things.

Rosalie.
You crazy?

Mary.
And the next time we go into town I'll let you wear my gold beads and my pearl pin. You'll like that, won't you, Rosalie?

Rosalie.
(*Draws back, moves her hands nervously*) I don't know what you're talking about, the devil knows.

Mary.
Oh, I'm not talking about anything in particular. You just run along now and remind me the next time to lend you—*lend* you—my beads and pin.

Rosalie.
(*Stares at her a moment. Slowly crosses toward* MARY) All right, I'll do it this time, but just 'cause I got a good disposition. But don't think you're going to boss me around, Mary Tilford.

Mary.
(*Smiling*) No, indeed. (ROSALIE *goes to* C. *door, opens it.* MARY *follows her.*) And get the things done neatly, Rosalie. Don't muss my white blouse. (ROSALIE *exits slamming door, as* MARY *laughs, opens the door, calls after her*) My tennis shoes need cleaning.

Evelyn.
Now what do you think of that? What made her so agreeable?

Mary.
(*Closes door, crosses downstage, sits in chair* R. *of desk*) Oh, a little secret we got. Go on, now, what else did she say?

Peggy.
Well, Mortar said that Dobie was jealous of them, and that she was like that when she was a little girl, and that she'd better get herself a beau of her own because

it was unnatural, and that she never wanted anybody to like Miss Wright, and that was unnatural. Boy! Did Miss Dobie get sore at that!

Evelyn.
Then we didn't hear any more. Peggy dropped some books.

Mary.
What'd she mean Dobie was jealous?

Peggy.
What's unnatural?

Evelyn.
Un for not. Not natural.

Peggy.
It's funny, because everybody gets married.

Mary.
A lot of people don't—they're too ugly.

Peggy.
(*Claps hand to her mouth*) Oh, my God! Rosalie'll find that copy of *Mademoiselle de Maupin*. She'll blab like the dickens.

Mary.
Ah, she won't say a word.

Evelyn.
(*Leans toward* MARY) Who gets the book when we move?

Mary.
You can have it. That's what I was doing this morning— finishing it. There's one part in it—

Peggy.
What part? (MARY *laughs.*)

Evelyn.
Well, what was it?

Mary.
Wait until you read it.

Evelyn.
Did you understand it? I don't always—

Peggy.
It's a shame about being moved, I don't want to go in with Helen, she's John's cousin you know, and I don't want to talk about the whole thing.

Evelyn.
What whole thing? You've only met him once.

Mary.
It was a dirty trick making us move. She just wants to

see how much fun she can take away from me. She
hates me.

Peggy.
No, she doesn't, Mary. She treats you just like the rest
of us—almost better.

Mary.
That's right, stick up for your crush. Take her side
against mine.

Peggy.
I didn't mean it that way.

Evelyn.
(*Looks at her watch. Rises*) We'd better get upstairs.

Mary.
I'm not going.

Peggy.
Rosalie isn't so bad.

Evelyn.
What you going to do about the kitten?

Mary.
I don't care about Rosalie and I don't care about the
kitten. (MARY *grabs what is left of kitten.* PEGGY *and*
EVELYN *take it away from her.*) I'm not going to be
here.

Peggy.
Not going to be here!

Evelyn.
What do you mean?

Mary.
(*Calmly*) I'm going home.

Peggy.
Oh, Mary—

Evelyn.
You can't do that.

Mary.
Oh, can't I? You just watch. I'm not staying here. (*Rises,
slowly crosses* L. *below desk to* U.L. *of chair* L. *of desk*)
I'm going home and tell grandma I'm not staying any
more. (*Smiles to herself*) I'll tell her I'm not happy.
They're scared of Grandma—she helped 'em when they
first started, you know—and when she tells them something, believe me, they'll sit up and listen. They can't
get away with treating me like this, and they don't have
to think they can.

Peggy.
(*Appalled*) You just going to walk out like that?

Evelyn.
What you going to tell your grandmother?

Mary.
Oh, who cares? I'll think of something to tell her. I can always do it better on the spur of the moment.

Peggy.
(*Rises*) She'll send you right back.

Mary.
(*Crosses to down* L. *table, fingers lamp*) You let me worry about that. Grandma's very fond of me, on account of my father was her favorite son. My father killed himself, but Grandma won't admit it. I can manage *her* all right.

Peggy.
I don't think you ought to go, really, Mary. It's just going to make an awful lot of trouble.

Evelyn.
What's going to happen about the kitten?

Mary.
Say I did it—it doesn't make a bit of difference any more to me. (*Crosses back to* U.L. *of chair,* L. *of desk*) Now listen, you two got to help. They won't miss me before dinner if you make Rosalie shut the door and keep it shut. Now, I'll go through the field to French's, and then I can get the bus to Homestead.

Evelyn.
How you going to get to the street car?

Mary.
Taxi, idiot.

Peggy.
How are you going to get out of here in the first place?

Mary.
(*Slowly moving downstage*) I'm going to walk out. I know where they keep the front door. Well, I'm going right out the door.

Evelyn.
Gee, I wouldn't have the nerve.

Mary.
Of course you wouldn't. You'd let 'em do anything to you they want. Well, they can't do it to me. (*Turns to them*) Who's got any money? (PEGGY *slowly crosses* R. *above desk, comes downstage between sofa and desk to below* L. *end of sofa*)

Evelyn.
(*Moves to above chair* R. *of desk*) Not me. Not a cent.

Mary.
I've got to have a dollar for the taxi and a dime for the bus.

Evelyn.
And where you going to find it?

Peggy.
(*Below* L. *end of sofa*) See? Why don't you just wait until you get your allowance on Monday, and then you can go any place you want. Maybe by that time—

Mary.
I'm going today. *Now.*

Evelyn.
You can't *walk* to Lancet.

Mary.
(*Slowly crosses* R. *below desk to* C. *To* PEGGY.) You've got money. You've got three dollars and twenty-five cents. Go get it for me.

Peggy.
(*Moves away* R. *below sofa*) No! No! I won't get it for you.

Evelyn.
(*Crosses to* C.) You can't have *that* money, Mary—

Mary.
(*Advances to below* L. *end of sofa*) Get it for me.

Peggy.
(*Cringes, her voice is scared*) I won't. I just won't. Mamma doesn't send me much allowance—not half as much as the rest of you get—I saved this so long—you took it from me last time—

Evelyn.
(*Comes down* L. *of* MARY) Ah, she wants that dress so bad.

Peggy.
I'll tell you a secret. I'd never even go to the movies if Miss Wright and Miss Dobie didn't give me money. I never have anything the rest of you get all the time. It took me so long to save that and I—

Mary.
Go upstairs and get me the money.

Peggy.
(*Hysterically, backing away from her*) I won't. I won't. I won't. (MARY *makes a sudden move to her, grabs her* L. *arm, and jerks it back, hard and expertly.* PEGGY

screams softly. EVELYN *tries to take* MARY's *arm away. Without releasing her hold on* PEGGY, MARY *slaps* EVELYN's *face.* EVELYN *backs away, begins to cry.*)

Mary.
Just say when you've had enough.

Peggy.
(*Softly, stiflingly*) All—all right—I'll get it.

Mary.
(*Smiles, nods her head, releases* PEGGY, *softly*) Go on, go on.

(PEGGY, *crying and rubbing her arm, slowly crosses* U.C. *toward door as the curtain falls.*)

from
THE CHILDREN'S HOUR
by Lillian Hellman

Act II, scene 2
MARY, ROSALIE

In this scene from the middle of the play, Mary is well
on her way to success in destroying the school. She has
run away from school to her grandmother and has related
several malicious and untrue incidents. Her distraught
grandmother has promised that Mary need not return to
school and she has called several parents, who have also
hurriedly sent for their children. In the following scene,
Rosalie has come to Mary's house for the night as her
mother cannot pick her up until the following day. As
Rosalie enters the living room, Mary is lying in front of a
love seat playing with a puzzle. She is hidden from Rosalie's
view. In the exchange between the two girls, some of
Mary's techniques become clear. (A little more background
can be gained by reading the introduction to the preceding
scene from the same play.)

Mary.
(*Loudly*) Whooooo! (ROSALIE *jumps up.*) Whooooo!
(ROSALIE *frightened, starts hurriedly for door.* MARY
sits up, laughs) You're a goose.
Rosalie.
(*Comes down to below* L. *end of* L. *love seat. Belligerent-
ly*) Oh, so it's you. Well, who likes to hear funny noises
at night? You could have been a werewolf.
Mary.
What would a werewolf do with you?
Rosalie.
(*Crossing* R. *to armchair*) Just what he'd do with any-
body else. (MARY *laughs*) Isn't it funny about school?

37

Mary.
What's funny about it?

Rosalie.
(*Crosses upstage, inspects sideboard*) Don't act like you can come home every night.

Mary.
Maybe I can from now on. (*Rolls over on her back luxuriously*) Maybe I'm never going back.

Rosalie.
Am I going back? I don't want to stay home.

Mary.
What'll you give to know?

Rosalie.
(*Takes a grape*) Nothing. I'll just ask my mother.

Mary.
Will you give me a free T.L. if I tell you?

Rosalie.
(*Comes to behind* R. *of love seat. Thinks for a moment*) All right. Lois Fisher told Helen that you were very smart.

Mary.
That's an old one. I won't take it.

Rosalie.
You got to take it.

Mary.
Nope.

Rosalie.
(*Laughs*) You don't know, anyway.

Mary.
I know what I heard, and I know Grandma phoned your mother in New York five dollars and eighty-five cents to come and get you right away. You're just going to spend the night here. I wish Evelyn could come instead of you.

Rosalie.
(*Comes down to* R. *of* R. *love seat*) But what's happened? Peggy and Helen and Evelyn and Lois went home tonight, too. Do you think somebody's got secret measles or something?

Mary.
No.

Rosalie.
Do *you* know what it is? How'd you find out? (*No answer*) You're always pretending you know everything. You're just faking. (*Flounces away. Sits on the ottoman*) Never mind, don't bother telling me. I think curiosity is very unladylike, anyhow. I have no concern with your

silly secrets, none at all. (*She twirls round on ottoman, stops and after long pause*) What did you say?

Mary.
I didn't say a thing.

Rosalie.
Oh. (*Twirls around again*)

Mary.
(*Laughs. Rises and puts the jigsaw puzzle in a drawer of the highboy*) But now suppose I told you that I just may have said that you were in on it?

Rosalie.
(*Stops twirling*) In on what?

Mary.
(*Comes down to* R. *of* R. *love seat*) The secret. Suppose I told you that I *may have* said that you told me about it?

Rosalie.
(*Rises*) Why, Mary Tilford! You can't do a thing like that. I didn't tell you about anything. (MARY *laughs*) Did you tell your grandmother such a thing?

Mary.
Maybe.

Rosalie.
(*Crosses to below* R. *love seat, turns to* MARY) Well, I'm going right up to your grandmother and tell her I didn't tell you anything—whatever it is. You're just trying to get me into trouble, like always, and I'm not going to let you. (*Starts for arch*)

Mary.
(*Crosses to below armchair*) Wait a minute, I'll come with you.

Rosalie.
(*Stops* U.L. *of armchair*) What for?

Mary.
I want to tell her about Helen Burton's bracelet.

Rosalie.
(*Slowly turns to* MARY) What about it?

Mary.
Just that you stole it.

Rosalie.
(*Crosses to* MARY) Shut up. I didn't do any such thing.

Mary.
Yes, you did.

Rosalie.
(*Tearfully*) You made it up. You're always making things up.

Mary.
You can't call me a liar, Rosalie Wells. That's a kind of dare and I won't take a dare. (*She starts for arch.* ROSALIE *blocks her way.*) I guess I'll go tell Grandma, anyway. Then she can call the police and they'll come for you and you'll get tried in court. (*She slowly backs* ROSALIE *to behind* R. *end of* L. *love seat. While she speaks, she pulls* ROSALIE's *glasses down on her nose and pulls her hair.*) And you'll go to one of those prisons, and you'll get older and older, and when you're good and old they'll let you out, but your mother and father will be dead and you won't have any place to go and you'll beg on the streets—

Rosalie.
(*Crying*) I didn't steal anything. I borrowed the bracelet and I was going to put it back as soon as I'd worn it to the movies. I never meant to keep it.

Mary.
Nobody'll believe that, least of all the police. You're just a common, ordinary thief. Stop that bawling. You'll have the whole house down here in a minute.

Rosalie.
You won't tell? Say you won't tell.

Mary.
Am I a liar?

Rosalie.
No.

Mary.
Then say: "I apologize on my hands and knees."

Rosalie.
I apologize on my hands and knees. Let's play with the puzzle.

Mary.
Wait a minute. Say: "From now on, I, Rosalie Wells— (*Crosses her wrists in front of her*) am the vassal of Mary Tilford and will do and say whatever she tells me under the solemn oath of a knight."

Rosalie.
(*Crosses downstage to below* R. *end of love seat*) I won't say that. That's the worst oath there is. (MARY *starts down right.*) Mary! Please don't— (*She quickly follows* MARY *and stops her below* R. *love seat*)

Mary.
Will you swear it?

Rosalie.
(*Sniffling*) But then you could tell me to do anything.
Mary.
(*Starts to move* R.) Say it quick or I'll—
Rosalie.
(*Hurriedly*) From now on— (*Slowly turns and crosses*
L. *to* L. *love seat, holding her wrists crossed in front of
her*) I, Rosalie Wells, am the vassal of Mary Tilford and
will do and say whatever she tells me under the solemn
oath of a knight.
Mary.
Don't forget that.

THE RAINY AFTERNOON
by William Inge

WILMA, BILLIE MAE, VIC

This is not a scene from a play, but the entire play. Although the cast consists solely of three children, the theme is mature and bitter. Upon viewing or reading the play, adults may become unnerved by the manner in which the children see and reflect the adult world. In terms of the acting for the children involved, the characters are real and not too difficult to identify with, and the dialogue is extremely natural.

The scene is the interior of an old barn in a small Midwestern town. Outside it is raining a slow, constant drizzle. Inside the barn, two little girls, dressed in stolen fragments of their mother's clothing, play at having tea, making the barn an imaginary house, using nail kegs and tool chests and barrels for furniture. At left is a crude stairway leading up to a loft that is totally darkened. Of the two girls, Wilma is the older and more aggressive. She is perhaps ten. Billie Mae is only seven or eight. She plays the game with some uncertainty, as though she were depending on Wilma for instruction. Both girls have their dolls beside them, treating the dolls like children.

Wilma.
You've got to spank your baby to make her behave.
Billie Mae.
Mine's behaving.
Wilma.
No she isn't. She's crying all the time. Spank her. I spank mine all the time. See?
(WILMA *demonstrates*)
Billie Mae.
Mine isn't crying.

Wilma.
She is, *too.* Spank her!

Billie Mae.
Well, all right! (*Timidly she spanks her doll*)

Wilma.
. . . and scold her.

Billie Mae.
You're a bad baby. You're a bad baby.

Wilma.
(*Resuming her role*) I guess you weren't invited to the big party at the country club yesterday. All the society people were there. I wore a beautiful new dress to it. Mrs. Sylvester Jones was there. She's a cow. She was dressed in horrible clothes. And her manners are terrible.

Billie Mae.
Are they?

Wilma.
Yes. Mrs. Sylvester Jones is a terrible woman. I don't know why anyone invites her any place. I didn't even speak to her.

Billie Mae.
I wanta go home.

Wilma.
(*Her own voice*) You can't.

Billie Mae.
Why not?

Wilma.
Because we're having a tea party, silly. You can't just get up and walk out of a tea party.

Billie Mae.
I'm not having any fun.

Wilma.
You don't know how to play. (VIC BATES, *a boy of* WILMA's *age, pulls up at the door on his bicycle.*)

Vic.
What're you crazy girls doin'?

Wilma.
What business is it of yours?

Vic.
I just asked. I don't care what you're doin'.

Wilma.
Then go away. Our mothers don't allow us to play with boys.

Billie Mae.
(*Affirming*) No. You go away.

Vic.
Am I hurtin' anyone, just sittin' here on my bike?

Wilma.
I thought you crazy boys were goin' on a hike.

Vic.
Don't you see it's raining?

Wilma.
(*Making a face*) Yah, yah, yah!

Vic.
What've you got on your mother's clothes for?

Wilma.
We can put on our mothers' clothes if we want to, can't we, crazy?

Vic.
I don't know what fun you crazy girls get outa playin' with dolls.

Wilma.
Girls have as much fun as boys do.

Billie Mae.
Yes. Girls have just as much fun as boys do.

Vic.
(*Getting off his bike, coming into the barn*) My father just got a new De Soto.

Wilma.
My father got a Pontiac.

Vic.
I like a De Soto better'n an old Pontiac.

Wilma.
Pontiac's the best car there *is*. I wouldn't have an old De Soto.

Billie Mae.
(*Spanking her doll*) Be good, you bad baby!

Wilma.
(*To VIC*) Wanta play house?

Vic.
How do ya play house?

Wilma.
I'll be the mother. You be the father, and Billie Mae will be our baby girl.

Vic.
What do we do?

Wilma.
You just pretend to be grownups. It's fun. Come on and try.

Vic.
It sounds stupid.

Wilma.
Come on and play.

Vic.
Nothin' else to do.

Billie Mae.
My mother says I'm not supposed to play with boys.

Wilma.
Your mother doesn't have to know, scaredy-cat!

Billie Mae.
(*Looking at* VIC) I don't like boys. Boys are rough.

Wilma.
Oh, they are *not*, silly.

Vic.
(*Coming into the barn*) O.K., I'll give it a try. What do you want me to do?

Wilma.
We just act like grownups. I know everything grownups do. I've watched my mother and daddy. I know everything they do.

Vic.
Like what?

Wilma.
You pretend like you're coming home from the office. You're real tired and I've got to get dinner.

Vic.
What fun'll that be?

Wilma.
(*Impatient with him*) It's just the way you play the game.

Vic.
O.K. (*Goes out and comes in again as a tired husband. He has no real gift for make-believe, but he tries to be convincing. He stretches his arms and flops into a chair.*) Sure had a busy day at the office today.

Wilma.
Did you, Hubby dear? I played bridge with the Van Uppingtons! And afterward we took a ride in their Rolls-Royce.

Vic.
(*Himself*) We supposed to be real rich?

Wilma.
Sure.

Vic.
(*Back into his role*) I made fifty million dollars this afternoon. On the stock market.

Wilma.
That's wonderful, dear. Now maybe I can get some new clothes. I'm so sick of all my old things.

Vic.
I think maybe I'll get another new car. I think I could use a racing car, maybe.

Wilma.
Would you like a cocktail, dear?

Vic.
Sure.

Wilma.
Baby's been very bad today, Hubby dear, I'm afraid you'll have to spank her.

Vic.
All right.

Wilma.
She just refused to do everything I told her to do, so you'll have to spank her to keep her from growing up to be a very bad girl.

Vic.
All right. (*He picks up* BILLIE MAE *and starts to put her over his knee*)

Billie Mae.
(*Accusingly, to* WILMA) I don't think this is fair.

Wilma.
It's just *pretending*, silly.

Vic.
(*Spanking her lightly*) You must be a good girl, Baby dear, and do everything your mother tells you.

Wilma.
You must spank her hard, Hubby dear. She's been a *very* bad girl. (VIC *spanks her harder*)

Billie Mae.
(*Jumping off* VIC's *lap*) I'm not going to play any more if you keep on spanking me.

Wilma.
I guess she's been punished enough, Hubby dear. We'll let Baby go back to bed now and go into the living room.

Vic.
O.K.

Billie Mae.
(*To herself*) I don't see why I have to be the baby.

Wilma.
(*To* VIC) Would you like a cocktail, dear?

Vic.
Sure.

Wilma.

(*Herself, to* BILLIE MAE) You be our maid now and bring us cocktails.

Billie Mae.

I'm not going to play any more. You didn't tell me I'd have to be the maid.

Wilma.

Just bring us a tray with something on it. Then you can go back to being Baby.

Billie Mae.

I'm not having any fun at all. (*Sets a couple of dirty old glasses on a board and serves drinks*) Here are your cocktails.

Wilma.

Thank you, Maid. (BILLIE MAE *returns to the chest and sits there resuming the role of Baby.* WILMA *continues to* VIC) I don't know what we're going to do with Maid, Hubby dear. She's just a terrible maid. She won't do anything I ask her.

Vic.

Tell her we're going to fire her.

Wilma.

But we can't fire her because help is so hard to get.

Vic.

Why don't *you* do the work?

Wilma.

Rich society women like me never do their own work. The Van Uppingtons have fifty maids, and butlers, too. And chauffeurs. And . . . all kinds of servants. Do you like your cocktail, dear?

Vic.

It's all right.

Wilma.

Are you ready for dinner, dear?

Vic.

I guess so.

Wilma.

(*Calling*) Maid! Maid! Hubby and I are ready for dinner now.

Billie Mae.

(*In her own voice*) You want me to be the Maid again?

Wilma.

Well, of course.

Billie Mae.

(*In her role*) Dinner is served.

Wilma.
Say "Madam."

Billie Mae.
Madam.

Wilma.
That's better. (*To* VIC) Will you take me to dinner, Hubby dear?

Vic.
(*Getting up*) O.K.

Wilma.
We're having roast turkey and banana salad and angelfood cake a la mode.

Vic.
Can't we have some sweet potatoes, too? I like sweet potatoes.

Wilma.
All right, dear. We'll have sweet potatoes too. (*They sit, one on either side of the barrel which serves as a table, and* BILLIE MAE *hands them imaginary dishes.*)

Vic.
That's awful good turkey.

Wilma.
It was the finest one I could buy. And isn't the banana salad good, too?

Vic.
(*Pretending to eat*) Sure. It's good, too.

Wilma.
(*To* BILLIE MAE) You can bring us the angel-food cake a la mode now.

Billie Mae.
O.K.

Wilma.
(*To* VIC) I certainly hope you like the dessert, Hubby dear.

Vic.
(*Himself*) My mother just calls my father by his real name.

Wilma.
I like to play the game the way *I'm* playing it.

Vic.
It just sounds kind of crazy, callin' me "Hubby dear" all the time. No one does that.

Wilma.
They do, too. (*Back in her role*) Have you had enough dinner, Hubby dear?

Vic.
I guess so.

Wilma.
Shall we go into the living room and look at television?

Vic.
I wanta go play poker.

Wilma.
You can't leave me alone with Baby.

Vic.
Oh, all right.

Wilma.
I'll put Baby to bed now. Will you come and kiss her good night?

Vic.
Have I gotta kiss her?

Wilma.
Well, sure, crazy! Are you afraid to kiss her?

Vic.
No. I'm not afraid. It's just kinda crazy. That's all.

Wilma.
(*To* BILLIE MAE) Daddy and I have come to say good night, Baby dear!

Billie Mae.
Good night!

Wilma.
Say your prayers and sleep tight.

Billie Mae.
O. K. (WILMA *kisses* BILLIE MAE *on the cheek, then turns to* VIC)

Wilma.
Now it's your turn. (VIC *leans over and kisses* BILLIE MAE *on the cheek*)

Vic.
Good night, Baby.

Billie Mae.
Good night, Daddy.

Wilma.
Shut your eyes real tight and go to sleep.

Billie Mae.
O.K.

Wilma.
Real tight.

Billie Mae.
I've got 'em shut as tight as I can.

Wilma.
I want Baby to grow up to be a very good girl, don't you, Hubby dear?

Vic.
Yeh . . . sure.

Wilma.
I don't think I want to look at television, after all.

Vic.
I don't care.

Wilma.
I've had such a busy day, I'm awfully tired. I think I'll go to bed.

Vic.
O.K.

Wilma.
Are you ready to go to bed, too, Hubby dear?

Vic.
Me? Oh . . .

Wilma.
You've had such a busy day at the office. I think you should go to bed now and be sure to get your rest.

Vic.
Well . . . I . . .

Wilma.
Come on, Hubby dear.

Vic.
(*He is not acting now*) Well . . . what do we do?

Wilma.
Our bedroom is in the hayloft. We'll go up there and leave Baby down here. (*She is completely self-possessed.*)

Vic.
(*Clearing his throat*) Uh . . . I don't think I wanta go to bed now. You go on to bed, and I . . . I'll go out for a walk.

Wilma.
You can't. It's raining outside.

Vic.
Oh!

Wilma.
You're *scared!*

Vic.
Who says so?

Wilma.
It sure looks like it.

Vic.
Well, I'm not, if you should happen to want to know.

Wilma.
Well, come on then. It's just a game.

Vic.
You mean . . . up there in the loft?

Wilma.
Sure.

Vic.
(*Completely at sea*) Well . . . I'm not gonna play this game any more. This is a crazy game. I'm not playing. (*He starts for his bike*)

Wilma.
I *told* you you're scared. (VIC *stops. He's not going to let himself be called scared.*) Boys are worse scaredy-cats than girls.

Vic.
Well . . . gee whiz!

Wilma.
And it's perfectly all right. There couldn't be anything wrong about it, cause we're just playing a game, aren't we? And we're doing everything our mothers and fathers do. So what could be wrong about it?

Vic.
Well . . . I don't know, but . . .

Wilma.
Unless you're just a plain old scaredy-cat.

Vic.
I told you, I'm not scared.

Wilma.
Then prove it!

Vic.
You're sure crazy.

Wilma.
Prove it!

Vic.
Well . . . (*With a nod at* BILLIE MAE, *lying on the chest with her eyes shut*) What about her?

Wilma.
(*Whispering*) She won't have to know anything.

Vic.
Well . . . gee!

Wilma.
Come on, scaredy-cat! (*She starts up the stairs to the loft.*)

Vic.
Gee!

Wilma.

If you don't follow me in two minutes, you're the biggest scaredy-cat that ever lived. So there! (*Continues up the stairs*)

Vic.

Shut up, will ya? I'm comin'.

Wilma.

(*Stops and turns around*) Then come along.

Vic.

(*Following her, against his better judgment*) I'm comin'. I'm coming. (*He follows* WILMA *into the darkness of the loft, and there is a silence of several minutes. Then* BILLIE MAE *sits up and looks about her.*)

Billie Mae.

What're you kids doin'? (*There is no response and she feels lonely and rejected.*) What's everyone doin'? (*Still no response.* BILLIE MAE *stands and walks around the barn, stopping at the foot of the stairs looking up.*) What're you crazy kids doin' up there in the loft? (*No response*) I bet you're doin' something bad. (*No response.* BILLIE MAE *begins to sob*) I don't like you any more, Wilma Wadsworth. I don't like you at all. (*Still no response*) I'm going home now and tell my mother . . . (*No response*) and I'll never come over to play with you again. (*Apparently* WILMA *is not concerned.* BILLIE MAE *moves to the door, as though hoping someone will stop her.*) I'm going. (*No response*) I'm going. (*No response. Now, the feeling of rejection is too strong for* BILLIE MAE *to hold. She bursts into sudden tears while she runs out of the barn.*) I'll never come back here to play with you again. I hate you Wilma Wadsworth. I'll never be your playmate any more. I hate you. I hate you.

(*The stage is empty now. There are several moments of absolute and mysterious silence.*)

Curtain

from
DEAD END
by Sidney Kingsley

Act I
PHILIP, TOMMY, DIPPY, ANGEL, T.B., SPIT, MIL-
TON

The story of *Dead End* is essentially the story of
poverty-stricken young men growing up in the shadow of
affluence. The boys, filled with the zest for living, manage
to make their own good times, pitching pennies, swimming
in the dirty river, and indulging in a great deal of horse-
play, which is often cruel. They are too young to ask
meaningful questions about their lives but some of the
adults in the play are trying to fight the system that
traps them into this kind of living, distorting and twisting
their values. A young man, Gimpty, says, "When I was
in school, they used to teach us that evolution made men
out of animals. They forgot to tell us it can also make
animals out of men."

The following scene portrays the crude humor created
by the boys through their bawdy language and their
horse play. It also contrasts the slum boys with a rich boy
growing up in refinement and isolation and with the new
boy on the block, a Jew and an eternal alien.

The scene takes place at the dead end of a New York
street, ending in a wharf over the East River. And here
on the shore, in the midst of slums, the very wealthy have
begun to establish their city residence in new palatial
apartments. The East River Terrace is one of these. A
gang of boys are swimming in the sewerage at the foot
of the wharf, splashing about and enjoying it immensely.
A well-dressed, delicate-featured little boy has come out
of the Terrace Apartments and is addressing his departing
governess.

There are two short deletions from the play which include adults and these are marked with asterisks.

Philip.
Oui, oui, mademoiselle.

Tommy.
Wee-wee! He's godda go wee-wee! (*All the boys shout with laughter.*)

Dippy.
Do a swan-dive, Tommy. At's wad I like.

Tommy.
O.K. Hole my butt. (*He hands his cigarette to* DIPPY.) Hey, kid! Hey, yew! Hey, wee-wee! (PHILIP *looks at him.*) Yuh wanna see sumpm? A swan-dive. Watch! (TOMMY *dashes off, under the hopper. We hear his "Whe-e-e" and a splash. The boys cluck approval.*)

Philip.
What's so wonderful about that?

Angel.
Aw, yuh fat tub a buttah, it's mor'n yew kin do.

Philip.
That shows how much you know.

T.B.
I bet a dollar he can't even swimn.

Philip.
I can, too.

T.B.
Ah, balonee!

Philip.
Balonee yourself! We've a pool in there and I swim every day. . . . with instruction.

Spit.
Aw, bushwah! (TOMMY *appears on the ladder.* DIPPY *hands him his cigarette.*)

Dippy.
He sez dey godda pool in ere.

Tommy.
How wuzat swan-dive?

Dippy.
He sez it wuz lousy.

Tommy.
(*Climbing over the parapet and crossing to* PHILIP,

belligerently) Oh yeah? What wuza mattuh wid it? Kin
yew do betta?

Philip.
A trillion times.

Tommy.
Awright. Lessee yuh.

Philip.
Where?

Tommy.
Heah!

Philip.
Here?

Tommy.
Yeah, heah. Yew hoid me. Yew ain' deef. (*Turns to the
others.*) His eahs ovuhlap, dat's it! (*They roar with
laughter.*)

Philip.
I wouldn't swim here.

T.B.
He's yelluh, dat's what! Dat's what! He's godda yelluh
streak up 'is back a mile wide.

Philip.
It's dirty here.

Dippy.
(*Shocked*) Doity!

T.B.
(*Very indignant*) Doity! He sez doity. He sez it's doity!
I'll sock 'im!

Angel.
Lil fairy!

Spit.
Wassamattuh? Yuh sca'd yuh git a lil doit on yuh?

Philip.
And besides, I haven't got my suit.

Tommy.
Well, go in bareass.

T.B.
Yeah, wassamattuh wid bareass?

Philip.
And besides, I'm not allowed to.

Dippy.
(*Sing-song*) Sissy, sissy, sucks his mamma's titty!

Philip.
Sticks and stones may break my bones, but names will
never hurt me. (*The boys crowd him back against the
gate.*) .

Tommy.
Ah, ahl spit in yuh eye an' drown yuh. Hey, what's at junk yuh got in yuh mout . . . like a hawse?

Philip.
It's a brace, to make my teeth straight.

Tommy.
Wha-a-at? I could do dat wit one wallop! (*The gang roars with laughter.*)

Philip.
You try and you'll be arrested.

Spit.
Yeah?

Tommy.
(*Contemptuously*) Look who's gonna arrest us!

Philip.
My uncle's a judge.

Tommy.
Balonee!

Philip.
Did you ever hear of Judge Griswald?

Angel.
So what? So I know a guy whose brudduh's a detective. He'll git us out.

T.B.
Yeah? Did yuh evuh hear a Judge Poikins! Well, he's a frien' a mine, see? He sent me to rifawm school once.

* * *

(*The doorman opens the gate and* PHILIP *goes in. The boys laugh and mock them.* DIPPY, *preoccupied with the phenomena of his body, suddenly discovers a lone hair on his chest.*)

Dippy.
Boy! Gee! Hey, I godda hair! (*He caresses it, proudly.* T.B. *comes over, inspects the hair, admires it, then suddenly plucks it out, and runs away laughing and holding up the trophy.* DIPPY *yips, first with pain, then with rage.* TOMMY *finds an old discarded broom in the litter under the hopper. He balances it skillfully on the palm of his hand.*)

Spit.
Gese, I'm hungry!

Tommy.
Me too!

Angel.
Boy, I'm so hungry I could eat a live dog.

Dippy.
(*Looks up from his wounded chest*) Boy, I could eat a hot dog.

Angel.
Wid sauerkraut!

Dippy.
Yeah.

Angel.
(*Licking his lips and patting his belly*) Yum.

Spit.
Hey, should we go tuh Schultzie's 'n see if we kin snitch sumpn?

Tommy.
(*Balancing the broom*) Nah, Schultzie's wise tuh us.

Angel.
We could try some udduh staws.

Tommy.
(*Still balancing the broom*) Nah, day're all wise tuh us. Duh minute we walk in 'ey asks us wadda we want. If we had some dough, while one uv us wuz buyin' sumpm de udduh guys could swipe some stuff, see? I got faw cents, but 'at ain' enough. (*He drops the broom, and becomes the man of action.*) Anybody got any dough hea? Hey, yew, Angel, yuh got some?

Angel.
No, I ain'.

Tommy.
Come on! Don' hole out.

Angel.
Honest! I didn't git no customuh dis mawnin'.

Tommy.
Wheah's 'is pants? Look in 'is pants! (*T.B. and SPIT rush to the hopper, grab ANGEL's pants, and start rifling the pockets. ANGEL follows them, yelling.*)

Angel.
Hey! Git outta deah! Git outta deah!

T.B.
Nuttn but a couple a stamps 'n a boy-scout knife.

Spit.
(*Taking the knife himself*) Oh baby, kin I have dis?

Angel.
(*Follows SPIT*) No, I need it.

Spit.
No, yuh don't.

Angel.
Aw, Spit, gimme my knife!

Spit.
(*Mocking his accent*) Watsa ma'? Piza Taliana? (*He spits at him.*) Right inee ear! Ha!

Angel.
(*Backs a step and wipes out his ear with a finger*) Ah, yuh louse? Ast me fuh sumpm sometime 'n' see watcha git.

Tommy.
Give 'im 'is knife!

Spit.
Da hell I will!

Angel.
Aw, Spit, gimme my knife! Tommy, make 'im, will yuh?

Tommy.
Gimme dat knife!

Spit.
What fuh?

Tommy.
(*Makes a fist and waves it in front of* SPIT's *nose*) Fuh dis . . . right in yuh bugle! (*He grabs the knife and examines it.*) Gese, dat's a knife! Five blades! Boy, I'd like one like 'at. (*Enter from the lower tenement door, a young* BOY *of about twelve, a bit timid, neatly dressed, obviously Semitic features.*)

Angel.
Aw, Tommy, I need it. I godda use it. Honest!

Tommy.
(*Gives him his knife*) Here! Stop squawkin'! Don't say I nevuh gave yuh nuttin'!

Angel.
Tanks, Tommy. Dat's white.

Tommy.
(*Good-naturedly*) Ah, shat ap! (*To* DIPPY, *who sits reflectively picking his nose*) Hey, Dippy! Pick me a big juicy one! (DIPPY *grins, rolls the resinous matter into a little ball, and flicks it at* TOMMY. TOMMY *laughs. . . .*)

* * *

T.B.
Hey, look! Deah's 'at new kid 'at moved aroun' a block.

Spit.
'At's 'at Jew kid! (*They rise and come down toward him.*)

Tommy.
 Hey, kid!
Angel.
 Hey, kid!
The Jewish Boy.
 (*Looks up.*) Wadda yuh want?
Spit.
 Come heah, Ikey! Come on! Don' be so slow. (*He comes over, eager to join them, yet scared.*)
Tommy.
 Yew do noo kid onna block, aintcha?
The Jewish Boy.
 Yeah.
Tommy.
 Whatsya name?
The Jewish Boy.
 Milton. Milton Schwartz.
Tommy.
 Yuh wanna belong tuh are gang?
Milty.
 (*Eagerly*) Yeah. Shuah.
Tommy.
 Got 'ny doug? Yuh godda be ineetiated.
Milty.
 I god tree sants.
Tommy.
 Gimme it!
Spit.
 (*Prodding him in the ribs.*) Give it tuh 'im!
T.B.
 (*Prodding him harder and pulling him around*) Go on!
Tommy.
 (*Pulling him back*) Come on! Don' hold out! (MILTY *fishes out three cents and hands them to* TOMMY) 'At's all yuh got?
Milty.
 Yeah.
Spit.
 Sure?
Milty.
 Hones'.
Tommy.
 Soich 'im. (*They start to go through his pockets.*)
Milty.
 (*Turns his pockets inside out*) Don'! You don' half tuh. Look!

Spit.
Ah, you punk.

Tommy.
Listen, yew! If yuh wanna belong to dis gang, yuh godda git a quatuh.

Milty.
A quatuh? Wheah ahm gonna git a quatuh fum?

Spit.
Fum yuh old lady.

Milty.
She woodn gimme no quahtuh.

Spit.
You know wheah she keeps huh money, doncha?

Milty.
Dat's a sin tuh steal.

Spit.
(*Mocking his accent*) Wassamattuh, Ikey?

Milty.
Don' make fun on me, I can' help it.

Spit.
(*Contemptuously*) Yuh scared tuh snitch a quatuh? Gese, she won' fin' out.

Milty.
Yes, she would.

Spit.
(*Still mocking him*) Oh, she counts huh money all a time, huh, Jakey Ikey?

Milty.
Stop dat! Gimme back my tree sants. I don't wanna hang out wid youse.

Tommy.
(*To* SPIT) Yuh godda watch-pocket, aintcha?

Spit.
Yeah.

Tommy.
Guard dis dough! (*He hands the money to* SPIT, *who puts it in his pocket. They walk away, completely ignoring* MILTY.)

Milty.
(*Follows them, murmuring tremulously*) Gimme back my tree sants.

Spit.
(*Whispers to the others*). Let's cockalize him.

Angel.
Wadda yuh say, Tommy?

Tommy.
> O.K.

T.B.
> Come on! (ANGEL *crosses nonchalantly behind* MILTY, *then crouches on his hands and knees unnoticed. The others turn and slowly approach him. Suddenly* TOMMY *pushes* MILTY, *who stumbles backward and trips over* ANGEL, *feet flying up. They all pounce on the prostrate boy . . . .*)

from
DEAD END
by Sidney Kingsley

Act III
TOMMY, ANGEL

In this play about boys growing up in the slums, the inevitable has happened. One of the boys, Tommy, is in trouble with the police for a stabbing and has been hiding. Tommy has been a definite leader of the group and though just as crude as the other boys, has given indication of a sense of fair play. This is probably due to the fact that his older sister has tried desperately to help him grow up with a decent set of values.

The scene takes place at the dead end of a New York street, ending in a wharf over the East River. There is a blaze of fire crackling out of an old iron ash-can in the center of the street. The boys have been roasting potatoes skewered on long sticks. They have just left Angel to stand guard for a few minutes. Angel fishes his kazoo from a pocket, relaxes by the fireside, and hums into the instrument. A shadow detaches itself from the hopper and creeps stealthily toward Angel. It whispers "Psst! Hey! Angel!" Angel wheels around, startled. (For further background on the play, read the introduction to the preceding scene.)

Angel.
Tommy! Gese!
Tommy.
(*His face glowing red as he leans over the fire toward* ANGEL.) Sh! Shat 'ap! (*In a hoarse whisper*) Wheah ah da guys? (*They both talk in whispers.*)
Angel.
Dey went tuh look fuh wood.

Tommy.
What?

Angel.
Fuh wood. Maw wood. Milty jus' took yuh sistuh . . .

Tommy.
Is Spit wit de guys?

Angel.
Yeah.

Tommy.
O.K.

Angel.
Milty jus' took yuh sistuh tuh yer hideout.

Tommy.
He did? De louse!

Angel.
Whatcha gonna do, Tommy?

Tommy.
Run away . . . so de bulls don' git me.

Angel.
(*Impressed*) Gese!

Tommy.
(*Quietly*) But foist I'm gonna ketch de guy who snitched.
Do yuh know who it wuz?

Angel.
Me? No.

Tommy.
(*Flaring*) Don' lie tuh me. . . . I'll kill yuh!

Angel.
Yew know me, Tommy.

Tommy.
O.K. I tink I'm wise tuh who done it.

Angel.
Who?

Tommy.
Spit.

Angel.
Yuh tink so?

Tommy.
Yeah.

Angel.
Gese!

Tommy.
Now I'm gonna hide, see? Right back a deah. (*Points up
behind the hopper*) If yuh let on I'm heah . . . (*Ominous-
ly*) I'll put yuh teet' down yuh troat!

Angel.
Aw, Tommy, yuh know me . . . yuh know me!

Tommy.
O.K. Den do like I tell yuh. When Spit comes back, yew tell 'im like dis . . . Duh guy I stabbed wuz down heah lookin' fuh Spit tuh givim five bucks fuh snitchin' on who done it. Yuh got dat straight?

Angel.
Duh guy what he got stabbled . . . wuz down heah lookin' fuh Spit . . . tuh givvim five bucks fuh snitchin' on who done it.

Tommy.
Right.

Angel.
O.K.

Tommy.
An' rememba . . . yew let on I'm heah, I'll. . . .

Angel.
Aw, Tommy, yew know me.

Tommy.
Aw right. Jus' do like I told yuh.

Angel.
Whadda yuh gonna do tuh Spit if 'ee done it?. (*TOMMY takes a knife from his pocket, and rips open the blade. The firelight runs along the blade. It looks bright and sharp and hard. TOMMY grimly draws it diagonally across his cheek. ANGEL grunts.*) Mark a de squealuh?

Tommy.
(*Snaps the blade home and pockets the knife.*) Right.

Angel.
Gese!

Tommy.
Now, go on playin' yuh kazoo like nuttn happened . . . like I wuzn't heah. (*Footsteps and voices from the gate. TOMMY ducks and melts into the shadows of the hopper. ANGEL plays his kazoo a bit ostentatiously.*)

from
ALICE IN WONDERLAND
Adapted for the stage by Eva Le Gallienne and Florida
Friebus from Lewis Carroll's ALICE IN WONDERLAND
and THROUGH THE LOOKING-GLASS

Act II, scene 1
ALICE, THE RED QUEEN

Though this scene is written for one child and one adult,
it can be played very successfully by two children because
it is fantasy. There are several scenes of this type included
in the collection because, as we all know, witches, fairies
and angels are ageless.

Alice in Wonderland is a timeless and familiar classic.
In this adaptation, Eva Le Gallienne has opened the play
with Alice seated in a chair in front of a fireplace, playing with the looking glass, through which she walks.
Alice's adventures continue as she finds a tiny golden key
that opens a little door to a small passage. She drinks from
a magic bottle and becomes so small that she can get
through the door into a lovely garden. In her wanderings
through Wonderland, she has met talking birds, a peculiar
caterpillar, the Cheshire Cat, the Mad Hatter, the Dor-
mouse, and many other fantastic characters.

In the following scene, Alice is running away from a
Whole Pack of Cards that is flying down upon her. Alice
is frightened by many things she has seen but she still
manages to be polite and she is always curious.

*At rise, Alice is seen still running, but now she is facing
left. She slows down wearily and comes to a stop. As lights
come up, she finds herself in a land that is marked out in
squares, like a huge chessboard, with a large tree at the
right. Presently, from the left, with a thump, thump of*

footsteps, the RED QUEEN *enters and comes face to face with* ALICE.

Red Queen.

Where do you come from and where are you going? Look up, speak nicely, and don't twiddle your fingers.

Alice.

(*Attending to all these directions as well as she can*) You see I've lost my way.

Red Queen.

I don't know what you mean by *your* way, all the ways about here belong to *me*—but why did you come out here at all? Curtsey while you're thinking what to say. It saves time.

Alice.

(*Aside*) I'll try it when I go home the next time I'm a little late for dinner.

Red Queen.

(*Looking at her watch*) It's time for you to answer now. Open your mouth a *little* wider when you speak and always say "Your Majesty."

Alice.

I only wanted to see what the garden was like, Your Majesty—

Red Queen.

(*Patting* ALICE *on the head which she doesn't like at all*) That's right, though when you say "garden"—*I've* seen gardens, compared with which this would be a wilderness.

Alice.

(*Going right on*) —and I thought I'd try and find my way to the top of that hill.

Red Queen.

When you say "hill"—*I* could show you hills, in comparison with which you'd call that a valley.

Alice.

No, I shouldn't, a hill *can't* be a valley, you know. That would be nonsense—

Red Queen.

You call it "nonsense" if you like, but *I've* heard nonsense, compared with which that would be as sensible as a dictionary! (ALICE *curtsies again as she is afraid by the* QUEEN's *tone that she is a little offended.*)

Alice.

(*Surveying the view*) I declare it's marked out just like a large chessboard. It's a great huge game of chess that's being played—all over the world—if this *is* the world at all, you know. Oh, what fun it is! How I *wish* I was part of it. I wouldn't mind being a Pawn, if only I might join—though of course I should *like* to be a queen, best. (*She glances shyly at the* QUEEN *who smiles pleasantly.*)

Red Queen.
That's easily managed. You can be the White Queen's Pawn, if you like, as Lily's too young to play; and you're in the Second Square to begin with: when you get to the Eighth Square, you'll be a Queen. (*They begin to run hand in hand—the scene does not change—the* QUEEN *runs so fast* ALICE *can scarcely keep up with her and still the* QUEEN *keeps crying*) Faster, faster!

Alice.
(*To herself*) I wonder if all the things move along with us?

Red Queen.
Faster! Don't try to talk! (ALICE *falters and falls back a little.*) Faster! Faster!

Alice.
(*At last getting her breath*) Are we nearly there?

Red Queen.
Nearly there! Why, we passed it ten minutes ago! Faster! (*They run on in silence for awhile.*) Now! Now! Faster, Faster! (*The* QUEEN *pulls* ALICE *up in line with herself again. They run on . . . then slowly come to a stop.* ALICE *drops to ground. The* QUEEN *seats* ALICE *under the tree. Kindly.*) You may rest a little now.

Alice.
(*Looking around in surprise*) Why, I do believe we've been under this tree the whole time! Everything's just as it was!

Red Queen.
Of course it is. What would you have it?

Alice.
Well, in *our* country, you'd generally get to somewhere else—if you ran very fast for a long time as we've been doing.

Red Queen.
A slow sort of country! Now, *here,* you see, it takes all the running *you* can do to keep in the same place. If you

want to get somewhere else, you must run at least twice as fast as that!

Alice.
I'd rather not try, please! I'm quite content to stay here—only I *am* so hot and thirsty!

Red Queen.
I know what *you'd* like. (*Takes a large, hard-wafer biscuit out of her pocket.*) Have a biscuit? (ALICE *takes it but finds it very dry. She chokes and puts remainder of biscuit in her pocket.*) While you're refreshing yourself, I'll just take the measurements. (*She marches to a point downstage,* right, *in front of the tree, where she begins to measure with a tape measure, taking little sidesteps from right to left, and marking the end of each "square" with a bounce in her knees, and a gesture of her hand, as though placing a peg.*) At the end of two yards . . . (*She takes two sidesteps left. Bounce.*) I shall give you your directions—Have another biscuit?

Alice.
No, thank you, one's *quite* enough.

Red Queen.
Thirst quenched, I hope? At the end of *three* yards . . . (*Business*) I shall repeat them for fear of your forgetting them. At the end of *four* . . . (*Business*) I shall say goodbye. And at the end of *five* . . . (*Business*) I shall go! (*She marches back to her starting point and begins walking slowly along the line that she has measured, describing each square with suitable gestures.*) A pawn goes two squares in its first move, you know. So you'll go *very* quickly through the Third Square . . . by railway, I should think . . . and you'll find yourself in the Fourth Square in no time. Well, *that* square belongs to Tweedledum and Tweedledee . . . the Fifth is mostly water . . . the Sixth belongs to Humpty Dumpty . . . But you make no remark?

Alice.
I . . . I didn't know I had to make one just then.

Red Queen.
You *should* have said, "It's extremely kind of you to tell me all this," . . . however, we'll suppose it said . . . the Seventh Square is all forest . . . however, one of the Knights will show you the way . . . and in the Eighth

Square we shall be Queens together, and it's all feasting and fun! (*She turns to* ALICE. ALICE *gets up and curtsies.*) Speak in French when you can't think of the English for a thing. Turn out your toes when you walk, and remember who you are! (*She turns left and starts running.*)

Alice.
She *can* run very fast!

Red Queen.
Good-bye. (*She exits, left.* Blackout. *Shrill whistle of a steam engine.*)

from
HEIDI
by Johanna Spyri
adapted from the novel by Lorraine Cohen

HEIDI, CLARA

The story of Heidi is a children's classic. Heidi, a curly-
haired child of five who has a sunny disposition, love,
warmth and humor, has been orphaned. She is taken to
her grandfather's hut in the Swiss Alps to live. He is at
first sullen over his new responsibility but eventually is
charmed by the child. Heidi is blissfully happy in the
mountains and makes friends with the goats, Peter, the
goatherd, and Peter's blind grandmother, but she is taken
away to Frankfurt to become educated and to serve as
companion to the invalid, Clara.

The following scene takes place in the parlor of the
Sesemann's in Frankfurt where Heidi is to stay. She has
been dressed in her peasant best. Clara, a few years older
than Heidi, dressed very sedately, is seated in her wheel
chair. Next to her is a table with a glass of milk and
a soft roll, a music box, and some books. Heidi is seated
very uncomfortably on the edge of a big chair and keeps
looking at the windows and the door. She has just arrived. The adults have left the room and this is the first
time she and Clara have been alone.

Clara.
I'm so glad you're here. (*Silence*) I have some lovely
dolls and so many books and games, I know you'll love
them. (*Silence*) You *do* know how to talk, don't you?
Heidi.
Fräulein Rottenmeier told me I mustn't chatter.
Clara.
You mustn't let Fräulein upset you. She doesn't mean to

be so harsh. (*Silence*) Wouldn't you like to see this book?
It has lovely illustrations.

Heidi.

Fräulein Rottenmeier also said I mustn't muss my dress or
get the room in disorder. (*Almost in tears*) And my feet
hurt.

Clara.

Why, what's wrong with your feet?

Heidi.

I don't know.

Clara.

Why don't you take your shoes off and see if something is
inside?

Heidi.

O, may I? (*Hurriedly takes her shoes and socks off and
happily wiggles her toes*) Oh, where is my basket? I must
have my basket!

Clara.

I think Fräulein took it.

Heidi.

Oh no, I must get it right away! Right now! I must have
it! I—

Clara.

Wait a minute, Heidi, there it is near the door. (HEIDI
runs to it, peeks inside.) What's in it, Heidi?

Heidi.

I—I—can't show you.

Clara.

Of course you can. I won't tell Fräulein. I'm your friend,
Heidi.

Heidi.

Look! (*Brings basket to* CLARA *and brings out a kitten*)

Clara.

Oh, how darling! Are they yours?

Heidi.

I couldn't leave them behind so I hid them in here. But
what shall I do? They're probably hungry.

Clara.

Here, give them some of my milk. (*They do.*) Do you
think if we broke up this roll they could eat that too?
(HEIDI *has the roll in her hands and hesitates.*) What's
the matter, Heidi?

Heidi.

May I keep this roll?

Clara.
Oh, Heidi, are you hungry? Please eat it.

Heidi.
(*Putting it in her pocket*) No, I'm going to save it for Peter's grandmother, it's so soft and she has lost all her teeth. But what shall I do with the kittens? Fräulein will never let me keep them.

Clara.
I'll think of a place to hide them. Maybe we can keep them in the attic. Fräulein never goes up there.

Heidi.
They won't like an attic. They love grass. Oh, what am I going to do? (*Puts kitten back in basket, heads for the door*)

Clara.
Where are you going, Heidi?

Heidi.
I must go home.

Clara.
Heidi, you can't. Not now. They won't let you past the front door. And you don't know your way. Frankfurt is a big city. You'll get lost.

Heidi.
(*Stopping at door, tearfully*) I must go home. (*Doggedly*)

Clara.
You just got here. Maybe you'll like it.

Heidi.
Oh, no! There are only walls here. I want to see the fir trees blowing in the wind like they do at Grandfather's. They make such lovely sounds. And I want to see the mountains touching the sky. Oh, Clara, and Grandfather, he needs me. And Peter's grandmother needs me. And the goats need me.

Clara.
Goats? Oh, Heidi, tell me about the goats. I've never even seen a real one. (*Silence*) Please Heidi, come here and tell me about them.

Heidi.
I have the loveliest little goat. His name is Little Swan. He must be wondering where I am.

Clara.
Why don't we call one of the kittens "Little Swan?"

Heidi.
(*Swallowing hard*) That'll be nice.

Clara.
I'm truly sorry you're so sad, Heidi.

Heidi.
I miss Little Swan. I miss the mountains. I miss the wind in the fir trees.

Clara.
Would you like to hear my music box? (*Plays it*)

Heidi.
It sounds a little like the wind in the mountains.

Clara.
I knew you would like it.

Heidi.
It makes me want to dance.

Clara.
Oh, do dance, Heidi. I would so much like to see it.

Heidi.
(*Begins to dance*) It's lovely. It makes me feel like I'm the wind at Grandfather's house.

Clara.
I wish I could dance.

Heidi.
(*Suddenly stopping*) You can't dance?

Clara.
I can't even walk.

Heidi.
Oh, Clara, everybody can walk.

Clara.
I can't.

Heidi.
Come, I'll help you.

Clara.
I can't, Heidi.

Heidi.
Of course you can.

Clara.
I'm afraid.

Heidi.
I'm strong. I'll help you. (*Helps* CLARA *stand up but* CLARA *falls back in chair*)

Clara.
I can't. I'm afraid. Maybe if you help me a little each day . . .

Heidi.
I won't be able to. I'm sorry, Clara, but I have to go.

Clara.
You can't go, Heidi. You have to stay here. You're such
a long way from your grandfather. (HEIDI *begins to
sob.*) Oh, Heidi, please don't cry. It makes me so sad to
see you cry. We could be such good friends and I need
you too, just as badly as Peter's grandmother. (HEIDI
continues crying.) Heidi, would you like to pray? Would
that help?

Heidi.
Pray?

Clara.
Don't you ever pray? When I have troubles and Papa isn't
here, it helps me to talk to God. Don't you ever want to
talk to Him?

Heidi.
A long, long time ago I used to pray with my grandmother but I've forgotten how to do it.

Clara.
There's no special way. Just talk to Him. Say all the
things in your heart.

Heidi.
Will He listen?

Clara.
Oh yes, Heidi. He always listens. (*Silence*) And if you
whisper I won't hear you.

Heidi.
He'll hear my whisper?

Clara.
(*Smiling*) Yes, Heidi, he will. And you'll feel so much
better. Try it.

Heidi.
Oh thank you, Clara. I do like you and I wish I could help
you. Yes, I'll pray now. (*Goes off to corner of room*)
Dear God, please let me see Grandfather soon, and the
grandmother and the goats and the mountains and the fir
trees blowing in the wind. I want to go home so much.
Please help me, please, please.

from
MACBETH
by William Shakespeare
adapted by Lorraine Cohen

THE THREE WITCHES

The following scene comprises passages from the various
witches' scenes in *Macbeth*. Although the witches' roles
were written for adults, they are exciting for children to
play. Children are, of course, familiar with witches and
they delight in the sound of the language Shakespeare has
given to the three in *Macbeth*.

*A heath in Scotland. Three witches are dancing around a
cauldron.*

All The Witches.
Double, double, toil and trouble;
Fire burn and cauldron bubble.
First Witch.
Thrice the black cat haw mewed.
Second Witch.
Thrice and once the hedge-hog whined.
Third Witch.
'Tis time, 'tis time.
First Witch.
Round about the cauldron go . . .
In the poisoned entrails throw.
All The Witches.
Double, double, toil and trouble . . .
Fire burn and cauldron bubble.
Second Witch.
Fillet of a fenny snake,
In the cauldron boil and bake.
Third Witch.
Eye of newt and toe of frog,

Wool of bat and tongue of dog,
Adder's fork and blind-worm's sting,
Lizard's leg and owlet's wing,
For a charm of powerful trouble,
Like a hell broth boil and bubble.

All The Witches.
Double, double, toil and trouble,
Fire burn and cauldron bubble.

Second Witch.
Cool it with a baboon's blood,
Then the charm is firm and good.

All The Witches.
The weird sisters, hand in hand,
Posters of the sea and land.
Thus do go about ... about ... thrice to thine,
And thrice to mine,
And thrice again to make up nine.
Peace! The charm's wound up!

First Witch.
When shall we three meet again,
In thunder, lightning, or in rain?

Second Witch.
When the hurly-burly's done,
When the battle's lost and won.

Third Witch.
That will be ere the set of sun.

First Witch.
Where has thou been, sister?

Second Witch.
Killing swine.

Third Witch.
Sister, where thou?

First Witch.
A sailor's wife and chestnuts in her lap,
And munched, and munched and munched.
"Give me some!" said I.
"Away with thee!" she cried.
Her husband is away at sea, and look what I have!

Second Witch.
Show me! Show me!

First Witch.
I have her husband's thumb,
Wrecked as homeward he did come.

Third Witch.
  By the picking of my thumbs,
  Something wicked this way comes.
All The Witches.
  Fair is foul, and foul is fair,
  Hover through the fog and filthy air.
  Show his eyes and grieve his heart.
  . . . . . Come like shadows, so depart.
                              (*They vanish.*)

from
the novel LITTLE WOMEN
by Louisa Mae Alcott
adapted by Lorraine Cohen

MEG, JO, AMY, BETH

The story of the March family, written in the nineteenth century, is still a favorite among young readers. The trials and tribulations of the lady-like Meg, the tomboyish Jo, the vain Amy and the gentle Beth, growing up poor but happy under the watchful eye of their mother while their father is in the army, have elicited chuckles and countless tears from readers over the years.

The following scene is adapted from the beginning of the book. The four girls are knitting.

Jo.
(*Lying on rug*) Christmas won't be Christmas without any presents.

Meg.
(*Looking at her old dress*) It's so dreadful to be poor!

Amy.
I don't think it's fair for some girls to have lots of pretty things, and other girls nothing at all.

Beth.
We've got Father and Mother, and each other.

Jo.
We haven't got Father and shall not have him for a long time. (*Silence*)

Meg.
You know the reason Mother proposed not having any presents this Christmas was because it's going to be a hard winter for everyone; and she thinks we ought not to spend money for pleasure, when our men are suffering so in the army. We can't do much, but we can make our

78

little sacrifices and ought to do it gladly. But I'm afraid I don't.

Jo.

But I don't think the little we should spend would do any good. We've each got a dollar, and the army wouldn't be much helped by our giving that. I agree not to expect anything from Mother or you, but I do want to buy a new book.

Beth.

I planned to spend mine in new music.

Amy.

I shall get a nice box of Faber's drawing pencils; I really need them.

Jo.

Mother didn't say anything about our money, and she won't wish us to give up everything. Let's each buy what we want, and have a little fun; I'm sure we grub hard enough to earn it.

Amy.

Jo, You do use such slang words, it's really very in-dignified. (*Jo begins to whistle.*) Don't Jo, it's so boyish.

Jo.

That's why I do it.

Amy.

I detest rude, unladylike girls.

Jo.

I hate affected, niminy piminy chits.

Beth.

Oh girls, don't argue.

Meg.

Beth is right. You are old enough to leave off boyish tricks, and behave better, Josephine. It didn't matter so much when you were a little girl, but now you are so tall, and turn up your hair, you should remember that you are a young lady.

Jo.

I ain't! and if turning up my hair makes me one, I'll wear it in two tails till I'm twenty. I hate to think I've got to grow up and be Miss March, and wear long gowns, and look as prim as a China aster. It's bad enough to be a girl, anyway, when I like boys' games and work, and manners. I can't get over my disappointment in not being a boy, and it's worse than ever now, for I'm dying to go and fight with papa, and I can only stay at home and

knit like a poky old woman! (*Throws her ball of wool
across the room*)

Beth.
Oh, poor Jo!

Meg.
As for you, Amy, you are altogether too particular and
prim. Your airs are funny now, but you'll grow up an
affected little goose if you don't take care. I like your
nice manners and refined ways of speaking, when you
don't try to be elegant, but your absurd words are as bad
as Jo's slang.

Amy.
I'm just trying to exprove my vocabulary. (JO *snorts
loudly.*) I'm just going to ignore such coarseness.

Jo.
Oh, how furious you make me!

Beth.
Oh, a letter is here. Maybe it's from father. (*Goes off*)

Meg.
I hope it's from father. (*Girls all chime in*) (BETH *returns with a letter.*)

Beth.
It is from Father. Shall we open it or wait till Mother
comes home?

Jo.
Oh, I could never wait.

Amy.
Meg, you are supposed to be Mother's helper when she's
not here. You read it. You have the authoritary. (JO
snorts and laughs again. AMY *sticks out her tongue.*)

Meg.
Oh, stop it, girls. All right, let me read it. Wouldn't it be
perfectly wonderful if he was coming home for Christmas?

Beth.
Oh, do you think that's what it could be? Read it Meg,
read it.

Meg.
(*Opening the letter, reading aloud*)
"My dear family,
    This will be a very short letter before we move camp
again but I do want to wish you all a Merry Christmas. I
would have liked more than anything else to spend this
holiday with you but it looks like it will be at least a year

before I see you all again. My dear daughters, help and obey your mother, do your duty faithfully so that when I come home to you, I may be prouder than ever of my little women."

(*Silence. Sniffing.*)

Amy.

I *am* a selfish pig! but I'll truly try to be better so he mayn't be disappointed in me.

Meg.

We all will! I think too much of my looks, and hate to work, but won't any more, if I can help it.

Jo.

I'll try and be what he loves to call me, "a little woman" and not be rough and wild.

Beth.

Remember all the lovely times we had with Father last summer? Remember when we went out there where our flowers and arbors are and there were so many pretty things, we all stood and sung for joy up there in the sunshine. (*Silence again as all the girls remember things. AMY is crying.*)

Jo.

Let's cheer up before Mommy comes home. I know, let's rehearse our play that we are going to do for her.

Meg.

You know what I made for the play? A bit of jewelry of gold-paper for me to wear. Won't that be perfect, Jo?

Jo.

Perfectly jolly! Let's rehearse. Come here, Amy, and do the fainting scene. You are stiff as a poker in that.

Amy.

I can't help it. I never saw anyone faint, and I don't choose to make myself all black and blue, tumbling flat as you do. If I can go down easily, I'll drop: if I can't, I shall fall into a chair and be graceful. I don't care if Hugo does come at me with a pistol.

Jo.

Do it this way. Clasp your hands so, and stagger across the room, crying frantically, "Roderigo! Save me! Save me!" (*JO does this with a melodramatic scream.*) (*AMY tries it but her hands are poked out stiffly and her scream at the end is funny. JO groans.*)

Jo.

It's no use! Do the best you can when the time comes, and if the audience shouts, don't blame me. Come on Meg, let's try your part.

Meg.

(*Very dramatically*) Ah me! I shall never marry you Hugo though you keep me prisoner till I am old and gray. Mine heart belongeth to Roderigo. Is that right, Jo?

Jo.

It's the best we've had yet.

Beth.

I don't see how you can write such splendid things, Jo. You're a regular Shakespeare!

Jo.

Not quite. I'd like to try to do Macbeth though, if we only had a trap-door for Banquo. I always wanted to do the killing part. "Is that a dagger that I see before me?" (*Rolling her eyes and clutching the air*)

Meg.

No, it's Beth's knitting needle with a ball of yarn stuck on it! (*Laughter*)

(*The doorbell rings*)

Amy.

I'll get it. (*Goes off*)

Meg.

We should practice the gong too. Start us Beth. (*The girls sing after BETH.*)

Amy.

(*Coming back with flowers, a basket of goodies*) Look at this! (*The girls crowd around, exclaiming.*)

Beth.

I never saw such a beautiful bouquet.

Meg.

Who sent it?

Jo.

And just look at these pastries! (*Stuffing one in her mouth*)

Meg.

Jo! (JO *sheepishly puts it back.*)

Amy.

It was a present from our new neighbor, the Lawrence boy. I do like his manners but he seemed very shy.

Jo.

Oh, I've met him already. When our cat ran away, he

brought her back and we talked over the fence, all about cricket but now Meg is so prim she won't let me speak to him when we pass.

Amy.

And you know what else? He invited us all over to a party at his house tomorrow evening? Isn't that elegant-ish?

Meg.

Won't it be marvelous to go to a party? But what shall we wear?

Jo.

What's the use of asking that, when you know we shall wear our poplins, because we haven't got anything else.

Amy.

If only I had a silk! I think I would die for a silk dress!

Jo.

I'm sure our pops look like silk, and they are nice enough for us. Yours is as good as new, but I forgot the burn and the tear in mine. Whatever shall I do? The burn shows horridly and I can't take it out.

Beth.

I'll try and fix it for you, Jo.

Amy.

That's what you get from standing so near the fire. You are so clumsy.

Meg.

You must sit still all you can, and keep your back out of sight. The front is all right.

Amy.

I shall put this ribbon in my hair and maybe Mother will lend me her little pearl pin, and my new slippers are love-ly, and my gloves will do, though they aren't as nice as I'd like.

Jo.

Mine are spoiled with lemonade, and I can't get any new ones, so I shall just have to go without them.

Meg.

You *must* have gloves, or I won't go. Gloves are more im-portant than anything else. You can't dance without them, and if you don't, I should be so mortified.

Jo.

Then I'll stay still.

Amy.

You can't ask Mother for new ones, they are so expensive,

and you are so careless. Can't you fix them in some way?

Jo.
I can hold them crunched up in my hand, so no one will know how stained they are, that's all I can do. No! I'll tell you how we can manage—each wear one good one and carry a bad one. Isn't that a nifty idea?

Meg.
Your hands are bigger than mine, and you will stretch my glove dreadfully.

Jo.
Then I'll go without them. I don't care what people say.

Meg.
You can wear my glove! Only don't stain it!

Amy.
And don't put your hands behind you, or say "Christopher Columbus," will you?

Jo.
Don't worry.

Amy.
Oh, I don't like this collar! Do you think I could borrow yours, Meg?

Meg.
Come on. Let's see what I have. (MEG *and* AMY *exit.*)

Beth.
I'll clean your glove too. I'm sure I can.

Jo.
Beth, what would we do without you? You know, you look like the essence of a flower. A rose, no, a violet I think. Sing for me Beth dear, please. (BETH *begins singing as the lights dim and go out.*)

from
STRAWBERRY ICE CREAM SODA
by Irwin Shaw
adapted from the short story by Lorraine Cohen

EDDIE 15, LAWRENCE 13

This is a story of two young brothers, working out the
conflict that arises over their different sets of values. In
the face of losing the respect of his older brother, Lawrence
redeems his honor by his willingness to make a personal
sacrifice.

The scene takes place on the front lawn of a summer
home in the Adirondack Mountains. Eddie Barnes is lying
on his stomach in the long grass. At the window, Lawrence
can be seen practicing the piano. The sound of musical
scales can be heard. Eddie is morosely regarding a grass-
hopper. Without interest, he puts out his hand and cap-
tures it.

Eddie.
Give honey, give honey or I'll kill yuh. . . . (*The grass-
hopper is unresponsive and* EDDIE *disgustedly throws it
away. He turns over on his back.*) God, why does anybody ever go to the country? (*He stands up, goes over
to the window.*) Lawrrrence, Lawrrrence, you stink. (*He
walks over to his radish patch, kicks away the loose dirt
and looks. Nothing.*) Damn crows! (*The piano music
stops and* LAWRENCE *comes out, flexing his fingers,
very neat in clean khaki shorts and a white shirt. He sits
down in the grape arbor.*)
Lawrence.
I would like a strawberry ice cream soda.
Eddie.
(*Hopefully*) Got any money? (LAWRENCE *shakes his
head.*) No strawberry ice cream soda.

85

Lawrence.
You got any money?

Eddie.
Some. (*Silence*) I gotta save my money. (*Harshly*) I got a date. I got thirty-five cents. How do I know she won't want a banana-split tonight?

Lawrence.
(*Nodding understandingly but sadly*) (*Uncomfortable silence for a few seconds*) All the time I was practicing, I kept thinking, "I would like a strawberry ice cream soda, I would like a strawberry ice cream soda . . ."

Eddie.
Aaah, shut up! (LAWRENCE *is flexing his fingers mechanically.*) Why don't you stop that fer once? Just fer once?

Lawrence.
This is good for my fingers. It keeps them loose.

Eddie.
Yuh give me a pain.

Lawrence.
All right. I won't do it now. It's nice here. It's very peaceful.

Eddie.
Aaah, yuh even talk like a pianist. (*Suddenly remembering something*) Hey, what happened this morning down at the lake?

Lawrence.
Oh, nothing.

Eddie.
What do you mean nothing? Andy said something happened.

Lawrence.
Well, it was nothing.

Eddie.
Well, yuh better tell me about this nothing. I'm your brother and I should know.

Lawrence.
I have to practice some more.

Eddie.
(*Stopping him*) Come on, you better tell me.

Lawrence.
Well, it was awfully stupid. The farmer's son wanted to fight.

Eddie.
Fight? With you? Why?

Lawrence.
Oh, I don't remember.

Eddie.
You don't remember? Someone wants to fight with you and you don't remember? Do you want me to go to him and ask him about it?

Lawrence.
Oh, I bumped into his boat a little. There was no damage but he got excited.

Eddie.
Gee kid, can't you even row a boat?

Lawrence.
It's bad for my hands. It stiffens the fingers but I had to get something for Mom from the village.

Eddie.
Well, what happened?

Lawrence.
Nothing. I tell you nothing happened.

Eddie.
That's not what Andy said. What did you do when he wanted to fight it out?

Lawrence.
You know I can't fight. (*Looking at hands*)

Eddie.
Andy heard the boy calling "Yella! Yella!"

Lawrence.
I guess he did.

Eddie.
Yella! Yella! Yella as a flower. My own brother. If it was me, I'da been glad to get killed before I let anybody call me that. I would let 'em cut my heart out first. My own brother. Yella as a flower. Just one in the eyes. Just one! Just to show 'im. But he stands there, takin' guff from a kid with holes in his pants. A pianist, Lawrrrrence! They knew what they were doin' when they called yuh Lawrrrrence! Don't talk to me! I don't want yuh ever to talk to me again as long as yuh live! Lawrrrrrence! Get out of here. I don't even want to see you. (LAWRENCE *looks at him silently, leaves. EDDIE chokes back tears.*) Damn, damn. (*There is a passing of time. EDDIE is moping on the grass when LAWRENCE appears with a black eye, a torn collar, smiling and whistling Brahms.*)

Lawrence.
It was a good fight. (*Starts to collapse*)

Eddie.
(*Helps him to bench, takes out hanky to clean LAW-RENCE's face.*) You don't whistle half bad. Yuh feelin' all right?

Lawrence.
Yes, I feel all right.

Eddie.
Well come on, let's go to town. I'll row. Let's get ice cream sodas. Let's get strawberry ice cream sodas.

from
JANE EYRE
by Charlotte Bronte
adapted from the novel by Lorraine Cohen

JANE, HELEN

The moody, romantic story of Jane Eyre has enchanted
generations of readers. The book opens with a portrayal of
the life of the orphaned Jane in a cruel relative's home.
She is finally sent to Lowood Institution, a charity school,
where though unhappy at its gloominess, rigidity, and
cruelty, she does become educated. When she grows up,
she becomes a governess for Mr. Rochester's ward in a
house haunted with mystery. She falls in love with Mr.
Rochester and after many frightening turns, the story ends
happily.

The following scene takes place in the darkening, gloomy
library-study of Lowood Institution the second day after
Jane's arrival. Jane has been wrongly accused of breaking
a slate, and then lying about it. She sits crying on top of a
high stool where she has been placed for a half hour's
punishment by the Director, Mr. Brocklehurst, and lectured
to on the evils of lying. While she is crying, Helen comes
in quietly. She is carrying something wrapped in a napkin.
She stands for a few moments without being noticed,
then suddenly has a short coughing spell. Jane, startled,
makes a furtive gesture to wipe her tears.

Jane.
  (*Gruffly*) What do you want?
Helen.
  I have something for you. (JANE *ignores her.* HELEN
  puts the small package on the table near JANE.) It's
  something to eat.

Jane.
How can I eat? I want to die.

Helen.
It's a muffin. With raisins.

Jane.
With raisins?

Helen.
Miss Temple put it aside for you.

Jane.
Miss Temple did? Why?

Helen.
She knew you would be hungry. You've missed lunch. (JANE *unwraps muffin, eats it ravenously.* HELEN *turns away, picks up book and begins to look at it.*)

Jane.
Are you being punished?

Helen.
Not now. (*Silence*) If you're feeling better, would you like to come to sewing class with me?

Jane.
No, I'll never go to any class in this school again. (*Silence*) If you're not being punished, why are you here?

Helen.
(*Shrugs her shoulders. A few minutes of silence*) Do you want me to go?

Jane.
No. (*Silence again,* HELEN *looking at book*)

Jane.
This is an awful place. (*Again no answer*) Why do they call this school an Institution? Is it different from other schools?

Helen.
It's partly a charity-school. You and I, and all the rest of us are charity children. I suppose you're an orphan. Are your mother and father both dead?

Jane.
Both died before I can remember.

Helen.
Well, all the girls here have lost either one or both parents and this is called an institution for educating orphans.

Jane.
Do we pay any money? Do they keep us for nothing?

Helen.
We pay, or our friends pay, fifteen pounds a year for each.

Jane.
Then why do they call us charity children?

Helen.
Because fifteen pounds is not enough for board and teaching. The rest is supplied by subscription.

Jane.
Who subscribes?

Helen.
Different benevolent-minded ladies and gentlemen in this neighborhood and in London. This house was built by Mrs. Naomi Brocklehurst and her son overlooks and directs everything here.

Jane.
Then this school does not belong to Miss Temple?

Helen.
To Miss Temple? Oh, no, I wish it did. She has to answer to Mr. Brocklehurst for all she does. Mr. Brocklehurst buys all our food and our clothes.

Jane.
I hate him.

Helen.
You mustn't. He is a clergyman and is said to do a great deal of good. (JANE *studies* HELEN.)

Jane.
Have you been here long?

Helen.
Two years.

Jane.
Are you an orphan?

Helen.
My mother is dead.

Jane.
You have a father.

Helen.
He is married again.

Jane.
Are you happy here?

Helen.
You do ask a lot of questions. (*Picks up her book again*)

Jane.
I'm sorry.

Helen.
That's all right.

Jane.

What is your name besides Burns?

Helen.

Helen.

Jane.

Do you come a long way from here?

Helen.

I come from a place further north; quite on the borders of Scotland.

Jane.

Will you ever go back?

Helen.

I hope so, but nobody can be sure of the future.

Jane.

You must want to get away from here, too.

Helen.

No, why should I? I was sent to Lowood to get an education. It would be silly to leave before that.

Jane.

But . . . I saw your punishment this morning. That teacher, Miss Scatcherd, is so cruel to you.

Helen.

She's not cruel. She dislikes my faults.

Jane.

If I were in your place, I should hate her. I should resist her. If she struck me with that rod, I should get it from her hand; I would break it under her nose.

Helen.

I don't think you would.

Jane.

But the worst part, making you stand in the middle of the classroom with everyone staring at you. How could you bear it so quietly? If I were in your place, it seems to me I would have wished the earth to open and swallow me up. But you looked as if you were thinking of something beyond the punishment, or something not near you. Were you daydreaming?

Helen.

I was thinking of Northumberland, and I thought that the noises I heard around me were the bubbling of a little brook which runs through Deepden, near our house. It happens to me so often. My mind wanders, I lose the sound of Miss Scatcherd's voice during lessons. I fall into a sort of dream. Then, when it comes to my turn to answer, I have no answer ready. It happened on Monday before you came. That afternoon, instead of dreaming of Deepden, I was wondering how a man who wished to do right could act so unjustly and unwisely as Charles the First sometimes did, and I thought what a pity it was with his wisdom, he had so little foresight. If he had been able to look ahead and understand the spirit of the age. Still, I like Charles—I respect him. I pity him, poor murdered king! (*Silence as* HELEN *is carried away with her thoughts again*)

Jane.
But it still isn't right for you to be punished in front of everybody. It's disgraceful. I couldn't bear it.

Helen.
Yet it would be your duty to bear it, if you couldn't avoid it. It's silly to say you cannot bear what you have to. (JANE *considers this with wonder.*)

Jane.
You say you have faults, Helen. What are they?

Helen.
Miss Scatcherd says I'm sloppy. I seldom keep my things in order. I'm careless, I forget rules, I read when I should be learning my lessons, I have no method, and sometimes, I say, like you, I cannot bear something. This is all very provoking to Miss Scatcherd who is naturally neat, punctual and particular.

Jane.
And cross and cruel. (*Silence*) Is Miss Temple as severe as Miss Scatcherd?

Helen.
Oh no, Miss Temple is so good, it hurts her to be severe to anyone, even the worst in the school. When she sees my errors, she tells me gently. When she teaches me, my thoughts never wander.

Jane.
Then with Miss Temple, you are always good?

Helen.
Yes, in a passive way, I don't even have to try. There really is no merit in such goodness.

Jane.
Oh yes, there is. You're good to those who are good to you. It's all I ever want to be. If people were always kind and obedient to those who are cruel and unjust, the

wicked people would have it all their own way, they
would never feel afraid, and so they would never change,
but would grow worse and worse. When we are struck
at with a reason, we should strike back again very hard.
I'm sure we should . . . so hard as to teach the person
who struck us never to do it again.

Helen.
You'll change your mind.

Jane.
But this is the way I feel. I hate those who hate me. I
must resist those who are unfair. It's natural that I should
love those who are kind.

Helen.
According to my history book, heathens and savage tribes
feel that way. That isn't Christian or civilized.

Jane.
Why? I don't understand.

Helen.
It's not violence that will overcome hate. And it's not
vengeance.

Jane.
What then?

Helen.
(*Slowly*) I think the answer must simply be love.

Jane.
Then I should love Mr. Brocklehurst. How can I? I hate
him! I should love Mrs. Reed and John but I just can't.
I never could. I'll hate them until I die!

Helen.
(*Softly*) Who are Mrs. Reed and John?

Jane.
Mrs. Reed is my uncle's wife. My uncle is dead, and he
left me to her care. She had to adopt me but she was
sorry to have to do it, but my uncle, as I have often
heard the servants say, got her to promise before he
died, that she would always keep me. But she has always
hated me. She let John bully me and when I hit him
back, she would lock me in that awful room upstairs.
She always told me I was worse than the servants, because the servants at least worked for their living. And
no matter what I did, it was wrong, even when I tried.
And I did try, Helen, I did try, honest! (*Close to tears*)
    (HELEN *begins to cough.*)

Are you all right? (HELEN *continues coughing.*) Let me get you a drink of water. (*Runs out, comes in with a small cup of water.* HELEN *drinks it.*)

Helen.
Thank you very much. I feel much better now, really. (JANE *sits again, quiet, thinking.*)

Helen.
Now, I must get to that sewing class.

Jane.
I'll come with you.
    (*Both girls exit.*)

from
THE CRUCIBLE
by Arthur Miller

Act I
ABIGAIL, MERCY, MARY WARREN, BETTY

The play takes place in Salem, Massachusetts, in 1692.
It is the time of the Salem Witch Trials, which affect the
lives of everyone—the innocent, the non-committed, the
well-meaning, the zealous. The story revolves around John
and Elizabeth Proctor who become caught up in the horror
when Elizabeth is accused of being a witch by Abigail, a
young girl who desires John. John goes to his death a
true hero, able to understand what is happening but power-
less to stop it.

The following scene shows how definitely the spirit of
repression and fear has molded the young people. The
girls have been secretly dancing in the woods and one of
them, Betty, has apparently fainted from fear. Stories of
witchcraft have already been circulating in the town. The
girls are in an upstairs bedroom in the home of Reverend
Samuel Parris and there is a great deal of commotion
downstairs. Abigail, although frightened, is clearly the
leader of the group, intense and calculating. Betty is lying
on the bed.

Abigail.
(*With hushed trepidation*) How is Ruth sick?
Mercy.
It's weirdish, I know not—she seems to walk like a dead
one since last night.
Abigail.
(*Turns at once and goes to* BETTY, *and now, with fear
in her voice*) Betty? (BETTY *doesn't move. She shakes
her.*) Now stop this! Betty! Sit up now!

(BETTY *doesn't stir.* MERCY *comes over.*)

Mercy.
Have you tried beatin' her? I gave Ruth a good one and it waked her for a minute. Here, let me have her.

Abigail.
(*Holding* MERCY *back*) No, he'll be comin' up. Listen, now; if they be questioning us, tell them we danced—I told him as much already.

Mercy.
Aye. And what more?

Abigail.
He knows Tituba conjured Ruth's sisters to come out of the grave.

Mercy.
And what more?

Abigail.
He saw you naked.

Mercy.
(*Clapping her hands together with a frightened laugh*) Oh, Jesus!

(*Enter* MARY WARREN, *breathless. She is seventeen, a subservient, naive, lonely girl.*)

Mary Warren.
What'll we do? The village is out! I just come from the farm; the whole country's talkin' witchcraft! They'll be callin' us witches, Abby!

Mercy.
(*Pointing and looking at* MARY WARREN) She means to tell, I know it.

Mary Warren.
Abby, we've got to tell. Witchery's a hangin' error, a hangin' like they done in Boston two year ago! We must tell the truth, Abby! You'll only be whipped for dancin', and the other things!

Abigail.
Oh, *we'll* be whipped!

Mary Warren.
I never done none of it, Abby. I only looked!

Mercy.
(*Moving menacingly toward* MARY) Oh, you're a great one for lookin' aren't you, Mary Warren? What a grand peeping courage you have!

(BETTY, *on the bed, whimpers.* ABIGAIL *turns to her at once.*)

Abigail.
Betty? (*She goes to* BETTY.) Now, Betty, dear, wake up now. It's Abigail. (*She sits* BETTY *up and furiously shakes her.*) I'll beat you, Betty! (BETTY *whimpers.*) My, you seem improving. I talked to your papa and I told him everything. So there's nothing to—

Betty.
(*Darts off the bed, frightened of* ABIGAIL, *and flattens herself against the wall*) I want my mama!

Abigail.
(*With alarm, as she cautiously approaches* BETTY) What ails you, Betty? Your mama's dead and buried.

Betty.
I'll fly to Mama. Let me fly! (*She raises her arms as though to fly, and streaks for the window, gets one leg out.*)

Abigail.
(*Pulling her away from the window*) I told him everything; he knows now, he knows everything we—

Betty.
You drank blood, Abby! You didn't tell him that!

Abigail.
Betty, you never say that again! You will never—

Betty.
You did, you did! You drank a charm to kill John Proctor's wife! You drank a charm to kill Goody Proctor!

Abigail.
(*Smashes her across the face*) Shut it! Now shut it!

Betty.
(*Collapsing on the bed*) Mama! Mama! (*She dissolves into sobs.*)

Abigail.
Now look you. All of you. We danced. And Tituba conjured Ruth Putnam's dead sisters. And that is all. And mark this. Let either of you breathe a word, or the edge of a word, about the other things, and I will come to you in the black of some terrible night and I will bring a pointy reckoning that will shudder you. And you know I can do it; I saw Indians smash my dear parents' heads on the pillow next to mine, and I have seen some reddish work done at night, and I can make you wish you had never seen the sun go down! (*She goes to* BETTY *and roughly sits her up*) Now, you—sit up and stop this!

(*But* BETTY *collapses in her hands and lies inert on the bed.*)

Mary Warren.
(*With hysterical fright*) What's got her? (ABIGAIL *stares in fright at* BETTY.) Abby, she's going to die! It's a sin to conjure, and we—

Abigail.
(*Starting for* MARY) I say shut it, Mary Warren!

from
THE DIARY OF ANNE FRANK
by Frances Goodrich and Albert Hackett

Act I, scene 2
ANNE, PETER

This play is adapted from the diary kept by Anne Frank as she and her family hid from the Nazis in Amsterdam, Holland, during World War II. In 1942 eight Jews—the Franks, the Van Daans and Dr. Dussel, a dentist—sought asylum in the attic of a warehouse belonging to Mr. Frank's firm. These hunted people lived together for two years, depending for food and necessities on four former employees of Mr. Frank. Anne began her diary at the age of 13, and has given the world a tender, beautiful document of a girl growing up and of the human spirit under terrible adversity. The attic hiding place was discovered in 1944 and its inhabitants were sent to concentration camps. In the next few months, they all died except for Otto Frank who was freed in 1945 by the Russians. When Amsterdam was liberated, he returned and was given the diary that Miep, one of their benefactors when they were hiding, had saved.

The following scene is from the beginning of the play when Anne is just getting acquainted with the Van Daans' son, Peter, who is seventeen. Anne is lively, friendly, almost excited about this new adventure of hiding. Peter is a quiet, unhappy boy.

Anne.
  What's your cat's name?
Peter.
  Mouschi.
Anne.
  Mouschi! Mouschi! Mouschi! (*She picks up the cat,*

walking away with it. To PETER) I love cats. I have
one . . . a darling little cat. But they made me leave her
behind. I left some food and a note for the neighbors to
take care of her . . . I'm going to miss her terribly.
What is yours? A him or a her?

Peter.
He's a tom. He doesn't like strangers.

(*He takes the cat from her, putting it back in its
carrier.*)

Anne.
(*Unabashed*) Then I'll have to stop being a stranger,
won't I? Is he fixed?

Peter.
(*Startled*) Huh?

Anne.
Did you have him fixed?

Peter.
No.

Anne.
Oh, you ought to have him fixed—to keep him from—
you know, fighting. Where did you go to school?

Peter.
Jewish Secondary.

Anne.
But that's where Margot and I go! I never saw you
around.

Peter.
I used to see you . . . sometimes . . .

Anne.
You did?

Peter.
. . . In the school yard. You were always in the middle of
a bunch of kids. (*He takes a penknife from his pocket.*)

Anne.
Why didn't you ever come over?

Peter.
I'm sort of a lone wolf. (*He starts to rip off his Star of
David.*)

Anne.
What are you doing?

Peter.
Taking it off.

Anne.
But you can't do that. They'll arrest you if you go out
without your star. (*He tosses his knife on the table.*)

Peter.
Who's going out?

Anne.
Why, of course! You're right! Of course, we don't need them any more. (*She picks up his knife and starts to take her star off.*) I wonder what our friends will think when we don't show up today?

Peter.
I didn't have any dates with anyone.

Anne.
Oh, I did, I had a date with Jopie this afternoon to go and play ping-pong at her house. Do you know Jopie de Waal?

Peter.
No.

Anne.
Jopie's my best friend. I wonder what she'll think when she telephones and there's no answer? . . . Probably she'll go over to the house . . . I wonder what she'll think . . . we left everything as if we'd suddenly been called away . . . breakfast dishes in the sink . . . beds not made. . . . (*As she pulls off her star the cloth underneath shows clearly the color and form of the star.*) Look! It's still there!(PETER *goes over to the stove with his star.*) What're you going to do with yours?

Peter.
Burn it.

Anne.
(*She starts to throw hers in, and cannot.*) It's funny, I can't throw mine away. I don't know why.

Peter.
You can't throw . . . ? Something they branded you with . . . ? That they made you wear so they could spit on you?

Anne.
I know. I know. But after all, it *is* the Star of David, isn't it?

from
THE DIARY OF ANNE FRANK
By Frances Goodrich and Albert Hackett

Act II, scene 2
ANNE, PETER

This next scene from the play takes place after the
Franks and their friends have been in hiding for a long
time and the fears and frictions of people living together
continually in a confined place is taking its toll. Peter's
parents are constantly arguing and Anne is having difficulty in her relationship to her mother. The two young
people are finding understanding and solace in each other's
company. The following scene in Peter's room is a young
love scene—Anne's first kiss.

Anne.
Aren't they awful? Aren't they impossible? Treating us
as if we're still in the nursery.
  (*She sits on the cot.* PETER *gets a bottle of pop and
  two glasses.*)
Peter.
Don't let it bother you. It doesn't bother me.
Anne.
I suppose you can't really blame them . . . they think
back to what *they* were like at our age. They don't realize
how much advanced we are . . . when I think what
wonderful discussions we've had! . . . Oh, I forgot. I
was going to bring you some more pictures.
Peter.
Oh, these are fine, thanks.
Anne.
Don't you want some more? Miep just brought me some
new ones.

103

Peter.

Maybe later. (*He gives her a glass of pop and, taking some for himself, sits down facing her.*)

Anne.

(*Looking up at one of the photographs*) I remember when I got that . . . I won it. I bet Jopie that I could eat five ice cream cones. We'd all been playing ping-pong . . . we used to have heavenly times . . . we'd finish up with ice cream at the Delphi, or the Oasis, where Jews were allowed . . . there'd always be a lot of boys . . . we'd laugh and joke . . . I'd like to go back to it for a few days or a week. But after that I know I'd be bored to death. I think more seriously about life now. I want to be a journalist . . . or something. I love to write. What do you want to do?

Peter.

I thought I might go off some place . . . work on a farm or something . . . some job that doesn't take much brains.

Anne.

You shoudn't talk that way. You've got the most awful inferiority complex.

Peter.

I know I'm not smart.

Anne.

That isn't true. You're much better than I am in dozens of things . . . arithmetic and algebra and . . . well, you're a million times better than I am in algebra. (*With sudden directness*) You like Margot, don't you? Right from the start you liked her, liked her much better than me.

Peter.

(*Uncomfortably*) Oh, I don't know.

Anne.

It's all right. Everyone feels that way. Margot's so good. She's sweet and bright and beautiful and I'm not.

Peter.

I wouldn't say that.

Anne.

Oh, no, I'm not. I know that. I know quite well that I'm not a beauty. I never have been and never shall be.

Peter.

I don't agree at all. I think you're pretty.

Anne.

That's not true!

Peter.

And another thing. You've changed . . . from at first, I mean.

Anne.

I have?

Peter.

I used to think you were awful noisy.

Anne.

And what do you think now, Peter? How have I changed?

Peter.

Well . . . er . . . you're . . . quieter.

Anne.

I'm glad you don't just hate me.

Peter.

I never said that.

Anne.

I bet when you get out of here you'll never think of me again.

Peter.

That's crazy.

Anne.

When you get back with all of your friends, you're going to say . . . now what did I ever see in that Mrs. Quack Quack?

Peter.

I haven't got any friends.

Anne.

Oh, Peter, of course you have. Everyone has friends.

Peter.

Not me, I don't want any. I get along all right without them.

Anne.

Does that mean you can get along without me? I think of myself as your friend.

Peter.

No. If they were all like you, it'd be different. (*He takes the glasses and the bottle and puts them away. There is a second's silence and then Anne speaks, hesitantly, shyly.*)

Anne.

Peter, did you ever kiss a girl?

Peter.

Yes. Once.

Anne.

(*To cover her feelings*) That picture's crooked. (*Peter*

goes over, straightening the photograph) Was she pretty?

Peter.
Huh?

Anne.
The girl that you kissed.

Peter.
I don't know. I was blindfolded. It was at a party. One of those kissing games.

Anne.
(*Relieved*) Oh, I don't suppose that really counts, does it?

Peter.
It didn't with me.

Anne.
I've been kissed twice. Once a man I'd never seen before kissed me on the cheek when he picked me up off the ice and I was crying. And the other was Mr. Kopphuis, a friend of Father's who kissed my hand. You wouldn't say those counted, would you?

Peter.
I wouldn't say so.

Anne.
I know almost for certain that Margot would never kiss anyone unless she was engaged to them. And I'm sure too that Mother never touched a man before Pim. But I don't know . . . things are so different now . . . what do you think? Do you think a girl shouldn't kiss anyone except if she's engaged or something? It's so hard to try to think what to do, when here we are with the whole world falling around our ears and you think . . . well . . . you don't know what's going to happen tomorrow and . . . what do you think?

Peter.
I suppose it'd depend on the girl. Some girls, anything they do's wrong. But others . . . well . . . it wouldn't necessarily be wrong with them. I've always thought that when two people—
(*The carillon starts to ring nine o'clock*)

Anne.
Nine o'clock. I have to go.

Peter.
That's right.

Anne.
(*Without moving*) Good night. (*There is a second's*

pause. Then PETER *gets up and moves towards the door.*)

Peter.
You won't let them stop you coming?

Anne.
No. (*She rises and starts for the door.*) Sometime I might bring my diary. There are so many things in it that I want to talk over with you. There's a lot about you.

Peter.
What kind of things?

Anne.
I wouldn't want you to see some of it. I thought you were a nothing, just the way you thought about me.

Peter.
Did you change your mind, the way I changed my mind about you?

Anne.
Well . . . you'll see . . . (*For a second* ANNE *stands looking up at* PETER, *longing for him to kiss her. As he makes no move, she turns away. Then suddenly* PETER *grabs her awkwardly in his arms, kissing her on the cheek.* ANNE *walks out, dazed.*)

from
THE DIARY OF ANNE FRANK
By Frances Goodrich and Albert Hackett

Act II, scene 4
ANNE, PETER

In this scene Anne is trying to comfort Peter in his room
where he has rushed in despair over an argument between
his parents. Anne now shows a developing maturity and
wisdom in trying to understand what it is that is happening to them and to the world. The scene can also be played
as a monologue for a girl.

Anne.
Look, Peter, the sky. (*She looks up through skylight*)
What a lovely, lovely day! Aren't the clouds beautiful?
You know what I do when it seems as if I couldn't stand
being cooped up for one more minute? I *think* myself
out. I think myself on a walk in the park where I used
to go with Pim. Where the jonquils and the crocus and
the violets grow down the slopes. You know the most
wonderful thing about *thinking* yourself out? You can
have it any way you like. You can have roses and violets
and chrysanthemums all blooming at the same time . . .
it's funny . . . I used to take it all for granted . . . and
now I've gone crazy about everything to do with nature.
Haven't you?

Peter.
I've just gone crazy. I think if something doesn't happen
soon . . . if we don't get out of here . . . I can't stand
much more of it!

Anne.
(*Softly*) I wish you had a religion, Peter.

Peter.
No, thanks! Not me!

Anne.
Oh, I don't mean you have to be Orthodox . . . or believe
in heaven and hell and purgatory and things . . . I just
mean some religion . . . it doesn't matter what. Just to
believe in something! When I think of all that's out
there . . . the trees . . . and flowers . . . and seagulls . . .
when I think of the dearness of you, Peter . . . and the
goodness of the people we know . . . Mr. Kraler, Miep,
Dirk, the vegetable man, all risking their lives for us
every day . . . when I think of these good things, I'm
not afraid any more . . . I find myself, and God, and
I . . .

(PETER *interrupts, getting up and walking away.*)

Peter.
That's fine! But when I begin to think I get mad! Look at
us, hiding out for two years. Not able to move! Caught
here like . . . waiting for them to come and get us . . . and
all for what?

Anne.
(*Going to him*) We're not the only people that've had
to suffer. There've always been people that've had to . . .
sometimes one race . . . sometimes another . . . and
yet. . . .

Peter.
That doesn't make me feel any better!

Anne.
I know it's terrible, trying to have any faith . . . when
people are doing such horrible . . . but you know what
I sometimes think? I think the world may be going through
a phase, the way I was with Mother. It'll pass, maybe
not for hundreds of years, but some day . . . I still believe, in spite of everything, that people are really good
at heart.

Peter.
I want to see something now . . . not a thousand years
from now. (*He goes over, sitting down again on the cot.*)

Anne.
But, Peter, if you'd only look at it as part of a great
pattern . . . that we're just a little minute in life . . . (*She
breaks off*) Listen to us, going at each other like a
couple of stupid grownups! Look at the sky now. Isn't
it lovely? (*She holds out her hand to him.* PETER *takes
it and rises, standing with her at the window looking*

out, his arms around her) Some day, when we're outside again I'm going to . . . (*She breaks off as she hears the sound of a car, its brakes squealing as it comes to a sudden stop.*)

from
THE DARK AT THE TOP OF THE STAIRS
by William Inge

Act III
REENIE, SONNY

The entire play takes place in the living room of the
Floods' house in a small Oklahoma town in the early
1920's. The action centers around the problems of Rubin
Flood, a seemingly robust and strong-willed man, his family
and some of their friends and relatives. As they talk,
argue and become reconciled, it becomes apparent that
they all have their own "dark at the top of the stairs"
of which they are frightened. Though there is sadness and
futility in some of the lives portrayed, Rubin, his wife
Cora, and their two children, Reenie and Sonny, begin
to come to grips with their fears.

In the following scene from the end of the play, Reenie,
16, and Sonny, 10, are able to reach out to each other
after years of childish bickering. Reenie's first date has
ended tragically; Sammy, her escort, has committed suicide.
The only factor that keeps her from total depression is her
father's return home after leaving because of an argument
with her mother. In this scene, Sonny attempts to deal
with his strong feelings for his mother as he begins to
assert independence. Rubin and Cora have just left the
room.

A few stage directions that involve Cora looking at the
children are deleted. They are marked by asterisks.

Sonny.
  They always want to be alone.
Reenie.
  All married people do, crazy.

111

(SONNY *impulsively sticks out his tongue at her. But she ignores him, picking up one of the favors, a reminder of* SAMMY, *and fondling it tenderly.* SONNY *begins to feel regret.*)

Sonny.
I'm sorry I made a face at you, Reenie.

Reenie.
(*Sobbing softly*) Go on and make as many faces as you like. I'm not going to fight with you any more.

Sonny.
Don't cry, Reenie.

Reenie.
I didn't know Sammy had even remembered the favors until I started to go. Then I went to find my coat, and there they were, sticking out of my pocket. At the very moment he was putting them there . . . he must have had in mind doing what he did.

Sonny.
(*With a burst of new generosity*) You! You keep the favors, Reenie.

Reenie.
He promised them to *you.*

Sonny.
Just the same . . . *you* keep them, Reenie.

Reenie.
Do you mean it?

Sonny.
Yes.

Reenie.
You never were thoughtful like this . . . before.

* * *

Sonny.
Reenie, do you want to go to the movie tonight? It's Mae Murray in *Fascination,* and there's an *Our Gang Comedy* first.

Reenie.
I don't feel I should.

Sonny.
When I feel bad, I just *have* to go to the movies. I just *have* to.

Reenie.
I was supposed to go to the library tonight.

Sonny.
Please go with me, Reenie. Please.

Reenie.
Do you really want me?

Sonny.
Yes, Reenie. Yes.

Reenie.
Where would you get the money to take *me*, Sonny? I have to pay adult admission. It's thirty-five cents.

Sonny.
I've got all the money we'll need.

* * *

(*He runs for his piggy bank . . .*)

Reenie.
Sonny! Mother told you you had to save that money.

Sonny.
I don't care. She's not going to boss me for the rest of my life. It's *my* money, and I've got a right to spend it. (*With an heroic gesture of defiance, he throws the piggy bank smashing against the fireplace, its pieces scattering on the floor.*)

Reenie.
Sonny!

Sonny.
(*Finding his five-dollar bill in the rubble*) And we'll have enough for popcorn, too, and for ice cream afterwards at the Royal Candy Kitchen.

* * *

Reenie.
I feel very proud to be treated by my little brother.

Sonny.
Let's hurry. The comedy starts at seven o'clock and I don't want to miss it.

Reenie.
We can stay for the second show if we miss the comedy.

Sonny.
Oh, I want to stay for the second show, anyway. I always see the comedy twice.

from
FIVE FINGER EXERCISE
by Peter Shaffer

Act I, scene 1
CLIVE, PAMELA, WALTER

Peter Shaffer, in his first play, has written a brilliant
metaphor of a five finger exercise, in this tightly-knit drama
of interpersonal relationships. Four of the people involved
are members of the Harrington family; Stanley, the father,
a successful self-made business man who seems incapable
of understanding anything but the hard "facts" of life;
his wife, Louise, clinging to a ridiculous image of culture
and refinement; their sensitive son, Clive, 19, who is caught
between their two conflicting sets of values and is in turn
frustrated and unable to make decisions; and their daughter
Pamela, 14, a precocious and frivolous young lady. The
fifth person is Walter, the young German the Harringtons
have just engaged as a tutor, who inadvertently becomes
the catalyst that forces all of them to confront each other
and then themselves in a painful and explosive climax.

The following scene takes place in the living room of
the Harringtons' summer cottage in Suffolk, England. One
of the rare light-hearted moments of the play, it too, has
overtones of the prevailing unhappiness of the characters.
Louise and Walter have just left the room, Louise having
extracted a promise from Walter to play the piano for
her. Clive is alone in the room when Pamela comes to the
door. She studies her brother for a few seconds and then
knocks at the door.

Pamela.
   (*In a coy, exaggerated voice*) General . . . General Harrington.

114

Clive.
(*Old Soldier's voice*) Eh? What's that? (*The following dialogue is conducted in these voices.*)

Pamela.
May I come in?

Clive.
Well, if it's not little Daphne! Spike me cannon! How very kind of you to call. Come in, me dear. Don't be afraid.

Pamela.
Thank you. (*She minces into the room.*)

Clive.
And how are you, eh? Eh?

Pamela.
Fine, thank you. And how's the—(*Whispers*)—you know what?

Clive.
(*Normal voice*) Do I?

Pamela.
(*Normal voice*) Gout.

Clive.
Ah. (*General's voice*) Oh, it comes and goes, y'know. Comes and goes.

Pamela.
(*Daphne's voice again, gushing.*) I think it's wonderful of you to take it so well. I'm sure I'd be complaining all the time. I'm a real silly-billy about pain.

Clive.
Nonsense, me dear. Lord, though, how yer remind me of yer dear mother. Hair just like hers. Yellow as a cornflower, I always used to say.

Pamela.
(*Normal voice*) There's something wrong about that.

Clive.
(*Normal voice*) Is there? What?

Pamela.
Cornflowers are blue.

Clive.
Well, your mother certainly didn't have blue hair.

Pamela.
(*Archly*) That's all you know . . . anyway, you've got to test my history.

Clive.
(*Beckoning*) Your ribbon.
   (*Automatically she goes to him for it to be tied. He*

sits on the couch: she kneels beside him. The sound of piano music from the music room.)

Pamela.
(*Listening*) He's the best, isn't he?

Clive.
Just about.

Pamela.
Oh, you can tell. I knew just as soon as he came in the door. (*They listen for a moment.*)

Clive.
How d'you get on together?

Pamela.
Oh, we simply adore each other.

Clive.
Is he going to teach you anything?

Pamela.
Everything, my dear. Just wait and see, I'll be the most erudine girl for my age in London.

Clive.
Dite.

Pamela.
What?

Clive.
Eru*dite*. Well, supposing we make a start. (PAMELA *hands over her list.* CLIVE *studies it earnestly for a moment.*) Which was the most uncertain dynasty in Europe?

Pamela.
I haven't the faintest.

Clive.
(*As if reading*) The Perhapsburgs.

Pamela.
Who?

Clive.
The Perhapsburgs.

Pamela.
Now, Clive, really—

Clive.
(*Enthusiastically*) I don't know much about them yet, but I'm working on it. I'll have them fixed by the end of the week. So far there's just Thomas the Tentative—a successor of Doubting Thomas, of course—and Vladimir—the Vague.

Pamela.
That's marvellous! How about a woman?

Clive.
By all means.

Pamela.
Dorothea.

Clive.
Nice.

Pamela.
Dorothea the—the Downright.

Clive.
But that's just the opposite. There's nothing Perhaps about her.

Pamela.
Well, she could be the black sheep of the family.

Clive.
We'll see . . . now. (*He consults the list.*) Pay attention. Who was known as the Crying Cavalier?

Pamela.
(*Protesting*) No, Clive, seriously—I've really got to—

Clive.
Answer me. Who?

Pamela.
I don't know.

Clive.
Who was the Unknown Civilian?

Pamela.
I don't know.

Clive.
Who was the Curable Romantic?

Pamela.
I don't know. I don't know . . . ! (*She throws herself at* CLIVE. *The music stops.*)

Clive.
Really, you are the most impossibly ignorant child . . . (*Struggling with her happily*) Hepcat! Hepcat!

Pamela.
(*Springing away from* CLIVE) Tell me a story!

Clive.
Sweet or sour?

Pamela.
Sour.

Clive.
All right. Once upon a time there was a little girl who lived all by herself in a prison.

Pamela.
Why? What had she done?

Clive.
Nothing: that's the whole point. They took away all her clothes and made her wear blankets instead.
(WALTER *enters from the kitchen.*)

Walter.
Mrs. Harrington was asking for her handbag.

Pamela.
Here it is. (*Takes handbag from armchair and hands it to* WALTER.) Stay with us. Clive's telling me a story.

Walter.
A story? About history?

Pamela.
About a prison.

Clive.
(*Showing off to* WALTER.) Yes, it's going to be brilliant! All Gothic darkness and calamities. It's called the "Black Hole of East Suffolk". (*Mock grave*) Sit down and I'll unfold.

Walter.
No, not now. Your mother is waiting. Excuse me. (*He goes back into the kitchen.*)
(CLIVE *stares after* WALTER. *His gaiety leaves him.*)

Pamela.
What's wrong?

Clive.
Nothing. (*In an everyday voice, almost brusque.*) Come on. Let's get on with your history.

from
THE SOUND OF MUSIC
Book by Howard Lindsay and Russell Crouse, Music by
Richard Rodgers and Lyrics by Oscar Hammerstein II

Act I, scene 6
LIESL, ROLF

This musical, suggested by the story of the Von Trapp
Family Singers, takes place in Austria before World War
II, and despite its music and sentimentality has political
undertones. Maria, a postulant at Nonnberg Abbey, has
been sent to be a governess for the seven motherless children of Captain von Trapp. The Captain, a stern father
and former naval hero, now finds himself opposing the
Germans. He eventually is forced to flee his beloved
homeland, but not before he marries Maria.

This short scene takes place outside his villa in the
evening. Liesl, the oldest daughter of sixteen, is secretly
meeting Rolf, a young boy from the village. Rolf's pro-
German attitude comes through in his bearing and speech
despite the young tenderness of the scene. By the end of
the play, Rolf has become a dedicated Nazi but his feelings
for Liesl aid in helping the von Trapps escape.

Liesl.
  Good night, Rolf.
Rolf.
  (*Walking on with his bicycle*) Liesl!
Liesl.
  (*Going to him*) Yes?
Rolf.
  You don't have to say good night this early just because
  your father's home—
Liesl.
  How did you know my father was home?
119

Rolf.
Oh, I have a way of knowing things.

Liesl.
You're wonderful.

Rolf.
(*Resting the bicycle on its stand*) Oh, no, I'm not—really.

Liesl.
Oh, yes you are. I mean—how did you know two days ago that you would be here at just this time tonight with a telegram for Franz?

Rolf.
Every year on this date he always gets a birthday telegram from his sister.

Liesl.
You see—you *are* wonderful.

Rolf.
Can I come again tomorrow night?

Liesl.
(*Sitting on the bench*) Rolf, you can't be sure you're going to have a telegram to deliver here tomorrow night.

Rolf.
(*Sitting beside her*) I could come here by mistake—with a telegram for Colonel Schneider. He's here from Berlin. He's staying with the Gauleiter but I— (*Suddenly concerned*) No one's supposed to know he's here. Don't you tell your father.

Liesl.
Why not?

Rolf.
Well, your father's pretty Austrian.

Liesl.
We're all Austrian.

Rolf.
Some people think we ought to be German. They're pretty mad at those who don't think so. They're getting ready to—well, let's hope your father doesn't get into any trouble. (*He goes to his bicycle.*)

Liesl.
(*Rising*) Don't worry about Father. He was decorated for bravery.

Rolf.
I know. I don't worry about him. The only one I worry about is his daughter.

Liesl.
  (*Standing behind the bench*) Me? Why? (*Rolf gestures to her to stand on the bench. She does and he studies her.*)
Rolf.
  How old are you, Liesl?
Liesl.
  Sixteen—What's wrong with that?
  (*They kiss, break away in confusion, and* ROLF *jumps on his bicycle and rides off.* LIESL *shouts with joy and runs off in the opposite direction.*)
                    Blackout

from
THE BEAUTIFUL PEOPLE
by William Saroyan

Act I, scene 2
OWEN, AGNES

This is a play about a family of eccentrics, living vaguely
beyond the law, avoiding the realities of the world, but
creating a gentle, beautiful life for themselves. In an old
house on Red Rock Hill, near Quintara Woods in the
Sunset District of San Francisco live Jonah Webster, a
"sort-of" philosopher; his son Owen, 15, a poet and
scientist; and his daughter, Agnes, 17, "St. Agnes of the
Mice," whom mice love so much they gather flowers to
spell her name.

In this scene Owen is asleep on his back in the window
seat. Small flowers on the floor spell the name Agnes. His
sister enters the living room and looks at her sleeping
brother. Then she sees a mousetrap set by Owen in the
middle of the floor, picks it up and throws it in the fireplace. One stage direction that involves Jonah has been
deleted and is marked by asterisks.

Agnes.
You've got no right. (*She stands near* OWEN.) Owen.
(*She shakes him.*)

Owen.
(*In his sleep*) Is that you, Saint?

Agnes.
Wake up, Owen. Wake up. (*Crosses to piano.* OWEN
sits up.)

Owen.
(*Quickly, as he wakes*) What's the matter? (OWEN
shakes his head and opens his eyes, then smiles foolishly.)
Oh hello, Saint. I thought it was you. (*Stretches sleepily,*

122

suddenly notices the flowers spelling her name on the ground and leaps. Crossing down Center) Hey, Saint— look! (*He points dramatically, going to the flowers.*) A-g-n-e-s. Agnes, St. Agnes, the Little Sister of the Mice. (*He turns to his sister, smiling foolishly. Her face is troubled.*) What's the matter?

Agnes.
(*Quietly by piano*) You ought to be ashamed.

Owen.
(*Innocently*) Why?

Agnes.
(*Crossing up* Right *by archway*) How could you put a trap out when they're so full of sorrow?

Owen.
I didn't know they were full of sorrow. What are they full of sorrow about?

Agnes.
One's lost.

Owen.
(*Snaps his fingers*) *That's* why one of them didn't come out. (*Pause, reflecting*) *Sure,* but after she *left,* one of them came out.

Agnes.
(*Sadly*) After *who* left?

Owen.
We had a visitor. An old lady. I wanted to entertain her, so I put the trap out. (*Goes up to her*) What's the matter?

Agnes.
(*Softly*) I met a man. (*Very softly and sadly*) Well, a boy.

Owen.
Well, what's the matter? Are you sorry you hit him?

Agnes.
I didn't hit him (*Softly. Crosses to chair down* Right. *Sits*) We just walked and talked. That's all.

Owen.
Ah, what's the matter?

Agnes.
I like him. (*Slowly*) He's not nearly what I thought I'd find, but I like him.

Owen.
Well, that's fine. It's nice to like somebody. *Anybody.* (AGNES *puts her hands over her eyes*) Hey! What are you bawling about?

Agnes.
I *like* him.

Owen.
(*Very much interested. On one knee*) Is that the way it makes you feel?

Agnes.
(*Slowly*) It makes you feel sick, like a whole world sick, and nothing to do about it, but to like him, more and more with every breath you take. All we did was walk and talk. (*Her hands on the sides of her chair, solemnly*) We didn't even talk *sense*. I came home feeling pity for everything. Not love—*pity*.

Owen.
(*Rises and as he touches her on the arm lovingly.*) Ah, Saint. Don't feel bad. Look at your name—in flowers.
(*Crosses below table*) I told the old lady about them, but she didn't believe me. Are you sure he's *lost*?

Agnes.
He's been gone a week.

Owen.
Where'd he go?

Agnes.
He went to St. Anne's.

Owen.
(*Angrily*) St. Anne's? Well, it's a nice state of affairs when one of our mice gets caught in a church trap and we can even *set* a trap in our own house.

Agnes.
What the church is pleased to do about mice is no affair of ours. (*Rises*) Owen? (*Pause*)

Owen.
(*Objecting. Crossing left.*) How am I going to find a mouse in a church?

Agnes.
Just go there and look around. He may not be caught, he may be lost—trapped in some small room. (*Leans on table. Faces front*)

Owen.
Are you sure that's what it's all about?

Agnes.
(*Down* Center *of table*) Yes, I am. They're all crying.

Owen.
(*As he tries to balance the chair on his head.*) Well, let 'em cry. What'd they expect—fun? Things end. They

change. They spoil. They're hurt. Or destroyed. (*He lowers chair to floor.*) Accidents happen. Without these things, there could be no—no felicity. (*Holds chair with one hand*) You ought to know that. Eventually even a tree ends. One at a time, each of them ends, but there are always *trees*. And that's the reason: because eventually each of them ends. If you're going to teach them things, teach them *everything*. I suppose it's an improvement for them to be crying over *one* mouse that's dead or lost, but sooner or later everybody's got to know that death is with us from the first breath we take. (*Sits; riding chair; facing front*) Are they crying *hard*?

Agnes.
(*Simply*) Yes, they are.

Owen.
I guess he's *dead*.

* * *

Agnes.
Maybe he isn't. Maybe he's only hungry and weak—caught in a room he can't get out of. Please hurry, Owen.

Owen.
(*Crosses to door* Left *and gets ready to leave*) All right. If he's alive and in the church, I'll find him. I'll bring him home.

from
TEA AND SYMPATHY
By Robert Anderson

Act II
TOM, AL

In this sensitive play set in a boy's boarding school in
New England, Laura, the new wife of the headmaster,
has befriended a young, shy boy, Tom. In their loneliness,
they have established a gentle, close relationship. During
the course of the play, because of an innocent incident
with a teacher at the school, Tom is considered a homo-
sexual. The harassment that follows causes a great deal
of agony to Tom and sends reverberations throughout the
school.

In the following scene Tom is sitting on the bed in his
room with his head in his hands. He has just discovered
that his roommate, Al, has signed to live in a different
dormitory for the next term. Al comes to the door and
stands there a few seconds.

Al.
(Outside TOM's bedroom door) Tom? (TOM moves
quietly away from door.) Tom? (He opens the door.)
Hey.
Tom.
I was sleeping.
Al.
Standing up, huh? (TOM turns away.) You want to be
alone?
Tom.
No. You want to look [at that woman nursing her baby
again?] Go ahead. (He indicates the window.)
Al.
No, I don't want to look. I . . . (He looks at TOM, not

126

knowing how to begin. He stalls . . . smiling) Nice tie
you got there.

Tom.

(Starts to undo tie) Yeah, it's yours. You want it?

Al.

No. Why? I can only wear one tie at a time. (TOM *leaves
it hanging around his neck. After an awkward pause)*
I . . . uh . . .

Tom.

I guess I don't need to ask you what's the matter?

Al.

It's been rough today, huh?

Tom.

Yeah. *(He turns away, very upset. He's been holding
it in . . . but here's his closest friend asking him to open
up.)* Jesus Christ! (AL *doesn't know what to say. He goes
to* TOM's *bureau and picks up his hairbrush, gives his
hair a few brushes.)* Anybody talk to you?

Al.

Sure. You know they would.

Tom.

What do they say?

Al.

(Yanks his tie off) Hell, I don't know.

Tom.

I went to a meeting of the dance committee. I'm no
longer on the dance committee. Said that since I'd backed
out of playing the girl part in the play, I didn't show the
proper spirit. That's what they *said* was the reason.

Al.

(Loud) Why the hell don't you do something about it?

Tom.

(Yelling back) About what?

Al.

About what they're saying.

Tom.

What the hell can I do?

Al.

Geez, you could. . . . *(He suddenly wonders what* TOM
could do.) I don't know.

Tom.

I tried to pass it off. Christ, you can't pass it off. You
know, when I went into the showers today after my
tennis match, everyone who was in there, grabbed a
towel and . . . and . . . walked out.

Al.
They're stupid. Just a bunch of stupid bastards. (*He leaves the room.*)

Tom.
(*Following him into sitting room.*) Goddamn it, the awful thing I found myself . . . Jesus, I don't know . . . I found myself self-conscious about things I've been doing for years. Dressing, undressing . . . I keep my eyes on the floor. (*Re-enters his own room*) Geez, if I even look at a guy that doesn't have any clothes on, I'm afraid someone's gonna say something, or . . . Jesus, I don't know.

Al.
(*During this, AL has come back into the room, unbuttoning his shirt, taking it off, etc. Suddenly he stops.*) What the hell am I doing? I've had a shower today. (*He tries to laugh.*)

Tom.
(*Looks at him a moment*) Undress in your own room, will ya? You don't want them talking about you too, do you?

Al.
No, I don't. (*He has said this very definitely and with meaning.*)

Tom.
(*Looks up at his tone of voice*) Of course you don't. (*He looks at AL a long time. He hardly dares say this.*) You . . . uh . . . you moving out?

Al.
(*Doesn't want to answer*) Look, Tom, do you mind if I try to help you?

Tom.
Hell, no. How?

Al.
I know this is gonna burn your tail, and I know it sounds stupid as hell. But it isn't stupid. It's the way people look at things. You could do a lot for yourself, just the way you talk and look.

Tom.
You mean to get my hair cut?

Al.
For one thing.

Tom.
Why the hell should a man with a crew cut look more manly than a guy who—

Al.
Look, I don't know the reasons for these things. It's just the way they are.

Tom.
(*Looking at himself in bureau mirror*) I tried a crew cut a coupla times. I haven't got that kind of hair, or that kind of head. (*After a moment*) Sorry, I didn't mean to yell at you. Thanks for trying to help.

Al.
(*Finds a baseball on the radiator and throws it at* TOM. TOM *smiles, and throws it back.*) Look Tom, the way you walk . . .

Tom.
Oh, Jesus.

Al.
(*Flaring*) Look, I'm trying to help you.

Tom.
No one gave a goddamn about how I walked till last Saturday!

Al.
(*Starts to go*) Okay. Okay. Forget it. (*He goes out.*)

Tom.
(*Stands there a few moments, then slams the baseball into the bed and walks out after* AL *into sitting room*) Al?

Al.
(*Off*) Yeah?

Tom.
Tell me about how I walk.

Al.
(*In the sitting room*) Go ahead, walk!

Tom.
(*Walks back into the bedroom.* AL *follows him, wiping his face on a towel and watching* TOM *walk. After he has walked a bit*) Now I'm not going to be able to walk any more. Everything I been doing all my life makes me look like a fairy.

Al.
Go on.

Tom.
All right, now I'm walking. Tell me.

Al.
Tom, I don't know. You walk sort of light.

Tom.
Light? (*He looks at himself take a step.*)

Al.
Yeah.

Tom.
Show me.

Al.
No, I can't do it.

Tom.
Okay, you walk. Let me watch you. I never noticed how you walked. (*AL stands there for a moment, never having realized before how difficult it could be to walk if you think about it. Finally he walks.*) Do it again.

Al.
If you go telling any of the guys about this. . . .

Tom.
Do you think I would? . . . (*AL walks again.*) That's a good walk. I'll try to copy it. (*He tries to copy the walk, but never succeeds in taking even a step.*) Do you really think that's gonna make any difference?

Al.
I dunno.

Tom.
Not now it won't. Thanks anyway.

Al.
(*Comes and sits on bed beside TOM. Puts his arm around TOM's shoulder and thinks this thing out*) Look, Tom . . . you've been in on a lot of bull sessions. You heard the guys talking about stopping over in Boston on the way home . . . getting girls . . . you know.

Tom.
Sure. What about it?

Al.
You're not going to the dance Saturday night?

Tom.
No, not now.

Al.
You know Ellie Martin. The gal who waits on table down at the soda joint?

Tom.
Yeah. What about her?

Al.
You've heard the guys talking about her.

Tom.
Come on, come on.

Al.
Why don't you drop in on Ellie Saturday night?

Tom.
What do you mean?

Al.
Hell, do you want me to draw a picture?

Tom.
(*With disgust*) Ellie Martin?

Al.
Okay. I know she's a dog, but. . . .

Tom.
So what good's that going to do? I get caught there, I get thrown out of school.

Al.
No one ever gets caught. Sunday morning people'd hear about it . . . not the Dean. . . . I mean the fellows. Hell, Ellie tells and tells and tells . . . boy, you'd be made!

Tom.
Are you kidding?

Al.
No.

Tom.
(*With disgust*) Ellie Martin!

Al.
(*After a long pause*) Look, I've said so much already, I might as well be a complete bastard. . . . You ever been with a woman?

Tom.
What do you think?

Al.
I don't think you have.

Tom.
So?

Al.
You want to know something?

Tom.
What?

Al.
Neither have I. But if you tell the guys, I'll murder you.

Tom.
All those stories you told. . . .

Al.
Okay. I'll be sorry I told you.

Tom.
Then why don't you go see Ellie Martin Saturday night?

Al.
Why the hell should I?

Tom.
You mean you don't have to prove anything?

Al.
Aw, forget it. It's probably a lousy idea anyway. (*He starts out.*)

Tom.
Yeah.

Al.
(*Stops*) Look, about next—(*Stops*)

Tom.
Next year? Yes?

Al.
Hap Hudson's asked me to come to his house. He's got a single there. A lot of the fellows from the team are over there, and . . . well. . . . (*He doesn't look at* TOM.)

Tom.
Sure, sure. . . . I understand.

Al.
Sorry I didn't tell you till now, after we'd made our plans. But I didn't know. I mean, I just found out about the . . . the opening.

Tom.
I understand!

Al.
(*Looks up at last. He hates himself but he's done it, and it's a load off his chest.*) See ya. (*He starts to go.*)

Tom.
(*As* AL *gets to door*) Al. . . . (AL *stops and looks back. Taking tie from around his neck*) Here.

Al.
(*Looks at tie, embarrassed*) I said wear it. Keep it.

Tom.
It's yours.

Al.
(*Looks at the tie for a long time, then without taking it, goes through the door*) See ya. (TOM *folds the tie neatly, dazed, then seeing what he's doing, he throws it viciously in the direction of the bureau, and turns and stares out the window . . .*)

from
EASTER
by August Strindberg

Act I
BENJAMIN, ELEONORA

This play was written in 1901 when Strindberg was on
the threshold of realism. However, his tortured life, his
passionate emotions and his soaring imagination gave even
his realistic plays a kind of mysticism and haunting beauty.
More than a half-century later, this play seems somewhat
heavy-handed and symbolic rather than realistic, but Strindberg was among the first playwrights to deal with the
distorted relationships between people resulting from the
quest for and absence of love. The play is rarely performed
in its entirety but it contains several beautiful scenes.

The play takes place in Sweden in 1901 at the beginning of the Easter holidays. Elis Heyst is a teacher, trying
to carry on his life in a small town where his father has
created a scandal by embezzling funds. His sixteen-year-old
sister, Eleonora, has been sent away to a mental institution. In spite of the deadly air of gloom around him, Elis
is engaged to a lovely young woman, Kristina, and is
trying to put the pieces of his life together. The spirit of
Easter and the Resurrection pervades the play and Eleonora
is very much a Christ figure.

In the following scene in the Heyst living room, Benjamin, a young student of Elis', is trying to study for his
Latin examinations. Eleonora, who has run away from
the institution, enters and is carrying an Easter lily in
a pot. She puts it down, looks at Benjamin and then sits
down at the table opposite him.

Some of the dialogue of the scene has been slightly
revised for the benefit of the actors who would undoubtedly
find the translated words dated, cumbersome and difficult
to speak with truth.

Eleonora.
(*Pointing at the Easter lily*) Do you know what *that* is?

Benjamin.
(*Childishly*) Don't I just! It's an Easter lily. . . . But who are you?

Eleonora.
(*Kindly, sadly*) Yes, who are you?

Benjamin.
(*As before*) My name is Benjamin and I am boarding here with Mrs. Heyst.

Eleonora.
I see! My name is Eleonora and I am a daughter of the house.

Benjamin.
How strange that they have never talked of you!

Eleonora.
One does not talk of the dead!

Benjamin.
The dead!

Eleonora.
I am dead in the eyes of the world, for I have done something very wicked.

Benjamin.
You!

Eleonora.
Yes, I have embezzled trustee funds—that didn't matter so much, for ill-gotten gains never thrive—but that my old father was blamed for it and put in prison; that, you see, can never be forgiven.

Benjamin.
How strangely and beautifully you speak—and it never occurred to me that my inheritance might have been ill-gotten?

Eleonora.
One should not hold men in bondage, but set them free.

Benjamin.
Well, you have delivered me from the mortification of having been cheated.

Eleonora.
So you are under a guardian. . . .

Benjamin.
Yes, one whose sad lot it is to do time for the crime of these poor people.

Eleonora.
You shouldn't use such hard words; if you do, I'll leave

you; I am so delicate that I cannot bear anything hard!
And yet you suffer all this for my sake?

Benjamin.
For your father's sake.

Eleonora.
That's all one, for he and I are one and the same person.
(*Pause*) I have been very ill . . . why are you so sad?

Benjamin.
I have had a bad set-back!

Eleonora.
Need you be sorry about that? "The rod and the chastisement teach wisdom, and he who hateth chastisement shall
die." What was your set-back?

Benjamin.
I failed in my Latin examination, thought I felt so sure.

Eleonora.
I see, I see, you were so sure, so sure that you could have
wagered you would pass.

Benjamin.
Yes, and I did.

Eleonora.
I thought so! Well, you see, it happened because you were
too sure.

Benjamin.
Do you think that was the reason?

Eleonora.
Of course it was! Pride goes before a fall!

Benjamin.
I'll remember that next time.

Eleonora.
That's right. And the sacrifice which pleases God is a
contrite heart.

Benjamin.
Are you religious?

Eleonora.
Yes, I'm religious!

Benjamin.
I mean really?

Eleonora.
And so do I. So much so that if you were to speak ill of
God, my benefactor, I wouldn't sit at the same table with
you.

Benjamin.
How old are you?

Eleonora.
For me there is neither time nor space. I am everywhere,
and of all times; I am in father's prison and in my
brother's schoolroom. I am in my mother's kitchen and in
my sister's shop far away in America. When things go
well for my sister and she sells much, I feel her joy, and
when things go badly with her I suffer, but I suffer most
when she does wrong. Benjamin, you are called Benjamin
because you are the youngest of my friends . . . Yes,
everybody is my friend . . . Will you let me mother you,
and I will suffer for you too?

Benjamin.
I don't really understand what you say, but I do seem to
grasp the meaning of your thoughts. And now I'll do anything you like.

Eleonora.
Will you stop judging people, to begin with, even those
who are convicted criminals? . . .

Benjamin.
Yes, but I must have a reason. You see, I have studied
philosophy!

Eleonora.
Oh, have you? Then you must help me to explain these
words of a great philosopher. He says: "Whosoever hateth
the righteous becometh himself a wrong-doer!"

Benjamin.
By all the laws of logic that means that we may be fore-
doomed to commit crime . . .

Eleonora.
And that crime itself is a punishment.

Benjamin.
That's really deep! One would almost think it was Kant or
Schopenhauer.

Eleonora.
I don't know!

Benjamin.
In what book have you read it?

Eleonora.
In the Scriptures!

Benjamin.
Really? Are there things like that in them?

Eleonora.
What an ignorant, neglected child you are! If only I
might bring you up!

Benjamin.
You dear little thing!

Eleonora.
But surely there's no evil in you! Rather, you look good . . . What's the name of your Latin teacher?

Benjamin.
Mr. Algren!

Eleonora.
I shall remember that! . . . Oh! Now my father is in great sorrow! They are cruel to him. (*Stands still, as if listening*) Do you hear the singing in the telephone wires . . . it is the hard words which the beautiful soft, red copper cannot bear . . . when people speak ill of each other on the telephone, the copper wails and accuses—(*Severely*) —and every word is written in the book . . . and at the end of time comes the reckoning!

Benjamin.
How severe you are!

Eleonora.
Not I! Not I! How could I dare to be? I? I? (*She goes to the stove, opens the door and takes out some torn pieces of white note-paper. BENJAMIN gets up and looks at the paper, which ELEONORA pieces together on the dining table.*)

Eleonora.
(*Aside*) That people can be so careless as to leave their secrets in stoves . . . Wherever I come I go straight to the stove! But I never put anything to a wrong use, I should never dare, for then evil would befall me! . . . Now what's this? (*Reads*)

Benjamin.
It's Mr. Peter writing to make an appointment with Kristina . . . I've expected this for some time!

Eleonora.
(*Covers the paper with her hand*) Oh! You! What have you expected? Tell me, you evil creature, who thinks only evil! This letter will bring nothing but good, for I know Kristina, who is going to be my sister-in-law. And this meeting will avert a misfortune from my brother Elis . . . Will you promise me to say nothing, Benjamin?

Benjamin.
I don't think I should dare to mention it!

Eleonora.

How wrong of people to have secrets . . . They think themselves wise, and are fools! . . . But what business had I to go there?

Benjamin.

Why are you so inquisitive?

Eleonora.

It's part of my illness, you see, that I must know everything, or else I get restless . . .

Benjamin.

Know everything?

Eleonora.

It is a fault I can't overcome. But anyhow I know what the starlings say.

Benjamin.

They can't talk, can they?

Eleonora.

Have you never heard of starlings that have been taught to talk?

Benjamin.

Oh yes! those that have been taught!

Eleonora.

Consequently starlings can learn to talk! Now there are some that teach themselves, they are autodidacts . . . they sit and listen, of course, without our knowing it, and then they say it after us. I heard two of them sitting talking in the walnut tree just now as I came along.

Benjamin.

How funny you are! But what did they say then?

Eleonora.

Well! "Peter" said the one, "Judas" said the other—"ditto" said the first, "fy, fy, fy" said the second. But have you noticed that the nightingales only sing in the garden of the deaf and dumb over there?

Benjamin.

Yes, everybody knows that! Why is it?

Eleonora.

Because those who have hearing do not hear what the nightingales say; but the deaf and dumb do hear it!

Benjamin.

Tell me some more fairy tales!

Eleonora.

I will, if you are a good boy!

Benjamin.

How do you mean, good?

Eleonora.

Well, you must never take up my words and never say at
one time you said this, at another time you said that. . . .
Shall I tell you something more about the birds? There is
an evil bird called the rat buzzard. As you can hear by its
name, it lives on rats. But because it is a bad bird it
has difficulty in catching the rats, and therefore it can
only say one word, which sounds like the "miaow" of a
cat. When the bird says "miaow" the rats run and hide,
but the buzzard itself doesn't understand what it says . . .
and must often go without food because it is a nasty
bird! Do you want to hear any more? Or shall I talk about
the flowers? Do you know, when I was ill I had to take a
drug made of henbane, which has the power of turning
the eye into a magnifying glass . . . But with belladonna
we see everything smaller . . . Well, anyhow, now I can
see further than most other people and I can see the stars
in broad daylight!

Benjamin.

But then the stars are not even up?

Eleonora.

How funny you are! The stars are always up . . . Don't
you know; and now I sit facing north and I see Cassiopeia
looking like a "w" placed in the middle of the Milky
Way . . . Can you see it?

Benjamin.

No, I can't.

Eleonora.

Notice that one person can see what another cannot see
. . . therefore don't be so sure of *your* eyes. . . . Now I will
tell you about this flower on the table. It is an Easter lily
which has its home in Switzerland . . . it has a cup which
has drunk the sunlight, that is why it is yellow and soothes
pain. . . . I passed a flower shop just now and saw it, and
wanted to give it to my brother Elis. When I tried to get
in through the door I found it locked . . . for this is confirmation day . . . but I had to get the flower, so I took
out my keys and tried them, and what do you think! My
latch key fitted . . . I went in . . . Well, do you understand the silent language of flowers? Every perfume expresses ever so many thoughts, and these thoughts
crowded in upon me; and with my magnifying eye I

looked into their workshops, which nobody has seen. And they spoke to me of the sorrows which the thoughtless gardener had caused them—I don't say cruel, for he was only careless . . . Then I put one krona and my card on the counter, took the flower, and went out.

Benjamin.
How careless! Supposing they miss the flower and don't find the money?

Eleonora.
That's true! You're right!

Benjamin.
A coin may disappear, and if they only find your card, you are lost!

Eleonora.
But surely nobody would believe that I meant to take anything?

Benjamin.
(*Looks fixedly at her*) No?

Eleonora.
(*Looks at him and rises*) Oh! I know what you mean! Like father, like child! How careless I was! How! . . . Well! What must be must be! (*Sits down*) So be it, then!

Benjamin.
Can't it be put right?

Eleonora.
Sh! Talk about something else! . . . Mr. Algren! . . . Poor Elis! Poor all of us! But it is Easter, and we must suffer. And isn't there a concert tomorrow? And aren't they playing Haydn's Sieben Worte des Ersosers, "Mother, behold thy son"! (*She covers her face with her hands and weeps.*)

Benjamin.
What was the illness you had?

Eleonora.
My illness is not "sickness unto death" but in honor of God! "I awaited good and evil came; I awaited the light and the darkness came!" . . . What kind of childhood had you, Benjamin?

Benjamin.
I don't know. Dismal! And yours?

Eleonora.
I never had one. I was born old . . . I knew of everything

when I was born, and when I learned things it was only
like remembering. I knew of people's . . . thoughtlessness
and foolishness when I was four years old, and that's why
people were unkind to me!

Benjamin.
Everything you say I seem to have thought too!

Eleonora.
And probably you have! What made you think that my
coin would disappear in the flower shop?

Benjamin.
Because the unpleasant must always happen!

Eleonora.
So you've noticed that too! Hush! somebody is coming!
(*Looks towards the back.*) I hear . . . it's Elis! Oh! I am
so happy! . . . my only friend on earth! (*Her face becomes clouded.*) But . . . he doesn't expect me! And he
will not be pleased to see me. No, he won't . . . certainly
not!—Benjamin, Benjamin, put on a friendly face and be
cheerful when my poor brother comes. I shall go so that
you may prepare him for my coming. But no hard words,
they hurt me so; do you hear! Give me your hand! (BEN-
JAMIN *offers his hand.* ELEONORA *kisses the top of
his head.*) That's it! Now you are my little brother! God
bless you and keep you! (*She goes out to the left and in
passing pats the sleeve of* ELIS' *overcoat affectionately.*)
Poor Elis!

from
EASTER
by August Strindberg

Act II
ELEONORA, BENJAMIN

Eleonora, who has just come home for the Easter holidays
from a mental institution, has stolen an Easter lily from the
florist as a gift to her brother. It has just been discovered
and she is confronted with the realization of what she has
done. (For further background on the play, see the preceding scene.)

Eleonora.
God help us, what have I done now? The police are look-
ing for the culprit, and if I am discovered . . . poor
Mother, and Elis!
Benjamin.
(*Childishly*) Eleonora, you must say that I did it!
Eleonora.
You, can you bear another's guilt, you child?
Benjamin.
That's easily done, when you know you are innocent!
Eleonora.
But we must never tell stories!
Benjamin.
Then let me telephone to the flower shop and tell them
how it happened!
Eleonora.
No, I have done wrong, and I must be punished with
fears. I have awakened their fear of thieves, and fear will
overtake *me.*
Benjamin.
But if the police come . . .
Eleonora.
Yes, that is hard . . . but then it is meant so!—Oh! that

142

this day were over! (*Goes to the pendulum clock on the dining table and moves the hands*) . . . Dear little clock, move a little faster! Tick, tick, ping, ping, ping. Now it's eight! Ping, ping, ping, now it's nine!—ten!—eleven!— twelve! Now it's Easter Eve! Now the sun will soon be rising and then we will write on the Easter eggs! I shall write this; "Behold, Satan hath desired to get possession of thee, that he may sift thee like wheat, but I have prayed for thee" . . .

Benjamin.
Why do you hurt yourself so, Eleonora?

Eleonora.
I, hurt! O Benjamin. Think of all the flowers that have opened out, the anemones and snowdrops which have been standing out in the snow all day and all night, shivering in the darkness! Think what they must suffer! The night's the worst, of course, when it is dark, and they get frightened of the darkness and can't run away . . . and they stand and wait for the daylight. Everything, everything suffers, but the flowers most of all; and the birds of passage that have come from the south! Where will they sleep tonight?

Benjamin.
(*Childishly*) They'll sit in hollow trees, of course!

Eleonora.
Surely there are not so many hollow trees that all of them can get in! I have only seen two hollow trees in the parks hereabouts, and there the owls live, as you know, and they kill the small birds. . . . Poor Elis, who thinks that Kristina has left him, but I know she will come back!

Benjamin.
If you know it, why didn't you say so?

Eleonora.
Because Elis must suffer, everybody must suffer today, on Good Friday, that they may remember Christ's suffering on the cross. (*The sound of a police whistle is heard from the street. Starts*) What was that?

Benjamin.
(*Rises*) Don't you know?

Eleonora.
No!

Benjamin.

It was the police!

Eleonora.

Oh! Yes, it sounded like that when they came to arrest Father . . . and then I fell ill! And now they are coming to take me!

Benjamin.

(*Places himself facing the door, in front of* ELEONORA)

No, they must not take you! I will defend you, Eleonora!

Eleonora.

That's noble, Benjamin, but you mustn't. . . .

Benjamin.

(*Looks through the curtains*) There are two of them! (ELEONORA *tries to push* BENJAMIN *away, but he resists gently.*) Not you, Eleonora, for then—I don't want to live any longer!

Eleonora.

Go and sit down in that chair! Child, go and sit down! (BENJAMIN *obeys reluctantly.*) (*Looks out from behind the curtains without concealing herself.*) It was only two boys! Oh! we of little faith! Do you think God is so cruel, when I have done no evil, and only acted thoughtlessly . . . I deserved it! Why did I doubt?

Benjamin.

But tomorrow someone will come and take the furniture.

Eleonora.

Let him come! And we shall have to go! Leave everything . . . all the old furniture which Father collected for us, and which I have seen since I was a little child! Yes, we ought not to possess anything which binds us to earth. Out on the stony paths and wander with wounded feet, for the road leads upwards, that is why it is toilsome. . . .

Benjamin.

Now you are tormenting yourself again, Eleonora!

Eleonora.

Let me! But do you know what I find most difficult to part from? It's the clock over there! It was there when I was born and it has measured out all my hours and days . . . (*She lifts the clock from the table.*) Listen! it beats like a heart—just like a heart . . . and it stopped at the hour when grandfather died, for we had it even then! Good-bye, little clock, stop soon again. . . . Do you know, it used to go fast when we had bad luck in the house, just as if it wished to get over it—for *our* sakes, of course! But when things were bright it went slow so that we might enjoy them longer. That was a kind clock! But we also had an unkind one . . . and that's why it must hang in the kitchen now! It could not bear music, for as soon as Elis played the piano it began to strike. We all noticed it, not only I. And that is why it must stay in the kitchen, for it was naughty! But Lina doesn't like it either, for it's not quiet at night and she can't cook eggs by it . . . they are always hard-boiled, Lina says. Now you are laughing!

Benjamin.
What else can I do?

Eleonora.
You are a nice boy, Benjamin, but you must be serious! Think of the birch standing behind the mirror there!

Benjamin.
But you talk so funnily that I can't help smiling. . . . And why should we always cry?

Eleonora.
If we are not to weep in the vale of sorrow where then shall we weep?

Benjamin.
Hm!

Eleonora.
You would like to smile all day long, and that is why you've suffered! And I only like you when you are serious. Remember that!

Benjamin.
Do you think we shall come through all this, Eleonora?

Eleonora.
Yes, most of it will clear away as soon as Good Friday is over, but not everything. Today the birch, tomorrow Easter eggs! Today snow, tomorrow thaw! Today death, tomorrow resurrection!

Benjamin.
How wise you are!

Eleonora.
Yes, already I feel that it is clearing up for fine weather outside; that the snow is melting . . . It smells of melting snow even in here . . . and tomorrow the violets will open against the south wall! The clouds have lifted, I can feel

it in my breathing. . . . Oh! I know so well when the heavens are open! Go and draw the curtains, Benjamin. I want God to see us! (BENJAMIN *rises and obeys; the moonlight falls into the room.*)

Eleonora.

Look at the full moon! It is the Easter moon! and the sun is still there you know, though the light comes from the moon!

from
EASTER
by August Strindberg

Act III
BENJAMIN, ELEONORA

In this last act of the play, there is a waiting, a fore-
shadowing, as the fate of the Heyst family hangs in the
balance. Along with the now known theft of the flower
by Eleonora is a re-opening of the old embezzlement
scandal. Eleonora, 16, is talking to a student of her
brother's. For further background, see the first scene from
the play.

Benjamin.
Why are they all asking for the newspaper?
Eleonora.
Don't you understand? There will be in it. . . .
Benjamin.
What?
Eleonora.
Everything! the burglary, the police, and more too . . .

* * *

Eleonora.
The paper, the paper . . . Oh! if only the printing
works had been smashed up, or if only the editor had
fallen ill . . . no, I mustn't say that! Do you know, I was
with Father last night . . .
Benjamin.
Last night?
Eleonora.
Yes, in my sleep . . . and I was in America with my
sister . . . The day before yesterday she sold 30 dollars
worth and had 5 dollars profit.
Benjamin.
Is that much or little? Eh?

Eleonora.
It's quite a lot!

Benjamin.
(*Slyly*) Did you meet anyone you knew in the market?

Eleonora.
Why do you ask? You mustn't be artful with me, Benjamin. You want to know my secrets, but you shan't!

Benjamin.
And you think you can learn mine that way!

Eleonora.
Do you hear how the telephone wires are singing? Now the newspaper is out, and people are telephoning! "Have you read it?" "Yes, I've read it!" "Isn't it awful?"

Benjamin.
What is awful?

Eleonora.
Everything! Life is altogether awful. But we must be content with our lot as it is! . . . Think of Elis and Kristina, they are fond of each other and they hate each other all the same, so that the thermometer falls when they pass through the room! She was at the concert last night, and today they don't speak to each other. . . . Why? Why?

Benjamin.
Because your brother is jealous!

Eleonora.
Don't say that word! Besides, what do you know about jealousy, except that it is a disease, and consequently a punishment. We should not touch evil, lest it defile us! Just look at Elis; haven't you noticed how changed he is since he began to read those papers . . .

Benjamin.
About the trial?

Eleonora.
Yes! Doesn't it seem as if all the evil in them had penetrated into his soul and were now shining out from his face and his eyes . . . Kristina feels it, and in order that the evil shan't touch her, she puts on armor of ice! Oh! those papers! . . . If only I might burn them. Malice and falsehood and revenge radiate from them. So, my child, you must keep yourself free from evil and impurity, both your lips and your heart!

Benjamin.
How clearly you see everything!

Eleonora.
Do you know what is in store for me if Elis and the others get to know that it was I who bought the daffodil in such an odd way?

Benjamin.
What will they do to you?

Eleonora.
I shall be sent back . . . where I came from, where the sun doesn't shine; where the walls are white and bare like a bathroom; where you only hear weeping and waiting; where I have wasted a year of my life.

Benjamin.
Where do you mean?

Eleonora.
Where you are tortured worse than in prison, where the accursed dwell, where unrest has its home and where despair watches night and day, and whence no one returns!

Benjamin.
Worse than prison, where do you mean?

Eleonora.
In prison one is condemned, but there one is damned! In prison one is examined and listened to! Over there one is not listened to . . . Poor daffodil, the cause of it all. I meant so well and acted so wrongly.

Benjamin.
But why don't you go to the shopkeeper and say, "This is how it happened." You are just like a lamb being led to the slaughter.

Eleonora.
When it knows it must be slaughtered, it doesn't complain and does not try to run away. What else can it do?

from
OH DAD, POOR DAD, MOMMA'S HUNG YOU IN THE CLOSET AND I'M FEELIN' SO SAD
by Arthur L. Kopit

Scene III
JONATHAN, ROSALIE

This play, like the title itself, has sad undertones but is so uninhibited, so wild, so full of contradictions, surprises and exaggerations that there is a pungent comic quality to it. "Poor Dad" is the stuffed corpse of Mr. Rosepettle, kept in the bedroom closet of his widow, Madame Rosepettle. She has other necrophiliac tendencies as well for she takes great joy in growing carniverous plants and fish and disturbing lovers on the beach. Jonathan, her seventeen-year-old son, is an extremely pathetic emotional cripple. He never leaves the lavish suite he and his mother share in a hotel in the Caribbean but works on his stamp collection and views the world through a handmade telescope. Rosalie, about 19, a feminine little slut who works as a baby sitter in the area becomes curious about Jonathan and obtains a key to the Rosepettle suite.

The following scene takes place at night in the hotel room suite. Rosalie has let herself in with her key and is visiting Jonathan. Madame Rosepettle is out.

Rosalie.
There's something bothering you, isn't there? (*Pause. JONATHAN does not answer at first, but stares off into space frightened, bewildered.*)

Jonathan.
(*Weakly*) I never thought I'd see you again. I never thought I'd talk to you again. I never thought you'd come.

Rosalie.
Did you really think that?

Jonathan.
She told me she'd never let you visit me again. She said no one would *ever* visit me again. She told me I had seen enough.

Rosalie.
But I had a key made.

Jonathan.
She—she hates me.

Rosalie.
What?

Jonathan.
She doesn't let me do anything. She doesn't let me listen to the radio. She took the tube out of the television set. She doesn't let me use her phone. She makes me show her all my letters before I seal them. She doesn't—

Rosalie.
Letters? What letters are you talking about?

Jonathan.
Just—letters I write.

Rosalie.
To *whom*?

Jonathan.
To people.

Rosalie.
Other girls? Could they be to other girls by any chance?

Jonathan.
No. They're just to people. No people in particular. Just people in the phone book. Just names. So far I've covered all the "A's" and "B's" up to Barrera.

Rosalie.
What is it you say to them? Can you tell me what you say to them—or is it private? Jonathan, just what do you say to them!?

Jonathan.
Mostly I just ask them what they look like. (*Pause. Suddenly he starts to sob in a curious combination of laughter and tears.*) But I don't think she ever mails them. She reads them, then takes them out to mail. But I don't think she ever does. I'll bet she just throws them away. Well, if she's not going to mail them, why does she say she will? I—I could save the stamps.

Rosalie.
Guess why I had this key made.

Jonathan.

I'll bet she's never even mailed one. From Abandono to Barrera, not one.

Rosalie.

Do you know why I had this key made? Do you know why I'm wearing this new dress?

Jonathan.

She tells me I'm brilliant. She makes me read and re-read books no one's ever read. She smothers me with blankets at night in case of a storm. She tucks me in so tight I can't even get out till she comes and takes my blankets off.

Rosalie.

Try and guess why I'm all dressed up.

Jonathan.

She says she loves me. Every morning, before I even have a chance to open my eyes, there she is, leaning over my bed, breathing in my face and saying, "I love you, I love you."

Rosalie.

Jonathan, isn't my dress pretty?

Jonathan.

But I heard everything tonight. I heard it all when she didn't know I was here. (*He stares off into space, bewildered.*)

Rosalie.

What's the matter? (*He does not answer.*) Jonathan, what's the matter?

Jonathan.

But she must have known I was here. She *must* have known! I mean—where could I have gone? (*Pause*) But—if that's the case—*why did she let me hear?*

Rosalie.

Jonathan, I do wish you'd pay more attention to me. Here, look at my dress. You can even touch it if you like. Guess how many crinolines I have on. Guess why I'm wearing such a pretty, new dress. *Jonathan!*

Jonathan.

(*Distantly.*) Maybe—it didn't make any difference to her —whether I heard or not. (*He turns suddenly to her and hugs her closely. She lets him hold her, then she steps back and away from him. Her face looks strangely old and determined under her girlish powder and pinkness.*)

Rosalie.
Come with me.

Jonathan.
What?

Rosalie.
Leave and come with me.

Jonathan.
(*Fearfully*) Where?

Rosalie.
Anywhere.

Jonathan.
Wha'—wha'—what do you mean?

Rosalie.
I mean, let's leave. Let's run away. Far away. Tonight.
Both of us, together. Let's run and run. Far, far away.

Jonathan.
You—mean, leave?

Rosalie.
Yes. Leave.

Jonathan.
Just like that?

Rosalie.
Just like that.

Jonathan.
But—but—but—

Rosalie.
You want to leave, don't you?

Jonathan.
I—I don't—don't know. I—I—

Rosalie.
What about the time you told me how much you'd like
to go outside, how you'd love to walk by yourself, anywhere you wanted?

Jonathan.
I—I don't—know.

Rosalie.
Yes, you do. Come. Give me your hand. Stop trembling
so. Everything will be all right. Give me your hand
and come with me. Just through the door. Then we're
safe. Then we can run far away, somewhere where she'll
never find us. Come Jonathan. It's time to go.

Jonathan.
There are others you could take.

Rosalie.
But I don't love them. (*Pause*)

Jonathan.
You—you *love* me?

Rosalie.
Yes, Jonathan. I love you.

Jonathan.
Wha—wha—why?

Rosalie.
Because you watch me every night.

Jonathan.
Well—can't we stay here?

Rosalie.
No!

Jonathan.
Wha—wha—whhhhy?

Rosalie.
Because I want you alone. (JONATHAN *turns from her and begins to walk about the room in confusion.*) I want you, Jonathan. Do you understand what I said? *I want you for my husband.*

Jonathan.
I—I—can't, I mean, I—I want to go—go with you very much but I—I don't think—I can. I'm—sorry. (*He sits down and holds his head in his hands, sobbing quietly.*)

Rosalie.
What time will your mother be back?

Jonathan.
Na—not for a while.

Rosalie.
Are you sure?

Jonathan.
Ya—yes.

Rosalie.
Where is she?

Jonathan.
The usual place.

Rosalie.
What do you mean, "the usual place"?

Jonathan.
(*With a sad laugh*) The beach. (ROSALIE *looks at* JONATHAN *quizzically.*) She likes to look for people making love. Every night at midnight she walks down to the beach searching for people lying on blankets and making love. When she finds them she kicks sand in their faces and walks on. Sometimes it takes her as

much as three hours to chase everyone away. (ROSALIE *smiles slightly and walks toward the master bedroom. JONATHAN freezes in fear. She puts her hand on the door knob.*) WHAT ARE YOU DOING!? (*She smiles at him over her shoulder. She opens the door.*) STOP!! You can't go in there!!! STOP!!

Rosalie.
(*She opens the door completely and beckons him to come.*) Come.

Jonathan.
Close it. Quickly!

Rosalie.
Come, Jonathan. Let's go inside.

Jonathan.
Close the door!

Rosalie.
(*With a laugh*) You've never been in here, have you?

Jonathan.
NO. And you can't go in, either. No one can go in there but Mother. It's her room. Now close the door!

Rosalie.
(*She flicks on the light switch. No lights go on.*) What's wrong with the lights?

Jonathan.
There are none. Mother's in mourning. (ROSALIE WALKS *into the room and pulls the drapes off the windows. Weird colored lights stream in and illuminate the bedroom in wild, distorted, nightmarish shadows and lights. They blink on and off, on and off. It's all like some strange, macabre fun house in an insane amusement park. Even the furniture in the room seems peculiarly prominent. It almost seems to tilt over the bed. Still in the main room*) What have you done!? (ROSALIE *walks back to the door and smiles to him from within the master bedroom.*) What have you done?

Rosalie.
Come in, Jonathan.

Jonathan.
GET OUT OF THERE!

Rosalie.
Will you leave with me?

Jonathan.
I can't!

Rosalie.
But you want to, don't you?

Jonathan.
Yes, yes, I want to, but I told you—I—I—I can't. I can't! Do you understand? I can't! Now come out of there.

Rosalie.
Come in and get me.

Jonathan.
Rosalie, *please*.

Rosalie.
(*Bouncing on the bed.*) My, what a comfortable bed.

Jonathan.
GET OFF THE BED!!!

Rosalie.
What soft, fluffy pillows. I think I'll take a nap.

Jonathan.
Rosalie, *please listen to me*. Come out of there. You're not supposed to be in that room. Please come out. Rosalie, *please*.

Rosalie.
Will you leave with me if I do?

Jonathan.
Rosalie—? I'll—I'll show you my stamp collection if you'll promise to come out.

Rosalie.
Bring it in here.

Jonathan.
Will you come out then?

Rosalie.
Only if you bring it in here.

Jonathan.
But I'm not allowed to go in there.

Rosalie.
(*Poutingly*) Then I shan't come out!

Jonathan.
You've got to!

Rosalie.
Why?

Jonathan.
Mother will be back.

Rosalie.
She can sleep out there. (ROSALIE *yawns.*) I think I'll take a little nap. This bed is so comfortable. Really, Jonathan, you should come in and try it.

Jonathan.
MOTHER WILL BE BACK SOON!!

Rosalie.
Give her your room then if you don't want her to sleep
on the couch. I find it very nice in here. Good night.
(*Pause.*)

Jonathan.
If I come in, will you come out?

Rosalie.
If you don't come in I'll never come out.

Jonathan.
And if I do?

Rosalie.
Then I may.

Jonathan.
What if I bring my stamps in?

Rosalie.
Bring them and find out.

Jonathan.
(*He goes to the dresser and takes out the drawer of
stamps. Then he takes out the drawer of coins.*) I'm
bringing the coins too.

Rosalie.
How good you are, Jonathan.

Jonathan.
(*He takes a shelf full of books.*) My books, too. How's
that? I'll show you my books and my coins and my
stamps. I'll show you them all. Then will you leave?

Rosalie.
Perhaps. (*He carries them all into the bedroom and sets
them down next to the bed. He looks about fearfully.*)
What's wrong?

Jonathan.
I've never been in here before.

Rosalie.
It's nothing but a room. There's nothing to be afraid of.

Jonathan.
(*He looks about doubtfully.*) Well, let me show you my
stamps. I have one billion, five—

Rosalie.
Later, Jonathan. We'll have time. Let me show you
something first.

Jonathan.
What's that?

Rosalie.
You're trembling.

Jonathan.
What do you want to show me?

Rosalie.
There's nothing to be nervous about. Come. Sit down.

Jonathan.
What do you want to show me?

Rosalie.
I can't show you if you won't sit down.

Jonathan.
I don't want to sit down! (*She takes hold of his hand. He pulls it away.*)

Rosalie.
Jonathan!

Jonathan.
You're sitting on Mother's bed.

Rosalie.
Then let's pretend it's my bed.

Jonathan.
It's not your bed!

Rosalie.
Come, Jonathan. Sit down here next to me.

Jonathan.
We've got to get out of here. Mother might come.

Rosalie.
Don't worry. We've got plenty of time. The beach is full of lovers.

Jonathan.
How do you know?

Rosalie.
I checked before I came. (*Pause.*)

Jonathan.
Let—let me show you my coins.

Rosalie.
Why are you trembling so?

Jonathan.
Look, we've got to get out! Something terrible will happen if we don't.

Rosalie.
Then leave with me.

Jonathan.
The bedroom?

Rosalie.
The hotel. The island. Your mother. Leave with me, Jonathan. Leave with me now, before it's too late.

Jonathan.
I—I—I—

Rosalie.
I love you, Jonathan, and I won't give you up. I want you . . . all for myself. Not to share with your mother, but for me, alone—to love, to live with, to have children by. I want you, Jonathan. You, whose skin is softer and whiter than anyone's I've ever known. Whose voice is quiet and whose love is in every look of his eye. I want you, Jonathan, and I won't give you up. (*Short pause.*)

Jonathan.
(*Softly, weakly.*) What do you want me to do?

Rosalie.
Forget about your mother. Pretend she never existed and look at me. Look at my eyes, Jonathan; my mouth, my hands, my skirt, my legs. Look at me, Jonathan. Are you still afraid?

Jonathan.
I'm not afraid. (*She smiles and starts to unbutton her dress.*) What are you doing!? No!

Rosalie.
(*She continues to unbutton her dress.*) Your mother is strong, but I am stronger. (*She rises and her skirt falls about her feet. She stands in a slip and crinolines.*) I don't look so pink and girlish any more, do I? (*She laughs.*) But you want me anyhow. You're ashamed but you want me anyhow. It's written on your face. And I'm very glad. Because I want you. (*She takes off a crinoline.*)

Jonathan.
PUT IT ON! *Please*, put it back on!

Rosalie.
Come, Jonathan. (*She takes off another crinoline.*) Lie down. Let me loosen your shirt.

Jonathan.
NO . . . NO . . . NO! STOP! *Please*, stop! (*She takes her last crinoline off and reaches down to take off her socks. The lights outside blink weirdly. Wild, jagged music with a drum beating in the background is heard.*)

Rosalie.
Don't be afraid, Jonathan. Come. Lie down. Everything will be wonderful. (*She takes her socks off and lies down in her slip. She drops a strap over one shoulder and smiles.*)

Jonathan.
Get off my mother's bed!

Rosalie.
I want you Jonathan, all for my own. Come. The bed is soft. Lie here by my side. (*She reaches up and takes his hand. Meekly he sits down on the edge of the bed. The closet door swings open suddenly and the* CORPSE *of Albert Edward Robinson Rosepettle III tumbles forward stiffly and onto the bed, his stone-stiff arms falling across* ROSALIE's *legs, his head against her side.* JONATHAN, *too terrified to scream, puts his hand across his mouth and sinks down onto the bed, almost in a state of collapse. Outside the music screams.*) Who the hell is this!?

Jonathan.
It-it-it-it—it—it's—

Rosalie.
What a stupid place to keep a corpse. (*She pushes him back in the closet and shuts the door.*) Forget it, Jonathan. I put him back in the closet. Everything's fine again.

Jonathan.
It's—it's—it's my—my—my—

Rosalie.
(*Kneeling next to him on the bed and starting to unbutton his shirt.*) It's all right, Jonathan. It's all right. Sshh. Come. Let me take off your clothes.

Jonathan.
(*Still staring dumbly into space.*) It's—it's my—ffffather.

(*The closet door swings open again and the* CORPSE *falls out, this time his arms falling about* ROSALIE's *neck.* JONATHAN *almost swoons.*)

Rosalie.
Oh, for God's sake. (*She pushes him off the bed and onto the floor.*) Jonathan . . . ? LISTEN TO ME JONATHAN! STOP LOOKING AT HIM AND LOOK AT ME! (*He looks away from his father, fearfully, his mouth open in terror.*) I love you, Jonathan, and I want you *now*. Not later and not as partner with your mother but now and by myself. I want you, Jonathan, as my husband. I want you to lie with me, to sleep with me, to be with me, to kiss me and touch me, to live with me, *forever*. Stop looking at him! He's dead! Listen to me. I'm alive. I want you for my husband! Now help me take my slip off. Then you can look at my body and

touch me. Come, Jonathan. Lie down. I want you forever.

Jonathan.

Ma—mother was right! You do let men do anything they
want to you.

Rosalie.

Of course she was right! Did you really think I was that
sweet and pure? Everything she said was right. (*She
laughs.*) Behind the bushes and it's done. Here's the
money. Thanks. Come again. Hah-hah! Come again!
(*Short pause*) So what!? It's only you I love. They make
no difference.

Jonathan.

You're dirty! (*He tries to get up but can't, for his father
is lying in front of his feet.*)

Rosalie.

No, I'm not dirty. I'm full of love and womanly feelings.
I want children. Tons of them. I want a husband. Is
that dirty? Take off your clothes.

Jonathan.

NO!!

Rosalie.

Forget about your father. Drop your pants on top of
him, then you won't see his face. Forget about your
mother. She's gone. Forget them both and look at me.
Love is so beautiful, Jonathan. Come and let me love
you; tonight and forever. Come and let me keep you
mine. Mine to love when I want, mine to kiss when I
want, mine to have when I want. Mine. All mine. So
come, Jonathan. Come and close your eyes. It's better
that way. Close your eyes so you can't see. Close your
eyes and let me lie with you. Let me show you how
beautiful it is . . . love.

(*She lies back in bed and slowly starts to raise her
slip. JONATHAN stares at her legs in horror. Then,
suddenly, he seizes her crumpled skirt and throws it over
her face, and smothers her to death. At last he rises and,
picking up his box of stamps dumps the stamps over her
limp body. He does the same with his coins and finally,
his books, until at last she is buried. . . . Then, done, he
throws his hands over his eyes and turns to run.*)

from
ROMEO AND JULIET
by William Shakespeare

Act II, scene 2
ROMEO, JULIET

The following scene is probably the world's best known
and most popular love scene. Romeo has seen Juliet at
a ball at her father's house and has fallen in love instantly.
It is after they have met that each discovers that their
beloved is a member of an opposing family. Their two
families, the Montagues and the Capulets, have been feud-
ing for many years. However, this does not stop Romeo.
After the ball he leaves his friends and goes to the Capulet
garden where under Juliet's window he overhears her
confess to the stars that she loves him. For the moment,
there is love and beauty but eventually the hatred between
the two families destroys the young lovers.

(*Capulet's orchard.* ROMEO *advances from the wall.*)
Romeo.
He jests at scars that never felt a wound.
(*Juliet appears above at her window.*)
But soft! What light through yonder window breaks?
It is the east, and Juliet is the sun!
Arise, fair sun, and kill the envious moon,
Who is already sick and pale with grief
That thou, her maid, art far more fair than she.
Be not her maid, since she is envious;
Her vestal livery is but sick and green,
And none but fools do wear it; cast it off.
It is my lady, O, it is my love!
Oh, that she knew she were!
She speaks, yet she says nothing; what of that?

Her eye discourses, I will answer it.—
I am too bold, 'tis not to me she speaks.
Two of the fairest stars in all the heaven,
Having some business, do entreat her eyes
To twinkle in their spheres till they return.
What if her eyes were there, they in her head?
The brightness of her cheek would shame those stars,
As daylight doth a lamp; her eyes in heaven
Would through the airy region stream so bright
That birds would sing and think it were not night.
See, how she leans her cheek upon her hand!
O, that I were a glove upon that hand,
That I might touch that cheek!

Juliet.
                        Ay me!

Romeo.
                                She speaks!

O, speak again, bright angel! For thou art
As glorious to this night, being o'er my head,
As a winged messenger of heaven
Unto the white-upturned wond'ring eyes
Of mortals that fall back to gaze on him
When he bestrides the lazy-pacing clouds
And sails upon the bosom of the air.

Juliet.
O Romeo, Romeo, wherefore art thou Romeo?
Deny thy father and refuse thy name,
Or, if thou wilt not, be but sworn my love
And I'll no longer be a Capulet.

Romeo.
(*Aside*) Shall I hear more, or shall I speak at this?

Juliet.
'Tis but thy name that is my enemy.
Thou art thyself, though not a Montague.
What's a Montague? It is nor hand, nor foot,
Nor arm, nor face, nor any other part
Belonging to a man. Oh, be some other name!
What's in a name? That which we call a rose
By any other name would smell as sweet;
So Romeo would, were he not Romeo call'd,
Retain that dear perfection which he owes
Without that title. Romeo, doff thy name,

And for thy name, which is no part of thee,
Take all myself.

Romeo.
                         I take thee at thy word.
Call me but love, and I'll be new baptiz'd;
Henceforth I never will be Romeo.

Juliet.
What man art thou that, thus bescreen'd in night,
So stumblest on my counsel?

Romeo.
                              By a name
I know not how to tell thee who I am.
My name, dear saint, is hateful to myself,
Because it is an enemy to thee.
Had I it written, I would tear the word.

Juliet.
My ears have yet not drunk a hundred words
Of thy tongue's uttering, yet I know the sound.
Art thou not Romeo, and a Montague?

Romeo.
Neither, fair saint, if either thee dislike.

Juliet.
How cam'st thou hither, tell me, and wherefore?
The orchard walls are high and hard to climb,
And the place death, considering who thou art,
If any of my kinsmen find thee here.

Romeo.
With love's light wings did I o'erperch these walls;
For stony limits cannot hold love out.
And what love can do, that dares love attempt;
Therefore thy kinsmen are no stop to me.

Juliet.
If they do see thee, they will murder thee.

Romeo.
Alack, there lies more peril in thine eye
Than twenty of their swords. Look thou but sweet,
And I am proof against their enmity.

Juliet.
I would not for the world they saw thee here.

Romeo.
I have night's cloak to hide me from their eyes,
And but thou love me, let them find me here.
My life were better ended by their hate,

Than death prorogued, wanting of thy love.

Juliet.

By whose direction found'st thou out this place?

Romeo.

By Love, that first did prompt me to inquire.
He lent me counsel, and I lent him eyes.
I am no pilot; yet wert thou as far
As that vast shore washed with the farthest sea,
I would adventure for such merchandise.

Juliet.

Thou know'st the mask of night is on my face,
Else would a maiden blush bepaint my cheek
For that which thou has heard me speak tonight.
Fain would I dwell on form, fain, fain deny
What I have spoke; but farewell compliment!
Dost thou love me? I know thou wilt say "Ay,"
And I will take thy word. Yet if thou swear'st,
Thou mayst prove false. At lovers' perjuries,
They say, Jove laughs. O gentle Romeo,
If thou dost love, pronounce it faithfully,
Or if thou think'st I am too quickly won,
I'll frown and be perverse and say thee nay,—
So wilt thou woo: but else, not for the world.
In truth, fair Montague, I am too fond,
And therefore thou mayst think my 'haviour light;
But trust me, gentleman, I'll prove more true
Than those that have more cunning to be strange.
I should have been more strange, I must confess,
But that thou overheard'st ere I was ware,
My true love's passion; therefore pardon me,
And not impute this yielding to light love,
Which the dark night hath so discover'd.

Romeo.

Lady, by yonder blessed moon I vow,
That tips with silver all these fruit-tree tops—

Juliet.

O, swear not by the moon, th' inconstant moon,
That monthly changes in her circled orb,
Lest that thy love prove likewise variable.

Romeo.

What shall I swear by?

Juliet.

                 Do not swear at all.
Or, if thou wilt, swear by thy gracious self,
Which is the god of my idolatry,
And I'll believe thee.

Romeo.

                 If my heart's dear love—

Juliet.

Well, do not swear. Although I joy in thee,
I have no joy of this contract tonight;
It is too rash, too unadvis'd, too sudden,
Too like the lightning, which doth cease to be
Ere one càn say "It lightens." Sweet, good night!
This bud of love, by summer's ripening breath,
May prove a beauteous flower when next we meet.
Good night, good night! As sweet repose and rest
Come to thy heart as that within my breast!

Romeo.

O, wilt thou leave me so unsatisfied?

Juliet.

What satisfaction canst thou have tonight?

Romeo.

Th' exchange of thy love's faithful vow for mine.

Juliet.

I gave thee mine before thou didst request it;
And yet I would it were to give again.

Romeo.

Wouldst thou withdraw it? For what purpose, love?

Juliet.

But to be frank, and give it thee again.
And yet I wish but for the thing I have.
My bounty is as boundless as the sea,
My love as deep; the more I give to thee,
The more I have, for both are infinite.
(NURSE *calls within.*)
I hear some noise within. Dear love, adieu!
Anon, good nurse! Sweet Montague, be true.
Stay but a little, I will come again. (*Exit*)

Romeo.

O, blessed, blessed night! I am afeard,
Being in night, all this is but a dream,
Too flattering-sweet to be substantial.
     (*Re-enter* JULIET *above.*)

Juliet.
Three words, dear Romeo, and good night indeed.
If that thy bent of love be honorable,
Thy purpose marriage, send me word tomorrow,
By one that I'll procure to come to thee,
Where and what time thou wilt perform the rite;
And all my fortunes at thy foot I'll lay,
And follow thee my lord throughout the world.

Nurse.
(*Within*) Madam!

Juliet.
I come, anon.— But if thou meanst not well, I do beseech
thee—

Nurse.
(*Within*) Madam!

Juliet.
              By and by, I come:—
To cease thy suit, and leave me to my grief.
Tomorrow will I send.

Romeo.
                   So thrive my soul—

Juliet.
A thousand times good night! (*Exit*)

Romeo.
A thousand times the worse, to want thy light.
Love goes toward love, as schoolboys from their books,
But love from love, toward school with heavy looks.
    (*Retiring slowly.*)
    (*Re-enter* JULIET, *above.*)

Juliet.
Hist! Romeo, hist!—O, for a falconer's voice,
To lure this tassel-gentle back again!
Bondage is hoarse, and may not speak aloud,
Else would I tear the cave where Echo lies
And make her airy tongue more hoarse than mine
With repetition of my Romeo's name.

Romeo.
It is my soul that calls upon my name.
How silver-sweet sound lovers' tongues by night,
Like softest music to attending ears!

Juliet.
Romeo!

Romeo.
       My dear?

Juliet.

                    What o'clock tomorrow
Shall I send to thee?

Romeo.

                          By the hour of nine.

Juliet.

I will not fail; 'tis twenty years till then.
I have forgot why I did call thee back.

Romeo.

Let me stand here till thou remember it.

Juliet.

I shall forget, to have thee still stand there,
Rememb'ring how I love thy company.

Romeo.

And I'll still stay, to have thee still forget,
Forgetting any other home but this.

Juliet.

'Tis almost morning. I would have thee gone;—
And yet no farther than a wanton's bird,
Who lets it hop a little from her hand,
Like a poor prisoner in his twisted gyves,
And with a silk thread plucks it back again,
So loving-jealous of his liberty.

Romeo.

I would I were thy bird.

Juliet.

                      Sweet, so would I;
Yet I should kill thee with much cherishing.
Good night, good night! Parting is such sweet sorrow
That I shall say good night till it be morrow. (*Exit*)

Romeo.

Sleep dwell upon thine eyes, peace in thy breast!
Would I were sleep and peace, so sweet to rest!
Hence will I to my ghostly father's cell,
His help to crave and my dear hap to tell. (*Exit*)

from
WINTERSET
by Maxwell Anderson

Act I, scene 3
MIO, CARR, MIRIAMNE

Winterset is a play in verse, compelling and tragic. Maxwell
Anderson used his command of poetic language to tell
a story based on the Sacco and Vanzetti case of the nineteen twenties. However, the theme of abstract justice is
an enduring one and the play still speaks to us today.
Guilt, love, vengeance and dignity also play their roles
as the story unfolds and realism emerges through the
soaring language.

A man has been executed for a crime he did not commit
and his son, Mio, comes back to New York with a burn-
ing desire to right the wrong and clear his father's name.
Shortly after his arrival he is hunted down by Trock, the
man who actually committed the crime, and Shadow, his
henchman. The following scene takes place on a riverbank
under a bridgehead. Mio, 17, and his friend Carr, also
17, come around an adjacent tenement building. Miriamne,
a girl of 15, is crying in front of the entrance.

Carr.
 Thought you said you were never coming east again.
Mio.
 Yeah, but—I heard something changed my mind.
Carr.
 Same old business?
Mio.
 Yes. Just as soon not talk about it.
Carr.
 Where did you go from Portland?

169

Mio.
Fishing—I went fishing. God's truth.

Carr.
Right after I left?

Mio.
Fell in with a fisherman's family on the coast and went after the beautiful mackerel fish that swim in the beautiful sea. Family of Greeks—Aristides Marinos was his lovely name. He sang while he fished. Made the pea-green Pacific ring with his Greek chanties. Then I went to Hollywood High School for a while.

Carr.
I'll bet that's a seat of learning.

Mio.
It's the hind end of all wisdom. They kicked me out after a time.

Carr.
For cause?

Mio.
Because I had no permanent address, you see. That means nobody's paying school taxes for you, so out you go. (*To* MIRIAMNE) What's the matter, kid?

Miriamne.
Nothing. (*She looks up at him, and they pause for a moment.*) Nothing.

Mio.
I'm sorry.

Miriamne.
It's all right. (*She withdraws her eyes from his and goes out past him. He turns and looks after her.*)

Carr.
Control your chivalry.

Mio.
A pretty kid.

Carr.
A baby.

Mio.
Wait for me.

Carr.
Be a long wait? (MIO *steps swiftly out after* MIRIAMNE, *then returns.*) Yeah?

Mio.
She's gone.

Carr.
Think of that.

Mio.

No, but I mean—vanished. Presto—into nothing—prodigioso.

Carr.

Damn good thing, if you ask me. The homely ones are bad enough, but the lookers are fatal.

Mio.

You exaggerate, Carr.

Carr.

I doubt it.

Mio.

Well, let her go. This riverbank's loaded with typhus rats, too. Might as well die one death as another.

Carr.

They say chronic alcoholism is nice but expensive. You can always starve to death.

Mio.

Not always. I tried it. After the second day I walked thirty miles to Niagara Falls and made a tour of the plant to get the sample of shredded wheat biscuit on the way out.

Carr.

Last time I saw you you couldn't think of anything you wanted to do except curse God and pass out. Still feeling low?

Mio.

Not much different. (*He turns away, then comes back.*) Talk about the lost generation, I'm the only one fits that title. When the State executes your father, and your mother dies of grief, and you know damn well he was innocent, and the authorities of your hometown politely inform you they'd consider it a favor if you lived somewhere else—that cuts you off from the world—with a meat-axe.

Carr.

They asked you to move?

Mio.

It came to that.

Carr.

God, that was white of them.

Mio.

It probably gave them a headache just to see me after all that agitation. They knew as well as I did my father

never staged a holdup. Anyway, I've got a new interest
in life now.

Carr.
Yes—I saw her.

Mio.
I don't mean the skirt.— No, I got wind of something,
out west, some college professor investigating the trial
and turning up new evidence. Couldn't find anything he'd
written out there, so I beat it east and arrived on this
blessed island just in time to find the bums holing up in
the public library for the winter. I know now what the
unemployed have been doing since the depression started.
They've been catching up on their reading in the main
reference room. Man, what a stench! Maybe I stank, too,
but a hobo has the stench of ten because his shoes are
poor.

Carr.
Tennyson.

Mio.
Right. Jeez, I'm glad we met again! Never knew anybody
else that could track me through the driven snow of
Victorian literature.

Carr.
Now you're cribbing from some half-forgotten criticism
of Ben Jonson's Roman plagiarisms.

Mio.
Where did you get your education, sap?

Carr.
Not in the public library, sap. My father kept a news-
stand.

Mio.
Well, you're right again. (*There is a faint rumble of
thunder.*) What's that? Winter thunder?

Carr.
Or Mister God, beating on His little tocsin. Maybe an-
nouncing the advent of a new social order.

Mio.
Or maybe it's going to rain coffee and doughnuts.

Carr.
Or maybe it's going to rain.

Mio.
Seems more likely. (*Lowering his voice*) Anyhow, I
found Professor Hobhouse's discussion of the Romagna
case. I think he has something. It occurred to me I might

follow it up by doing a little sleuthing on my own account.

Carr.
Yes?

Mio.
I have done a little. And it leads me to somewhere in
that tenement house that backs up against the bridge.
That's how I happen to be here.

Carr.
They'll never let you get anywhere with it, Mio. I told
you that before.

Mio.
I know you did.

Carr.
The State can't afford to admit it was wrong, you see.
Not when there's been that much of a row kicked up
over it. So for all practical purposes the State was right
and your father robbed the payroll.

Mio.
There's still such a thing as evidence.

Carr.
It's something you can buy. In fact, at the moment I
don't think of anything you can't buy, including life,
honor, virtue, glory, public office, conjugal affection and
all kinds of justice, from the traffic court to the immortal
nine. Go out and make yourself a pot of money and you
can buy all the justice you want. Convictions obtained,
convictions averted. Lowest rates in years.

Mio.
I know all that.

Carr.
Sure.

Mio.
This thing didn't happen to you.
They've left you your name
and whatever place you can take. For my heritage
they've left me with one thing only, and that's to be
my father's voice crying up out of the earth
and quicklime where they stuck him. Electrocution
doesn't kill, you know. They eviscerate them
with a turn of the knife in the dissecting room.
The blood spurts out. The man was alive. Then into
the lime pit, leave no trace. Make it short shrift
and chemical dissolution. That's what they thought

of the man that was my father. Then my mother—
I tell you these county burials are swift and cheap
and run for profit! Out of the house
and into the ground, you wife of a dead dog. Wait,
here's some Romagna spawn left. Something crawls here—
something they called a son. Why couldn't he die
along with his mother? Well, ease him out of town,
ease him out, boys, and see you're not too gentle.
He might come back. And, by their own living Jesus,
I will go back and hang the carrion
around their necks that made it!
Maybe I can sleep then.
Or even live.

Carr.
You have to try it?

Mio.
Yes.
Yes. It won't let me alone. I've tried to live
and forget it—but I was birthmarked with hot iron
into the entrails. I've got to find out who did it
and make them see it till it scalds their eyes
and make them admit it till their tongues are blistered
with saying how black they lied!

from
WINTERSET
by Maxwell Anderson

Act I, scene 3
MIO, MIRIAMNE

This next scene is one of young love blooming amidst
squalor, hate, death and vengeance. A policeman has just
broken up a spontaneous street dance and party by inhabitants of this New York river slum area. Everyone
has drifted away except for Mio, 17, and Miriamne, 15.
He has seen her earlier and they have danced together
briefly. (For further introduction to the play, see the
preceding scene.)

Mio.
  Looks like rain.
  (*She is silent.*)
  You live around here?
  (*She nods gravely.*)
  I guess
  you thought I meant it—about waiting here to meet me.
  (*She nods again.*)
  I'd forgotten about it till I got that winter
  across the face. You'd better go inside.
  I'm not your kind. I'm nobody's kind but my own.
  I'm waiting for this to blow over.
  (*She rises.*)
  I lied. I meant it—
  I meant it when I said it—but there's too much black
  whirling inside me—for any girl to know.
  So go on in. You're somebody's angel child
  and they're waiting for you.

Miriamne.
Yes. I'll go. (*She turns.*)

Mio.
And tell them
when you get inside where it's warm,
and you love each other,
and mother comes to kiss her darling, tell them
to hang on to it while they can, believe while they can
it's a warm safe world, and Jesus finds his lambs
and carries them in his bosom.— I've seen some lambs
that Jesus missed. If they ever want the truth
tell them that nothing's guaranteed in this climate
except it gets cold in winter, nor on this earth
except you die sometime.
(*He turns away.*)

Miriamne.
I have no mother.
And my people are Jews.

Mio.
Then you know something about it.

Miriamne.
Yes.

Mio.
Do you have enough to eat?

Miriamne.
Not always.

Mio.
What do you believe in?

Miriamne.
Nothing.

Mio.
Why?

Miriamne.
How can one?

Mio.
It's easy if you're a fool. You see the words
in books. Honor, it says there, chivalry, freedom,
heroism, enduring love—and these
are words on paper. It's something to have them there.
You'll get them nowhere else.

Miriamne.
What hurts you?

Mio.
Just that.

You'll get them nowhere else.

Miriamne.
Why should you want them?

Mio.
I'm alone, that's why. You see those lights,
along the river, cutting across the rain—?
those are the hearths of Brooklyn, and up this way
the love-nests of Manhattan—they turn their points
like knives against me—outcast of the world,
snake in the streets.—I don't want a hand-out.
I sleep and eat.

Miriamne.
Do you want me to go with you?

Mio.
Where?

Miriamne.
Where you go. (*A pause. He goes nearer to her.*)

Mio.
Why, you goddamned little fool—
what made you say that?

Miriamne.
I don't know.

Mio.
If you have a home
stay in it. I ask for nothing. I've schooled myself
to ask for nothing, and take what I can get,
and get along. If I fell for you, that's my look-out,
and I'll starve it down.

Miriamne.
Wherever you go, I'd go.

Mio.
What do you know about loving?
How could you know?
Have you ever had a man?

Miriamne.
(*After a slight pause*)
No, but I know.
Tell me your name.

Mio.
Mio. What's yours?

Miriamne.
Miriamne.

Mio.
There's no such name.

Miriamne.
  But there's no such name as Mio!
  M.I.O. It's no name.

Mio.
  It's for Bartolomeo.

Miriamne.
  My mother's name was Miriam,
  so they called me Miriamne.

Mio.
  Meaning little Miriam?

Miriamne.
  Yes.

Mio.
  So now little Miriamne will go in
  and take up quietly where she dropped them all
  her small housewifely cares.— When I first saw you,
  not a half-hour ago, I heard myself saying,
  this is the face that launches ships for me—
  and if I owned a dream—yes, half a dream—
  we'd share it. But I have no dream. This earth
  came tumbling down from chaos, fire and rock,
  and bred up worms, blind worms that sting each other
  here in the dark. These blind worms of the earth
  took out my father—and killed him, and set a sign
  on me—the heir of the serpent—and he was a man
  such as men might be if the gods were men—
  but they killed him—
  as they'll kill all others like him
  till the sun cools down to the stabler molecules,
  yes, till men spin their tent-worm webs to the stars
  and what they think is done, even in the thinking,
  and they are the gods, and immortal, and constellations
  turn for them all like mill wheels—still as they are
  they will be, worms and blind. Enduring love,
  oh gods and worms, what mockery!—And yet
  I have blood enough in my veins. It goes like music,
  singing, because you're here. My body turns
  as if you were the sun, and warm. This men called love
  in happier times, before the Freudians taught us
  to blame it on the glands. Only go in
  before you breathe too much of my atmosphere
  and catch death from me.

Miriamne.
  I will take my hands
  and weave them to a little house, and there
  you shall keep a dream—

Mio.
  God knows I could use a dream
  and even a house.

Miriamne.
  You're laughing at me, Mio!

Mio.
  The worms are laughing.
  I tell you there's death about me
  and you're a child! And I'm alone and half mad
  with hate and longing. I shall let you love me
  and love you in return, and then, why then
  God knows what happens!

Miriamne.
  Something most unpleasant?

Mio.
  Love in a box-car—love among the children.
  I've seen too much of it. Are we to live
  in this same house you make with your two hands
  mystically, out of air?

Miriamne.
  No roof, no mortgage!
  Well, I shall marry a baker out in Flatbush,
  it gives hot bread in the morning! Oh, Mio, Mio,
  in all the unwanted places and waste lands
  that roll up into the darkness out of sun
  and into sun out of dark, there should be one empty
  for you and me.

Mio.
  No.

Miriamne.
  Then go now and leave me.
  I'm only a girl you saw in the tenements,
  and there's been nothing said.

Mio.
  Miriamne. (*She takes a step toward him.*)

Miriamne.
  Yes. (*He kisses her lips lightly.*)

Mio.
  Why, girl, the transfiguration on the mount
  was nothing to your face. It lights from within—

a white chalice holding fire, a flower in flame,
this is your face.

Miriamne.
And you shall drink the flame
and never lessen it. And round your head
the aureole shall burn that burns there now,
forever. This I can give you. And so forever
the Freudians are wrong.

Mio.
They're well-forgotten
at any rate.

Miriamne.
Why did you speak to me
when you first saw me?

Mio.
I knew then.

Miriamne.
And I came back
because I must see you again. And we danced together
and my heart hurt me. Never, never, never,
though they should bind me down and tear out my eyes,
would I ever hurt you now. Take me with you, Mio,
let them look for us, whoever there is to look,
but we'll be away.

(MIO *turns away toward the tenement.*)

Mio.
When I was four years old
we climbed through an iron gate, my mother and I,
to see my father in prison. He stood in the death-cell
and put his hand through the bars and said, My Mio,
I have only this to leave you, that I love you,
and will love you after I die. Love me then, Mio,
when this hard thing comes on you, that you must live
a man despised for your father. That night the guards,
walking in flood-lights brighter than high noon,
led him between them with his trousers slit
and a shaven head for the cathodes. This sleet and rain
that I feel cold here on my face and hands
will find him under thirteen years of clay
in prison ground. Lie still and rest, my father,
for I have not forgotten. When I forget
may I lie blind as you. No other love,

time passing, nor the spaced light-years of suns
shall blur your voice, or tempt me from the path
that clears your name—
till I have these rats in my grip
or sleep deep where you sleep.
(*To* MIRIAMNE)
I have no house,
nor home, nor love of life, nor fear of death,
nor care for what I eat, or who I sleep with,
or what color of calcimine the Government
will wash itself this year or next to lure
the sheep and feed the wolves. Love somewhere else,
and get your children in some other image
more acceptable to the State! This face of mine
is stamped for sewage!
(*She steps back, surmising.*)

Miriamne.
Mio—

Mio.
My road is cut
in rock, and leads to one end. If I hurt you, I'm sorry.
One gets over hurts.

Miriamne.
What was his name—
your father's name?

Mio.
Bartolomeo Romagna
I'm not ashamed of it.

Miriamne.
Why are you here?

Mio.
For the reason
I've never had a home. Because I'm a cry
out of a shallow grave, and all roads are mine
that might revenge him!

Miriamne.
But Mio—why here—why here?

Mio.
I can't tell you that.

Miriamne.
No—but—there's someone
lives here—lives not far—and you mean to see him—
you mean to ask him—

(She pauses.)

Mio.
Who told you that?

Miriamne.
His name
is Garth—Garth Esdras—

Mio.
(After a pause, coming nearer)
Who are you, then? You seem
to know a good deal about me—Were you sent
to say this?

Miriamne.
You said there was death about you! Yes,
but nearer than you think! Let it be as it is—
let it all be as it is, never see this place
nor think of it—forget the streets you came
when you're away and safe! Go before you're seen
or spoken to!

Mio.
Will you tell me why?

Miriamne.
As I love you
I can't tell you—and I can never see you—

Mio.
I walk where I please—

Miriamne.
Do you think it's easy for me
to send you away?
(She steps back as if to go.)

Mio.
Where will I find you then
if I should want to see you?

Miriamne.
Never— I tell you
I'd bring you death! Even now. Listen!

*(SHADOW and TROCK enter between the bridge and
the tenement house. MIRIAMNE pulls MIO back into
the shadow of the rock to avoid being seen)*

from
WINTERSET
by Maxwell Anderson

Act III
MIO, MIRIAMNE, CARR

The following scene, at almost the end of the play, takes
place at the riverbank outside the tenement, under the
bridgehead. Mio, on a quest for the people responsible for
his father's death, is hiding from gunmen. The man who
could clear his father's name turns out to be the brother
of the girl he has fallen in love with. She now comes out
of the building. It is raining.

For more background on this play, see pages 169 and
175. There are several short deletions in this scene marked
by asterisks.

Mio.
   This rather takes one off his high horse.— What I mean,
   tough weather for a hegira. You see, this is my sleeping
   suit, and if I get it wet—basta!
Miriamne.
   If you could only hide here.
Mio.
   Hide?
Miriamne.
   Lucia would take you in. The street-piano man.
Mio.
   At the moment I'm afflicted with claustrophobia. I prefer
   to die in the open, seeking air.
Miriamne.
   But you could stay there till daylight.
Mio.
   You're concerned about me.
Miriamne.
   Shall I ask him?

Mio.

No. On the other hand there's a certain reason in your concern. I looked up the street and our old friend Trock hunches patiently under the warehouse eaves.

Miriamne.

I was sure of that.

Mio.

And here I am, a young man on a cold night, waiting the end of the rain. Being read my lesson by a boy, a blind boy—you know the one I mean. Knee-deep in the salt-marsh, Miriamne, bitten from within, fought.

Miriamne.

Wouldn't it be better if you came back in the house?

Mio.

You forget my claustrophobia.

Miriamne.

Let me walk with you, then. Please. If I stay beside you he wouldn't dare.

Mio.

And then again he might.— We don't speak the same language, Miriamne.

Miriamne.

I betrayed you. Forgive me.

Mio.

I wish I knew this region. There's probably a path along the bank.

Miriamne.

Yes. Shadow went that way.

Mio.

That's true, too. So here I am, a young man on a wet night, and blind in my weather eye. Stay and talk to me.

Miriamne.

If it happens—it's my fault.

Mio.

Not at all, sweet. You warned me to keep away. But I would have it. Now I have to find a way out. It's like a chess game. If you think long enough there's always a way out.— For one or the other.— I wonder why white always wins and black always loses in the problems. White to move and mate in three moves. But what if white were to lose—ah, what then? Why, in that case, obviously black would be white and white would be black.—As it often is.—As we often are.—Might makes

white. Losers turn black. Do you think I'd have time to
draw a gun?

Miriamne.
No.

Mio.
I'm a fair shot. Also I'm fair game.

* * *

Mio.
There was a war in heaven
once, all the angels on one side, and all
the devils on the other, and since that time
disputes have raged among the learned, concerning
whether the demons won, or the angels. Maybe
the angels won, after all.

Miriamne.
And again, perhaps
there are no demons or angels.

Mio.
Oh, there are none.
But I could love your father.

Miriamne.
I love him. You see,
he's afraid because he's old. The less one has
to lose the more he's afraid.

Mio.
Suppose one had
only a short stub end of life, or held
a flashlight with the batteries run down
till the bulb was dim, and knew that he could live
while the glow lasted. Or suppose one knew
that while he stood in a little shelter of time
under a bridgehead, say, he could live, and then,
from then on, nothing. Then to lie and turn
with the earth and sun, and regard them not in the least
when the bulb was extinguished or he stepped beyond
his circle into the cold? How would he live
that last dim quarter-hour, before he went,
minus all recollection, to grow in grass
between cobblestones?

Miriamne.
Let me put my arms around you, Mio.
Then if anything comes, it's for me, too.
(*She puts both arms round him.*)

Mio.

Only suppose
this circle's charmed! To be safe until he steps
from this lighted space into dark! Time pauses here
and high eternity grows in one quarter-hour
in which to live.

Miriamne.

Let me see if anyone's there—
there in the shadows.

(*She looks toward the right.*)

Mio.

It might blast our eternity—
blow it to bits. No, don't go. This is forever,
here where we stand. And I ask you, Miriamne,
how does one spend a forever?

Miriamne.

You're frightened?

Mio.

Yes.
So much that time stands still.

Miriamne.

Why didn't I speak—
tell them—when the officers were here? I failed you
in that one moment!

Mio.

His life for mine? Oh, no.
I wouldn't want it, and you couldn't give it.
And if I should go on living we're cut apart
by that brother of yours.

Miriamne.

Are we?

Mio.

Well, think about it.
A body lies between us, buried in quicklime.
Your allegiance is on the other side of that grave
and not to me.

Miriamne.

No, Mio! Mio, I love you!

Mio.

I love you, too, but in case my life went on
beyond that barrier of dark—then Garth
would run his risk of dying.

Miriamne.

He's punished, Mio.

His life's been torment to him. Let him go,
for my sake, Mio.

Mio.
I wish I could. I wish
I'd never seen him—or you. I've steeped too long
in this thing. It's in my teeth and bones. I can't
let go or forget. And I'll not add my lie
to the lies that cumber his ground. We live our days
in a storm of lies that drifts the truth too deep
for path or shovel; but I've set my foot on a truth
for once, and I'll trail it down!

(*A silence.* MIRIAMNE *looks out to the right.*)

Miriamne.
There's someone there—
I heard—

(CARR *comes in from the right.*)

Mio.
It's Carr.

Carr.
That's right. No doubt about it.
Excuse me.

Mio.
Glad to see you. This is Miriamne.
Carr's a friend of mine.

Carr.
You're better employed
than when I saw you last.

Mio.
Bow to the gentleman,
Miriamne. That's meant for you.

Miriamne.
Thank you, I'm sure.
Should I leave you, Mio? You want to talk?

Mio.
Oh no,
we've done our talking.

Miriamne.
But—

Carr.
I'm the one's out of place—
I wandered back because I got worried about you,
that's the truth.— Oh—those two fellows with the hats
down this way, you know, the ones that ran
after we heard the shooting—they're back again,

lingering or malingering down the bank,
revisiting the crime, I guess. They may mean well.

Mio.
I'll try to avoid them.

Carr.
I didn't care
for the way they looked at me.— No luck, I suppose,
with that case history? The investigation
you had on hand?

Mio.
I can't say. By the way,
the stiff that fell in the water and we saw swirling
down the eddy, he came trudging up, later on,
long enough to tell his name. His name was Shadow,
but he's back in the water now. It's all in an evening.
These things happen here.

Carr.
Good God!

Mio.
I know.
I wouldn't believe it if you told it.

Carr.
But—
the man was alive?

Mio.
Oh, not for long! He's dunked
for good this time. That's all that's happened.

Carr.
Well,
if you don't need me—

Miriamne.
You had a message to send—
have you forgotten—?

Mio.
I?— Yes, I had a message—
but I won't send it—not now.

Miriamne.
Then I will—!

Mio.
No.
Let it go the way it is! It's all arranged
another way. You've been a good scout, Carr,
the best I ever knew on the road.

Carr.
  That sounds
  like making your will.
Mio.
  Not yet, but when I do
  I've thought of something to leave you. It's the view
  of Mt. Rainier from the Seattle jail,
  snow over cloud. And the rusty chain in my pocket
  from a pair of handcuffs my father wore. That's all
  the worldly goods I'm seized of.
Carr.
  Look, Mio—hell—
  if you're in trouble—
Mio.
  I'm not. Not at all. I have
  a genius that attends me where I go,
  and guards me now. I'm fine.
Carr.
  Well, that's good news.
  He'll have his work cut out.
Mio.
  Oh, he's a genius.
Carr.
  I'll see you then.
  I'll be at the Grand Street place. I'm lucky tonight,
  and I can pay. I could even pay for two.
Mio.
  Thanks, I may take you up.
Carr.
  Good night.
Mio.
  Right, Carr.
Carr.
  (*To* MIRIAMNE) Good night.
Miriamne.
  (*After a pause*) Good night. (CARR *goes out to the left.*)
  Why did you do that? He's your genius, Mio,
  and you let him go.
Mio.
  I couldn't help it.
Miriamne.
  Call him.
  Run after him and call him!
Mio.
  I tried to say it

and it strangled in my throat. I might have known
you'd win in the end.

Miriamne.
Is it for me?

Mio.
For you?
It stuck in my throat, that's all I know.

Miriamne.
Oh, Mio,
I never asked for that! I only hoped
Garth could go clear.

Mio.
Well, now he will.

Miriamne.
But you—
It was your chance!

Mio.
I've lost
my taste for revenge if it falls on you. Oh, God,
deliver me from the body of this death
I've dragged behind me all these years! Miriamne!
Miriamne!

Miriamne.
Yes!

Mio.
Miriamne, if you love me
teach me a treason to what I am, and have been,
till I learn to live like a man! I think I'm waking
from a long trauma of hate and fear and death
that's hemmed me from my birth—and glimpse a life
to be lived in hope—but it's young in me yet, I can't
get free, or forgive! But teach me how to live
and forget to hate!

Miriamne.
He would have forgiven.

Mio.
He?

Miriamne.
Your father.
(*A pause*)

Mio.
Yes.
(*Another pause*)

You'll think it strange, but I've never
remembered that.

Miriamne.
How can I help you?

Mio.
You have.

Miriamne.
If I were a little older—if I knew
the things to say! I can only put out my hands
and give you back the faith you bring to me
by being what you are. Because to me
you are all hope and beauty and brightness drawn
across what's black and mean!

Mio.
He'd have forgiven—
Then there's no more to say—I've groped long enough
through this everglades of old revenges—here
the road ends.— Miriamne, Miriamne,
the iron I wore so long—it's eaten through
and fallen from me. Let me have your arms.
They'll say we're children— Well—the world's made up
of children.

Miriamne.
Yes.

Mio.
But it's too late for me.

Miriamne.
No.
(*She goes into his arms, and they kiss for the first time.*)
Then we'll meet again?

Mio.
Yes.

Miriamne.
Where?

Mio.
I'll write—
or send Carr to you.

Miriamne.
You won't forget?

Mio.
Forget?
Whatever streets I walk, you'll walk them, too,
from now on, and whatever roof or stars
I have to house me, you shall share my roof

and stars and morning. I shall not forget.

Miriamne.
God keep you!

Mio.
And keep you. And this to remember!
if I should die, Miriamne, this half-hour
is our eternity. I came here seeking
light in darkness, running from the dawn,
and stumbled on a morning.

* * *

Mio.
(*Looking up*) Now all you silent powers
that make the sleet and dark, and never yet
have spoken, give us a sign, let the throw be ours
this once, on this longest night, when the winter sets
his foot on the threshold leading up to spring
and enters with remembered cold—let fall
some mercy with the rain. We are two lovers
here in your night, and we wish to live.

Miriamne.
Oh, Mio—
if you pray that way, nothing good will come!
You're bitter, Mio.

Mio.
How many floors has this building?

Miriamne.
Five or six. It's not as high as the bridge.

Mio.
No, I thought not. How many pomegranate seeds did
you eat, Persephone?

Miriamne.
Oh darling, darling,
if you die, don't die alone.

Mio.
I'm afraid I'm damned
to hell, and you're not damned at all. . . .

* * *

Miriamne.
Mio, see, that path between the rocks—
they're not watching that—they're out at the river—
I can see them there—they can't watch both—
It leads to a street above.

Mio.
I'll try it, then.

Kiss me. You'll hear. But if you never hear—
then I'm the king of hell, Persephone,
and I'll expect you.

Miramne.
Oh, lover, keep safe.

Mio.
Good-bye.
(*He slips out quickly between the rocks. There is a quick
machine gun rat-tat. MIRIAMNE runs toward the path.
MIO comes back quickly, a hand pressed under his heart.*)
It seems you were mistaken.

Miriamne.
Oh, God, forgive me!
(*She puts an arm round him. He sinks to his knees.*)
Where is it, Mio? Let me help you in! Quick, quick,
let me help you!

Mio.
I hadn't thought to choose—this—ground—
but it will do.
(*He slips down.*)

Miriamne.
Oh, God, forgive me!

Mio.
Yes?
The king of hell was not forgiven then,
Dis is his name, and Hades is his home—
and he goes alone—

Miramne.
Why does he bleed so? Mio, if you go
I shall go with you.

Mio.
It's better to stay alive.
I wanted to stay alive—because of you—
I leave you that—and what he said to me dying:
I love you, and will love you after I die.
Tomorrow, I shall still love you, as I've loved
the stars I'll never see, and all the mornings
that might have been yours and mine. Oh, Miriamne,
you taught me this.

Miriamne.
If only I'd never seen you
then you could live—

Mio.

That's blasphemy— Oh, God.

there might have been some easier way of it.

You didn't want me to die, did you, Miriamne—?

You didn't send me away—?

Miriamne.

Oh, never, never—

Mio.

Forgive me—kiss me—I've got blood on your lips—

I'm sorry—it doesn't matter—I'm sorry—

* * *

Miriamne.

Mio—

I'd have gone to die myself—you must hear this, Mio,

I'd have died to help you—you must listen, sweet,

you must hear it—

(*She rises.*)

I can die, too, see! You! There!

You in the shadows! You killed him to silence him!

(*She walks toward the path.*)

But I'm not silenced! All that he knew I know,

and I'll tell it tonight! Tonight—

tell it and scream it

through all the streets—that Trock's a murderer

and he hired you for this murder!

Your work's not done—

and you won't live long! Do you hear?

You're murderers, and I know who you are!

(*The machine gun speaks again. She sinks to her
knees . . .*)

* * *

(*She crawls toward* MIO)

Look, Mio! They killed me, too. Oh, you can believe me

now, Mio. You can believe I wouldn't hurt you,

because I'm dying! Why doesn't he answer me?

Oh, now he'll never know!

(*She sinks down, her hand over her mouth, choking. . . .*)

from
WEST SIDE STORY
Book by Arthur Laurents, Music by Leonard Bernstein,
Lyrics by Stephen Sondheim, directed and choreographed
by Jerome Robbins

Act I, scene 2
TONY, RIFF

This much-acclaimed, long-running musical is based on
Jerome Robbins' conception of young street gangs on the
West Side of New York City in the 1950's. The story of
Romeo and Juliet is echoed in this story of Tony and Maria,
the two young lovers whose lives are destroyed by the
hatred of rival gangs.

The following scene takes place in a back yard late in
the afternoon of a summer day. Tony is on a small ladder
painting a sign while his friend, Riff, is talking to him
from below. Both boys are members of the Jets and there
is talk of a rumble between them and a gang called the
Sharks.

Riff.
  Riga tiga tum tum. Why not? . . . You can't say ya won't,
  Tony boy, without sayin' why not?
Tony.
  (*Grins*) Why not?
Riff.
  Because it's me askin': Riff. Womb to tomb!
Tony.
  Sperm to worm! (*Surveying the sign*) You sure this looks
  like sky-writin'?
Riff.
  It's brilliant.
Tony.
  Twenty-seven years the boss has had that drugstore. I
  wanna surprise him with a new sign.

Riff.
(*Shaking the ladder*) Tony, this is important!

Tony.
Very important: Acemen, Rocketmen.

Riff.
What's with you? Four and one-half years I live with a buddy and his family. Four and one-half years I think I know a man's character. Buddy boy, I am a victim of disappointment in you.

Tony.
End your sufferin', little man. Why don't you pack up your gear and clear out?

Riff.
'Cause your ma's hot for me. (TONY *grabs his arm and twists it.*) No! 'Cause I hate livin' with my buggin' uncle uncle UNCLE! (TONY *releases him and climbs back up the ladder.*)

Tony.
Now go play nice with the Jets.

Riff.
The Jets are the greatest!

Tony.
Were.

Riff.
Are. You found somethin' better?

Tony.
No. But—

Riff.
But what?

Tony.
You won't dig it.

Riff.
Try me.

Tony.
O.K. . . . Every single damn night for the last month, I wake up—and I'm reachin' out.

Riff.
For what?

Tony.
I don't know. It's right outside the door, around the corner. But it's comin'!

Riff.
What is? Tell me!

Tony.
I don't know! It's—like the kick I used to get from bein'
a Jet.

Riff.
. . . Or from bein' buddies.

Tony.
We're still buddies.

Riff.
The kick comes from people, buddy boy.

Tony.
Yeah, but not from being a Jet.

Riff.
No? Without a gang you're an orphan. With a gang you
walk in twos, threes, fours. And when your gang is the
best, when you're a Jet, buddy boy, you're out in the sun
and home free home!

Tony.
Riff, I've had it. (*Pause*)

Riff.
Tony, the trouble is large: the Sharks bite hard! We got
to stop them now, and we need *you!* (*Pause. Quietly*)
I never asked the time of day from a clock, but I'm
askin' you: Come to the dance tonight . . . (TONY
turns away) . . . I already told the gang you'd be there.

Tony.
(*After a moment, turns to him with a grin*) What time?

Riff.
Ten?

Tony.
Ten it is.

Riff.
Womb to tomb!

Tony.
Sperm to worm! And I'll live to regret this.

Riff.
Who knows? Maybe what you're waitin' for'll be
twitchin' at the dance! (*He runs off.*)

Tony.
Who knows?
(*Music starts and he sings*)
Could be! . . .
Who knows? . . .
There's something due any day;

I will know right away
Soon as it shows.

It may come cannonballin' down through the sky,
Gleam in its eye,
Bright as a rose!
Who knows? . . .
It's only just out of reach,
Down the block, on a beach,
Under a tree.
I got a feeling there's a miracle due,
Gonna come true,
Coming to me!

Could it be? Yes, it could.
Something's coming, something good,
If I can wait!
Something's coming, I don't know what it is
But it is
Gonna be great!

With a click, with a shock,
Phone'll jingle, door'll knock,
Open the latch!
Something's coming, don't know when, but it's soon—
Catch the moon,
One-handed catch!

Around the corner,
Or whistling down the river,
Come on—deliver
To me!

Will it be? Yes, it will.
Maybe just by holding still
It'll be there!
Come on, something, come on in, don't be shy,
Meet a guy,
Pull up a chair!

The air is humming,
And something great is coming!

Who knows?
It's only just out of reach,
Down the block, on a beach . . .
Maybe tonight . . . .

                          (The lights dim.)

from
WEST SIDE STORY
by Laurents, Bernstein, Sondheim. Directed and choreographed by Robbins

Act I, scene 3
MARIA, ANITA, BERNARDO, CHINO

This scene takes place in a bridal shop. Anita, a rather sophisticated young Puerto Rican girl, is sewing a dress for Maria who is younger and very lovely. They are preparing for a dance in the neighborhood, which will be Maria's first since she came to the United States from Puerto Rico a month before. (For further background on the play, see the introduction to the preceding scene.)

Maria.
(*Holding out scissors*) *Por favor*, Anita. Make the neck lower!
Anita.
Stop it, Maria.
Maria.
One inch. How much can one little inch do?
Anita.
Too much.
Maria.
(*Exasperated*) Anita, it is now to be a dress for dancing, no longer for kneeling in front of an altar.
Anita.
With those boys you can start in dancing and end up kneeling.
Maria.
Querida, one little inch; *una poca poca*—
Anita.
Bernardo made me promise—
Maria.
Ai! Bernardo! One month have I been in this country—

200

do I ever even touch excitement? I sew all day, I sit all
night. For what did my fine brother bring me here?

Anita.
To marry Chino.

Maria.
When I look at Chino, nothing happens.

Anita.
What do you expect to happen?

Maria.
I don't know: something. What happens when you look
at Bernardo?

Anita.
It's when I don't look that it happens.

Maria.
I think I will tell Mama and Papa about you and 'Nardo
in the balcony of the movies.

Anita.
I'll rip this to shreds!

Maria.
No. But if you perhaps could manage to lower the neck—

Anita.
Next year.

Maria.
Next year I will be married and no one will care if it is
down to here!

Anita.
Down to where?

Maria.
Down to here. (*Indicates her waist*) I hate this dress!

Anita.
Then don't wear it and don't come with us to the dance.

Maria.
(*Shocked*) Don't come! (*Grabs the dress*) Could we
not dye it red, at least?

Anita.
No, we could not. (*She starts to help* MARIA *into the
dress.*)

Maria.
White is for babies. I will be the only one there in a
white—

Anita.
Well???

Maria.
Ahhh-*sí!* It is a beautiful dress: I love you! (*As she hugs

ANITA, BERNARDO *enters, followed by a shy, gentle sweet-faced boy:* CHINO.)

Bernardo.
Are you ready?

Maria.
Come in, 'Nardo. (*Whirls in the dress*) Is it not beautiful?

Bernardo.
(*Looking only at* MARIA's *face*) Yes. (*Kisses her*) Very.

Anita.
I didn't quite hear . . .

Bernardo.
(*Kissing* ANITA *quite differently*) Very beautiful.

Maria.
(*Watches them a second, then turns to* CHINO) Come in, Chino. Do not be afraid.

Chino.
But this is a shop for ladies.

Bernardo.
Our ladies!

Maria.
'Nardo, it is most important that I have a wonderful time at the dancing tonight.

Bernardo.
(*As* ANITA *hooks up* MARIA) Why?

Maria.
Because tonight is the real beginning of my life as a young lady of America! (*She begins to whirl in the dress* . . .)

from
WEST SIDE STORY
by Laurents, Bernstein & Sondheim

Act I, scene 5
TONY, MARIA

It is now 11:00 P.M. after the dance. (See the introductory
comments to the preceding scene.) Tony and Maria have
met, danced, and fallen in love, much to the dismay of
Maria's brother, Bernardo, who is the leader of the Sharks.
A fight is brewing between the two gangs but Tony thinks
only of Maria and wanders to the building she lives in. In a
back alley, on a fire escape, the two profess their love for
each other.

*11:00 P.M. A back alley. A suggestion of buildings: a fire
escape climbing to the rear window of an unseen flat.
As TONY sings, he looks for where MARIA lives, wishing
for her. And she does appear, at the window above him,
which opens onto the fire escape. Music stays beneath most
of the scene.*

(TONY *sings*) Maria, Maria. . . .
Maria.
  Ssh!
Tony.
  Maria!
Maria.
  Quiet!
Tony.
  Come down.
Maria.
  No.
Tony.
  Maria. . . .

Maria.
Please. If Bernardo—

Tony.
He's at the dance. Come down.

Maria.
He will soon bring Anita home.

Tony.
Just for a minute.

Maria.
(*Smiles*) A minute is not enough.

Tony.
(*Smiles*) For an hour, then.

Maria.
I cannot.

Tony.
Forever!

Maria.
Ssh!

Tony.
Then I'm coming up.

Woman's Voice.
(*From the offstage apartment*) Maria!

Maria.
Momentito, Mama. . . .

Tony.
(*Climbing up*) Maria, Maria—

Maria.
Cállate! (*Reaching her hand out to stop him*) Ssh!

Tony.
(*Grabbing her hand*) Ssh!

Maria.
It is dangerous.

Tony.
I'm *not* "one of them."

Maria.
You are; but to me, you are not. Just as I am one of them— (*She gestures toward the apartment.*)

Tony.
To me, you are all the— (*She covers his mouth with her hand.*)

Man's Voice.
(*From the unseen apartment*) Maruca!

Maria.
Sí ya vengo, Papa.

Tony.
Maruca?

Maria.
His pet name for me.
Tony.
I like him. He will like me.
Maria.
No. He is like Bernardo: afraid. (*Suddenly laughing*)
Imagine being afraid of you!
Tony.
You see?
Maria.
(*Touching his face*) I see you.
Tony.
See only me.

(MARIA *sings*)
Only you, you're the only thing I'll see forever.
In my eyes, in my words and in everything I do,
Nothing else but you
Ever!

(TONY)
And there's nothing for me but Maria,
Every sight that I see is Maria.

(MARIA)
Tony, Tony . . .

(TONY)
Always you, every thought I'll ever know,
Everywhere I go, you'll be.

(MARIA)
All the world is only you and me! (*And now the build-ings, the world, fade away, leaving them suspended in space*)

Tonight, tonight,
It all began tonight,
I saw you and the world went away.
Tonight, tonight,
There's only you tonight,
What are you, what you do, what you say.

(TONY)
Today, all day I had the feeling
A miracle would happen—
I know now I was right.
For here you are
And what was just a world is a star
Tonight!

(BOTH)
Tonight, tonight,
The world is full of light,
With suns and moons all over the place.
Tonight, tonight,
The world is wild and bright,
Going mad, shooting sparks into space.
Today the world was just an address,
A place for me to live in,
No better than all right,
But here you are
And what was just a world is a star
Tonight!

Man's Voice.
    (*Offstage*) Maruca!

Maria.
Wait for me! (*She goes inside as the buildings begin to come back into place.*)

(TONY *sings*)
Tonight, tonight,
It all began tonight,
I saw you and the world went away.

Maria.
(*Returning*) I cannot stay. Go quickly!

Tony.
I'm not afraid.

Maria.
They are strict with me. Please.

Tony.
(*Kissing her*) Good night.

Maria.
Buenas noches.

Tony.
I love you.

Maria.
Yes, yes. Hurry. (*He climbs down.*) Wait! When will I see you? (*He starts back up.*) No!

Tony.
Tomorrow.

Maria.
I work at the bridal shop. Come there.

Tony.
At sundown.

Maria.
Yes. Good night.

Tony.
Good night. (*He starts off.*)

Maria.
Tony!

Tony.
Ssh!

Maria.
Come to the back door.

Tony.
Sí. (*Again, he starts out.*)

Maria.
Tony! (*He stops. A pause*) What does Tony stand for?

Tony.
Anton.

Maria.
Te adoro, Anton.

Tony.
Te adoro, Maria.

(BOTH *sing as music starts again*)
Good night, good night,
Sleep well and when you dream,
Dream of me
Tonight.
(*She goes inside. He ducks out into the shadows. . . .*)

from
A VIEW FROM THE BRIDGE
by Arthur Miller

Act II
CATHERINE, RODOLPHO

Arthur Miller based this play on a story told him by a
water-front worker. Eddy Carbone, an uneducated long-
shoreman, is driven by an unconscious passion for his
niece, Catherine, who has been raised in his home. When
she falls in love with Rodolpho, a young Italian immigrant who is in the country illegally, Eddy begins to
lose all sense of values and commits the ultimate sin of
his society. He informs on Rodolpho and his brother
Marco, who are relatives of his wife. His world falls
dizzyingly apart and reaches a terrifying climax when he is
killed by Marco in the street in front of his family and
neighbors.

The following scene takes place in the Carbones' living
room in a tenement house in New York. Catherine, 17, is
ironing. Rodolpho, blonde and about 20, watches her,
then comes and sits near her. It is the first time Catherine
and Rodolpho have been alone in the apartment.

Catherine.
  You hungry?
Rodolpho.
  Not for anything to eat. (*He leans his chin on the back
  of his hand on the table, watching her iron.*) I have nearly
  three hundred dollars. (*He looks up at her.*) Catherine?
Catherine.
  I heard you.

  (RODOLPHO *reaches out and takes her hand and
  kisses it, then lets it go. She resumes ironing. He rests
  his head again on the back of his hand.*)

Rodolpho.
You don't like to talk about it any more?

Catherine.
Sure, I don't mind talkin' about it.

Rodolpho.
What worries you, Catherine?

(CATHERINE *continues ironing. He now reaches out and takes her hand off the iron, and she sits back in her chair, not looking directly at him.*)

Catherine.
I been wantin' to ask you about something. Could I?

Rodolpho.
All the answers are in my eyes, Catherine. But you don't look in my eyes lately. You're full of secrets. (*She looks at him. He presses her hand against his cheek. She seems withdrawn.*) What is the question?

Catherine.
Suppose I wanted to live in Italy.

Rodolpho.
(*Smiling at the incongruity*) You going to marry somebody rich?

Catherine.
No, I mean live there—you and me.

Rodolpho.
(*His smile is vanishing*) When?

Catherine.
Well—when we get married.

Rodolpho.
(*Astonished*) You want to be an Italian?

Catherine.
No, but I could live there without being Italian. Americans live there.

Rodolpho.
Forever?

Catherine.
Yeah.

Rodolpho.
You're fooling.

Catherine.
No, I mean it.

Rodolpho.
Where do you get such an idea?

Catherine.
Well, you're always saying it's so beautiful there, with the mountains and the ocean and all the—

Rodolpho.
You're fooling me.

Catherine.
I mean it.

Rodolpho.
Catherine, if I ever brought you home
With no money, no business, nothing,
They would call the priest and the doctor
And they would say Rodolpho is crazy.

Catherine.
I know, but I think we would be happier there.

Rodolpho.
Happier! What would you eat? You can't cook the view!

Catherine.
Maybe you could be a singer, like in Rome or—

Rodolpho.
Rome! Rome is full of singers.

Catherine.
Well, I could work then.

Rodolpho.
Where?

Catherine.
God, there must be jobs somewhere!

Rodolpho.
There's nothing! Nothing, nothing.
Nothing. Now tell me what you're talking about.
How can I bring you from a rich country
to suffer in a poor country?
What are you talking about?
    (*She searches for words.*)
I would be a criminal stealing your face;
In two years you would have an old, hungry face.
When my brothers' babies cry they give them water,
Water that boiled a bone.
Don't you believe that?

Catherine.
    (*Quietly*) I'm afraid of Eddy here. (*A slight pause*)

Rodolpho.
We wouldn't live here.
Once I am a citizen I could work anywhere,
And I would find better jobs,
And we would have a house, Catherine.
If I were not afraid to be arrested
I would start to be something wonderful here!

Catherine.

(*Steeling herself*) Tell me something. I mean just tell me, Rodolpho—would you still want to do it if it turned out we had to go live in Italy? I mean just if it turned out that way.

Rodolpho.

This is your question or his question?

Catherine.

I would like to know, Rodolpho. I mean it.

Rodolpho.

To go there with nothing?

Catherine.

Yeah.

Rodolpho.

No. (*She looks at him wide-eyed.*) No.

Catherine.

You wouldn't?

Rodolpho.

No; I will not marry you to live in Italy.
I want you to be my wife
And I want to be a citizen.
Tell him that, or I will. Yes.
   (*He moves about angrily.*)
And tell him also, and tell yourself, please,
That I am not a beggar,
And you are not a horse, a gift,
A favor for a poor immigrant.

Catherine.

Well, don't get mad!

Rodolpho.

I am furious!
Do you think I am so desperate?
My brother is desperate, not me.
You think I would carry on my back
the rest of my life a woman I didn't love
just to be an American? It's so wonderful?
You think we have no tall buildings in Italy?
Electric lights? No wide streets? No flags?
No automobiles? Only work we don't have.
I want to be an American so I can work,
That is the only wonder here—work!
How can you insult me, Catherine?

Catherine.

I didn't mean that—

Rodolpho.
My heart dies to look at you.
Why are you so afraid of him?

Catherine.
(*Near tears*) I don't know!
      (RODOLPHO *turns her to him.*)

Rodolpho.
Do you trust me, Catherine? You?

Catherine.
It's only that I—
He was good to me, Rodolpho.
You don't know him; he was always the sweetest guy to
    me.
Good. He razzes me all the time,
But he don't mean it. I know.
I would—just feel ashamed if I made him sad.
'Cause I always dreamt that when I got married
He would be happy at the wedding, and laughin'.
And now he's—mad all the time, and nasty.
      (*She is weeping.*)
Tell him you'd live in Italy—just tell him,
And maybe he would start to trust you a little, see?
Because I want him to be happy; I mean—
I like him, Rodolpho—and I can't stand it!
      (*She weeps and he holds her.*)

Rodolpho.
Catherine—oh, little girl.

Catherine.
I love you, Rodolpho, I love you.

Rodolpho.
I think that's what you have to tell him, eh? Can't you
tell him?

Catherine.
I'm ascared, I'm so scared.

Rodolpho.
Ssssh. Listen, now. Tonight when he comes home
We will both sit down after supper
And we will tell him—you and I.
      (*He sees her fear rising.*)
But you must believe me yourself, Catherine.
It's true—you have very much to give me:
A whole country! Sure, I hold America when I hold you.
But if you were not my love,

If every day I did not smile so many times
When I think of you,
I could never kiss you, not for a hundred Americas.
Tonight I'll tell him,
And you will not be frightened any more, eh?
And then in two, three months I'll have enough,
We will go to the church, and we'll come back to our
     own—
     (*He breaks off, seeing the conquered longing in her
     eyes, her smile.*)
Catherine—

Catherine.
     Now. There's nobody here.

Rodolpho.
     Oh, my little girl. Oh God!

Catherine.
     Now. (*kissing his face*)
     (*He turns her upstage. They walk embraced, her head
     on his shoulder, and he sings to her softly. They go into a
     bedroom.*)

from
GOLDEN BOY
by Clifford Odets

Act I, scene 4
JOE, LORNA

This play, understood superficially, may appear dated; a
relic from the thirties. Harold Clurman, who directed it on
Broadway, interpreted it as an allegory. It is the story of a
young man who decides to forego his musical aspirations
and his simple family values to become a fighter. His quest
for personal success, fame and money inevitably lead him
to destruction. Mr. Clurman writes that the golden boy is
fighting for a place in the world as an individual. He, like
all of us, wants acceptance from an uncaring world. The
inevitable conflict is between what a man might be and
what he becomes, and the two worlds a man lives with.

   In the following scene, Lorna, a young woman, has
been sent to try to convince Joe not to go back to his
music but to pursue a boxing career. They are sitting on a
park bench on a summer evening.

Lorna.
   Success and fame! Or just a lousy living. You're lucky
   you won't have to worry about those things. . . .
Joe.
   Won't I?
Lorna.
   Unless Tom Moody's a liar.
Joe.
   You like him, don't you?
Lorna.
   (*After a pause*) I like him.
Joe.
   I like how you dress. The girls look nice in the summer-
214

time. Did you ever stand at the Fifth Avenue Library and watch those girls go by?

Lorna.
No, I never did. (*Switching the subject*) That's the carousel, that music. Did you ever ride on one of those?

Joe.
That's for kids.

Lorna.
Weren't you ever a kid, for God's sake?

Joe.
Not a happy kid,

Lorna.
Why?

Joe.
Well, I always felt different. Even my name was special—Bonaparte—and my eyes . . .

Lorna.
I wouldn't have taken that too serious. . . . (*There is a silent pause. JOE looks straight ahead.*)

Joe.
Gee, all those cars . . .

Lorna.
Lots of horses trot around here. The rich know how to live. You'll be rich . . .

Joe.
My brother Frank is an organizer for the C.I.O.

Lorna.
What's that?

Joe.
If you worked in a factory you'd know. Did you ever work?

Lorna.
(*With a smile*) No. When I came out of the cocoon I was a butterfly and butterflies don't work.

Joe.
All those cars . . . whizz, whizz. (*Now turning less casual*) Where's Mr. Moody tonight?

Lorna.
He goes up to see his kid on Tuesday nights. It's a sick kid, a girl. His wife leaves it at her mother's house.

Joe.
That leaves you free, don't it?

Lorna.
What are you hinting at?

Joe.
I'm thinking about you and Mr. Moody.

Lorna.
Why think about it? I don't. Why should you?

Joe.
If you belonged to me I wouldn't think about it.

Lorna.
Haven't you got a girl?

Joe.
No.

Lorna.
Why not?

Joe.
(*Evasively*) Oh . . .

Lorna.
Tokio says you're going far in the fighting game.

Joe.
Music means more to me. May I tell you something?

Lorna.
Of course.

Joe.
If you laugh I'll never speak to you again.

Lorna.
I'm not the laughing type.

Joe.
With music I'm never alone when I'm alone— Playing music . . . that's like saying, "I am man. I belong here. How do you do, World—good evening!" When I play music nothing is closed to me. I'm not afraid of people and what they say. There's no war in music. It's not like the streets. Does this sound funny?

Lorna.
No.

Joe.
But when you leave your room . . . down in the street . . . it's war! Music can't help me there. Understand?

Lorna.
Yes.

Joe.
People have hurt my feelings for years. I never forget. You can't get even with people by playing the fiddle. If music shot bullets I'd like it better—artists and people like that are freaks today. The world moves fast and they sit around like forgotten dopes.

Lorna.
You're loaded with fireworks. Why don't you fight?

Joe.
You have to be what you are—!

Lorna.
Fight! See what happens—

Joe.
Or end up in the bughouse!

Lorna.
God's teeth! Who says you have to be one thing?

Joe.
My nature isn't fighting!

Lorna.
Don't Tokio know what he's talking about? Don't Tom?
Joe, listen: be a fighter! Show the world! If you made
your fame and fortune—and you can—you'd be anything
you want. Do it! Bang your way to the lightweight
crown. Get a bank account. Hire a great doctor with a
beard—get your eyes fixed—

Joe.
What's the matter with my eyes?

Lorna.
Excuse me, I stand corrected. (*After a pause*) You get
mad all the time.

Joe.
That's from thinking about myself.

Lorna.
How old are you, Joe?

Joe.
Twenty-one and a half, and the months are going fast.

Lorna.
You're very smart for twenty-one and a half "and the
months are going fast."

Joe.
Why not? I read every page of the Encyclopaedia Britannica. My father's friend, Mr. Carp, has it. A shrimp with
glasses has to do something.

Lorna.
I'd like to meet your father. Your mother dead?

Joe.
Yes.

Lorna.
So is mine.

Joe.
Where do you come from? The city is full of girls who look as if they never had parents.

Lorna.
I'm a girl from over the river. My father is still alive—shucking oysters and bumming drinks somewhere in the wilds of Jersey. I'll tell you a secret: I don't like you.

Joe.
(*Surprised*) Why?

Lorna.
You're too sufficient by yourself . . . too inside yourself.

Joe.
You like it or you don't.

Lorna.
You're on an island.

Joe.
Robinson Crusoe . . .

Lorna.
That's right—"me, myself and I." Why not come out and see the world?

Joe.
Does it seem that way?

Lorna.
Can't you see yourself?

Joe.
No . . .

Lorna.
Take a bird's-eye view; you don't know what's right or wrong. You don't know what to pick, but you won't admit it.

Joe.
Do you?

Lorna.
Leave me out. This is the anatomy of Joe Bonaparte.

Joe.
You're dancing on my nose, huh?

Lorna.
Shall I stop?

Joe.
No.

Lorna.
You're a miserable creature. You want your arm in *gelt* up to the elbow. You'll take fame so people won't laugh or scorn your face. You'd give your soul for those things. But every time you turn your back your little soul kicks you in the teeth. It don't give in so easy.

Joe.
And what does your soul do in its perfumed vanity case?

Lorna.
Forget about me.

Joe.
Don't you want—?

Lorna.
(*Suddenly nasty*) I told you forget it!

Joe.
(*Quietly*) Moody sent you after me—a decoy! You made a mistake, Lorna, for two reasons. I make up my own mind to fight. Point two, he doesn't know you don't love him—

Lorna.
You're a fresh kid.

Joe.
In fact he doesn't know anything about you at all.

Lorna.
(*Challengingly*) But you do?

Joe.
This is the anatomy of Lorna Moon: she's a lost baby. She doesn't know what's right or wrong. She's a miserable creature who never knew what to pick. But she'd never admit it. And I'll tell you why you picked Moody!

Lorna.
You don't know what you're talking about.

Joe.
Go home, Lorna. If you stay, I'll know something about you . . .

Lorna.
You don't know anything.

Joe.
Now's your chance—go home!

Lorna.
Tom loves me.

Joe.
(*After a long silence, looking ahead*) I'm going to buy a car.

Lorna.
They make wonderful cars today. Even the lizzies—

Joe.
Gary Cooper's got the kind I want. I saw it in the paper, but it costs too much—fourteen thousand. If I found one second-hand—

Lorna.
And if you had the cash—

Joe.
I'll get it—

Lorna.
Sure, if you'd go in and really fight!

Joe.
(*In a sudden burst*) Tell your Mr. Moody I'll dazzle the eyes out of his head!

Lorna.
You mean it?

Joe.
(*Looking out ahead*) Those cars are poison in my blood. When you sit in a car and speed you're looking down at the world. Speed, speed, everything is speed—nobody gets me!

Lorna.
You mean in the ring?

Joe.
In or out, nobody gets me! Gee, I like to stroke that gas!

Lorna.
You sound like Jack the Ripper.

Joe.
(*Standing up suddenly*) I'll walk you back to your house —your hotel, I mean. (LORNA *stands*. JOE *continues*.) Do you have the same room?

Lorna.
(*With sneaking admiration*) You're a fresh kid!

Joe.
When you're lying in his arms tonight, tell him, for me, that the next World's Champ is feeding in his stable.

Lorna.
Did you really read those Britannica books?

Joe.
From A to Z.

Lorna.
And you're only twenty-one?

Joe.
And a half.

Lorna.
Something's wrong somewhere.

Joe.
I know ... (*They slowly walk out as Fadeout*)

from
SUMMER BRAVE
by William Inge

Act I
ALAN, HAL

Summer Brave is the rewritten and final version of the romantic comedy *Picnic*. As William Inge himself explains it, he was never completely satisfied with *Picnic* even after it had won prizes on Broadway and was a successful film. He apparently wrote the ending of *Picnic* under a deadline and several years later, for his own satisfaction, reworked it to fulfill his original intentions.

The play centers on desire and frustration. The setting is the front porch and lawn of a small frame house in a small Kansas town. In the background is the back entrance to the house of a neighbor, Mrs. Potts. The house belongs to Flo Owens, a widow who rents rooms to support herself and her two daughters, Madge and Millie. Madge, the elder girl, is the town beauty. She is engaged to a wealthy young man, Alan. Millie, the younger, is a tomboy, shy, and very intelligent, with aspirations for greater things. They are in the midst of plans for a Labor Day picnic when Hal, a boisterous drifter and lady killer, enters the scene and perks things up considerably. He is doing odd jobs for Mrs. Potts when he is spied by Alan with whom he had spent a short time in college. In the following scene, the lawn has been temporarily deserted except for the two young men. Alan calls to Hal. His feelings at seeing his old friend are mixed.

Alan.
  Hal! Hal! Come on over.
Hal.
  (*Before coming on*) Hi 'ya, Al!

221

Alan.
You've given the ladies quite a shock.

Hal.
(*Comes on, putting on a T-shirt. There is soot on his face and body.*) Well, I always do *that*, Al. (ALAN *isn't prepared to be amused.*)

Alan.
(*Straight to the point*) What're you doing *here*?

Hal.
Aren't you even gonna say hello?

Alan.
(*In one word*) Hello!

Hal.
(*Realizing all is not well*) Oh! (*Innocently*) I didn't figure I was stealin' your car, Al.

Alan.
What name did *you* invent for it?

Hal.
Well, I knew you had insurance. Right?

Alan.
(*Belligerent*) Of course!

Hal.
So I knew you'd get yourself a *new* car without putting out any dough. I even figured I might be doin' you a favor, helpin' you to get a new car. (ALAN *shrugs his shoulders hopelessly.* HAL *continues urgently*) And I *had* to get to California, Al. I just *had* to. Once I got out there, I was tellin' myself, I'd soon be able to pay you back. Yah! I'd pay you back double.

Alan.
You mean . . . once you crashed the movies!

Hal.
(*A little embarrassed*) Well . . . other guys have done it, Al.

Alan.
Did you finally get out?

Hal.
Yah, I got out.

Alan.
How?

Hal.
After I smashed your car, I went home. The old man died, Al.

Alan.
Oh . . . (*He's not ready yet to say he's sorry.*)

Hal.

He left me a little insurance. I used that.

Alan.

Did you get a test?

Hal.

Yah! I got the test okay.

Alan.

That's more than I expected.

Hal.

I don't see why one of those talent scouts'd come to see me play football and tell me he'd get me a screen test . . . if he didn't mean it.

Alan.

It happens at school every year.

Hal.

(*Reliving the experience enthusiastically*) I was about to have a big career, Al! Yah! They were gonna call me *Brush* Carter. How ya like that? They took a lotta pictures of me with my shirt off. Real rugged. Then they dressed me up like a pirate, like the Foreign Legion, then put me in a pair of tights and a cape, gave me a sword and big hat with lots of plumes, and there I was . . . (*Pantomime.*) makin' with the swordplay. You shoulda seen me, Al.

Alan.

Didn't they give you any lines to read?

Hal.

Yah. That part went okay. It was my teeth.

Alan.

Your teeth?

Hal.

Yah! You see, out there you gotta have a certain kind of teeth, or they can't use you. They told me, they'd have to pull all my teeth, for some reason, and gimme new ones. Yah!

Alan.

(*Coming to his own conclusion*) Oh!

Hal.

This babe explained the whole thing to me.

Alan.

What babe?

Hal.

That babe that finally got me the test.

Alan.

(*Putting two and two together*) Oh!

Hal.
Well . . . I was just *nice* to her. That's all. Anything wrong with *that*?

Alan.
(*Suddenly*) Let's get to the point, Hal. You're *broke*. You've come all the way back here to . . .

Hal.
I hitchhiked, Al.

Alan.
. . . to borrow money off me because you figured I'd be a big enough sap to give it to you.

Hal.
Gee, Al, I don't see why you have to put everything in black and white like that.

Alan.
I can't help you, Hal.

Hal.
All I want is a *job*.

Alan.
Look Hal, I'm *out* of college now. I'm beginning to settle down, and . . .

Hal.
I'm a good worker, Al.

Alan.
Maybe you are!

Hal.
I was on a ranch *all* summer, Al. Out in Nevada. Workin' hard, too. In bed every night at ten, up at six. No liquor! No babes! You'd been proud of me, Al.

Alan.
Well. . . . (*Not knowing what to do*)

Hal.
Come across, Al. Give a guy a break.

Alan.
I'm not Henry J. Kaiser. I don't have jobs at my fingertips that I can distribute to everyone who comes along.

Hal.
(*Abashed*) Sure, Al!

Alan.
(*Suddenly wanting an explanation*) Why do you come to *me*, Hal? Always to *me*!

Hal.
(*Embarrassed*) 'Cause . . .

Alan.
Tell me!

Hal.
(*A sad fact he hates to admit*) You're the only friend I
got, Al.

Alan.
(*Resisting any appeal to his sympathy*) Cut it!

Hal.
It's a fact! You know how it was in the fraternity. All
those other bastards always looking down their noses at
me! Makin' sure I used a fork instead of a knife! You're
the only decent guy I know in this whole fouled-up world.

Alan.
(*A little dubious*) Gee . . . thanks!

Hal.
It's *true*! You're the only friend I got, whether you wanta
be or not.

Alan.
Well, why don't you go *home*?

Hal.
Not since the old man died. *Huh-uh!*

Alan.
Maybe your mother *needs* you.

Hal.
Needs me? Not *her*. She's doin' O.K. She took over the
old man's filling station. She's in the gravy.

Alan.
Then get a job from *her*.

Hal.
(*Full of deep misgiving*) I can't even look her in the face,
Al . . . without gettin' *sick*.

Alan.
Hal, that's not fair to your own mother.

Hal.
The old man left the filling station to *me*. . . .

Alan.
Then go back and settle with your mother and. . . .

Hal.
But she told the lawyers he was bughouse, so *she* could
take over.

Alan.
(*Wincing*) Oh! Golly!

Hal.
See . . . the old man had started drinkin' again.

Alan.
Yah! You told me once he . . .

Hal.
(*Obviously he loved his father*) He'd been sober for six
years. It looked like he was gonna stay that way. But
the old lady had to have one more good fight out of
him. . . . So he went on his last bender.

Alan.
(*Thoughtfully*) Gee, Hal, I'm awfully sorry.

Hal.
(*His face is set with determination. A few tears begin to
well in his eyes. He grits his teeth and clenches his fists.*)
It's the kinda thing that . . . (*He gropes for the words.*)

Alan.
Easy, Hal!

Hal.
I gotta *amount* to something, Al. I *gotta*!

Alan.
(*Warm but reasonable.*) You're not going to do it over-
night, Hal. You're not going to do it by playing football
or trying to get in the movies.

Hal.
Yah! I know.

Alan.
I'll get you a job, Hal.

Hal.
That's all I want, Al. Just a job. A *good* job. I wanta be
like *you*.

Alan.
Like *me*?

Hal.
Yah, I'd like a job in a nice office, where I could wear a
sharp suit, and give dictation to a secretary, and talk
over the phone about . . . *enter*prises, and things.

Alan.
Look, Hal, I'm not much more than an errand boy, taking
orders from everyone at the bank. I earn two hundred
dollars a month.

Hal.
Is that all?

Alan.
I know Dad has plans for me, but right now I'm content
to stay here and *learn* the business, from the bottom up.

Hal.
(*Thinking*) It makes sense.

Alan.
   If you wanta get somewhere, Hal, you just have to work hard and be *patient*.
Hal.
   (*Taking it all in*) Yah! That's something I gotta learn . . . *patience!*

from
SUMMER BRAVE
by William Inge

Act II
MADGE, MILLIE

The next scene from *Summer Brave* takes place in the late
afternoon on the Owens' lawn just before a small town
evening picnic. Millie, 16, usually in a pair of dungarees
has dressed herself in a pretty dress and is wearing some
make-up. She feels awkward but is also somewhat pleased
with her appearance. Music is coming from a radio on
the porch and as Millie is dancing playfully around the
porch with an imaginary partner, her sister appears from
the kitchen. Madge, even in a housedress and apron, is
strikingly beautiful. (For further comments on the play,
see the introduction to the preceding scene.)

Madge.
I don't know why you couldn't have helped us in the
kitchen.
Millie.
(*Lightly, giving her own version of the sophisticated
belle*) I had to dress for the ball.
Madge.
I had to make the potato salad, and stuff the eggs, and
make three dozen bread and butter sandwiches. I feel
like an old kitchen slavey.
Millie.
(*In a very affected accent*) I had to *bathe* . . . and dust
my limbs with powder . . . and slip into my frock . . .
Madge.
Did you clean the bathtub?
Millie.
Yes, I cleaned the bathtub.

Madge.
It's a wonder.

Millie.
(*Shyly now, daring to ask the question*) Madge?

Madge.
What?

Millie.
How do I look? Tell me the truth.

Madge.
You look all right.

Millie.
(*Having hoped for a little more*) Do I, Madge?

Madge.
I guess so.

Millie.
I feel sorta funny.

Madge.
The dress is pretty.

Millie.
It was *yours*. Do *I* ever get any new dresses? No. "Here's an old dress of Madge's. It'll do for Millie." (*Serious again*) Madge?

Madge.
What?

Millie.
How do you talk to boys?

Madge.
Why, you just talk, silly.

Millie.
But how d'ya think of things to say?

Madge.
I don't know. I guess you just say the things that come into your head.

Millie.
But nothing ever comes into my head.

Madge.
Talk to boys the same as you'd talk to anyone else.

Millie.
Somehow . . . it's different. (*Another long pause*) Madge?

Madge.
What?

Millie.
Do you think Hal's good lookin'?

Madge.
(*If she does, she's not letting anyone know it.*) Maybe . . . in a sort of way.

Millie.
I think he's a big show-off. You should have seen him this afternoon at the swimming pool. He got up on the high diving board and did real graceful swan dives, and a two and a half gainer, and a back flip . . . and all the girls stood around clapping. He ate it up.

Madge.
(*Her mind elsewhere*) I think I'll paint my toenails to-night and wear sandals.

Millie.
And he was bragging all afternoon. He said he used to be a deep-sea diver off Catalina Island.

Madge.
Honest?

Millie.
And he says he used to make hundreds of dollars doing parachute jumps out of a balloon. Do you believe it?

Madge.
I don't see why not.

Millie.
You never hear Alan bragging that way.

Madge.
Alan never jumped out of a balloon.

Millie.
Madge, I think he's girl crazy too.

Madge.
You think every boy you see is something horrible.

Millie.
Alan took us into the Hi Ho for Cokes and there was a gang of girls in the back booth. Juanita Badger and her gang. When they saw him, they started giggling and tee-heeing and saying all sorts of crazy things. Then Juanita Badger comes up to me and whispers, "He's the cutest thing I ever saw." Is he, Madge?

Madge.
I certainly wouldn't say he was "the cutest thing I ever saw."

Millie.
Juanita Badger's an old floozy. She sits in the back row at the movies so the boys that come in will see her and sit with her. One time she and Rubberneck Krauss were asked by the management to leave. And they weren't just kissin' either.

Madge.
(*With a feeling of superiority*) I never speak to Juanita Badger.

Millie.
(*Approaching the real question she has been leading up to*) Madge?

Madge.
What is it?

Millie.
Do you . . . think he'll like me?

Madge.
I don't know.

Millie.
I . . . I just wonder.

from
PRIDE AND PREJUDICE
dramatized by Helen Jerome from the novel of Jane Austen

Act I, scene 2
CHARLOTTE, ELIZABETH

Pride and Prejudice was billed as a sentimental comedy
when it was performed in New York in 1935. But it is
more than that, and has captured the witty quality of the
Regency novel and the conflicting emotions of the heroine,
Elizabeth Bennet, a young woman with a mind of her
own in a day when it was neither expected nor desired.
The play, like the novel, centers on Mrs. Bennet's determined efforts to find husbands for her daughters. The
following scene takes place in the Bennets' living room at
Longbourn in Hertfordshire where a party is in progress.
Elizabeth and a friend, Charlotte, have slipped away from
the festivities.

Elizabeth.
Is it not a relief to get away from all those dancing
dervishes? Will you have some of this shrub, Charlotte?
(*Places fan on table* c., *her scarf on chair; goes to punch
bowl!*)
Charlotte.
(*Crosses to table* c.) Mr. Bingley was saying what a good
idea it was to have this away from the supper room
"where a fellow could have his tipple in peace." Nice
young gentleman, isn't he?
Elizabeth.
Quite charming! Jane seems to think so too. How lovely
the darling looks tonight. Her eyes are like stars. I
wonder if her shyness is such an asset, though?
Charlotte.
You fear Bingley might need encouragement?

Elizabeth.
Few men possess enough heart to be really in love without it, Charl.

Charlotte.
I imagine Bingley will get the needed encouragement this evening. He seems to be enjoying himself immensely.

Elizabeth.
I hope so. For myself, I call it deadly dull. All I can see is a number of brainless young men and eager young ladies prancing about awkwardly to the strains of tepid music. Do you think this sort of thing fun, Charl?
(*Crosses to chair below* L. *fireplace; sits*)

Charlotte.
(*Crosses to chair opposite* ELIZABETH; *sits*) It's a means to an end. Surely Miss Caroline Bingley is warning enough against spinsterhood.

Elizabeth.
Is a warning necessary?

Charlotte.
Did you notice the fair young Lydia's triumphant progress in the ballroom—right under the maternal nose too, and your mother just beamed on her.

Elizabeth.
Yes, Mamma is shocked if a gentleman glimpses our ankles, but to let him understand that he may attain complete possession is perfectly proper.

Charlotte.
(*Rubbing her feet*) Dear me, my feet ache.

Elizabeth.
What do you think of that new man, Mr. Wickham? Very attractive, isn't he? (*music stops*)

Charlotte.
(*Feeling one of her slippered feet tenderly*) That delectable Collins trod all over me.

Elizabeth.
But are you trying to evade my question, Charlotte?

Charlotte.
About Wickham? I noticed Miss Bingley refused to stand up with him.

Elizabeth.
(*Mocking the proper* DARCY) I expect she models herself on Darcy and only stands up with members of the peerage.

Charlotte.

(*Laughs*) To be quite sincere—I feel there's something not "right" about this Wickham. (*Looks searchingly at* ELIZABETH) Don't waste your time, dear. Concentrate on Darcy—rich, aristocratic—

Elizabeth.

(*Rises*) —priggish and snobbish.

Charlotte.

Well, we must take what offers, my dear. When do we ever meet the knights of our dreams? Men were put into the world to teach women the law of compromise.

Elizabeth.

(*Laughs*) Don't be ridiculous, Charlotte. Come, we must speed the few remaining guests.

(CHARLOTTE *rises; goes to* ELIZABETH. *Music starts*)

from
PRIDE AND PREJUDICE
dramatized by Helen Jerome from the novel of Jane Austen

Act II, scene 1
ELIZABETH, JANE

This next short scene from the play portrays some of the
tribulations of a young girl in love. Although the actual
problems are those of a former age, the emotions are as
familiar as today.

The scene takes place in the living room at Longbourn.
Elizabeth and Jane Bennet have just been told by their
mother that Charles Bingley, a suitor of Jane's, has left
quite suddenly for London. Jane is crying. (For further
comments on the play, see page 232.)

Elizabeth.
(*Taking* JANE *to sofa*) Don't—darling—he'll come back.
(BOTH *sit.*)
Jane.
(*Through her tears*) But Lizzie, he hasn't sent one word
—not one! I can't understand it. Caroline merely tells me
they are not coming back until the spring—
Elizabeth.
Nonsense. You'll see, he will be here to see Papa before
the week is out. Only, darling, don't trust Caroline
Bingley. She's fond of you, I know—but she doesn't want
you as her brother's wife.
Jane.
Oh no, Lizzie, Caroline has been so sweet to me. She is
incapable of deceit!
Elizabeth.
(*Tenderly*) All right, my sweet; believe in her as you do
everyone. One comfort—even *she* can't persuade Charles
that he doesn't love you.

Jane.

(*After a pause*) But how can I marry him if his sister is against it?

Elizabeth.

That you must decide for yourself, my dearest little saint. If—you decide that the anguish of disobliging his cat of a sister is more than equal to the joy of marrying him— then I advise you to refuse him.

Jane.

(*Laughing through her tears*) You naughty girl, Lizzie. You know very well that I should marry him if it vexed every relative he has. But if he doesn't come back . . . Lizzie, Lizzie . . . I couldn't bear it. (*Wistfully*) I think I should die.

Elizabeth.

He *must* come back . . . he won't be able not to— (BOTH *look towards door as* MRS. BENNET *re-enters* . . .)

from
LOOK HOMEWARD, ANGEL
by Ketti Frings
from the novel by Thomas Wolfe

Act I, scene 2
EUGENE, LAURA

In this play, Ketti Frings has accomplished what would
seem to be an impossible task; to mold Thomas Wolfe's
densely populated, densely worded, monumental novel into
the confines of three acts. She has caught the essence of
the novel in the characterizations of the members of the
Gant family and their boarders. Gant is a lusty giant with
enormous appetites that have been eroded by drink. His
wife, Eliza, manages to keep the family fed and sheltered
by renting rooms and dealing in real estate. She is shrewd
and acquisitive and totally incapable of understanding
her husband or her children. Her youngest is Eugene,
seventeen in this play, tall, awkward, hungry for learning.

The following scene takes place on the lawn in front
of the Gants' Dixieland Boarding House in Altamont,
North Carolina in the fall of 1916. It is a warm humid
evening and Eugene is sitting listlessly on the steps when
Laura enters. She is an attractive young woman, a new
boarder.

There is a short deletion from the play which involves
another boarder. It is marked by asterisks.

Laura.
  Good evening.
Eugene.
  What!
Laura.
  I said good evening.

Eugene.
(*Flustered*) Goodyado.

Laura.
I beg your pardon?

Eugene.
I mean—I meant to say good evening, how do you do?

Laura.
Goodyado! I like that much better. Goodyado! (*They shake hands,* LAURA *reacting to* EUGENE's *giant grip.*) Don't you think that's funny?

Eugene.
(*Sits on yard seat*) It's about as funny as most things I do.

Laura.
May I sit down?

Eugene.
(*Leaping up*) Please.

Laura.
(*As they both sit*) I'm Laura James.

Eugene.
I know. My name's Eugene Gant.

Laura.
You know, I've seen you before.

Eugene.
Yes, earlier this afternoon.

Laura.
I mean before that. I saw you throw those advertising cards in the gutter.

Eugene.
You did?

Laura.
I was coming from the station. You know where the train crosses the street? You were just standing there staring at it. I walked right by you and smiled at you. I never got such a snub before in my whole life. My, you must be crazy about trains.

Eugene.
You stood right beside me? Where are you from?

Laura.
Richmond, Virginia.

Eugene.
Richmond! That's a big city, isn't it?

Laura.
It's pretty big.

Eugene.
How many people?

Laura.
Oh, about a hundred and twenty thousand, I'd say.

Eugene.
Are there a lot of pretty parks and boulevards?

Laura.
Oh yes ...

Eugene.
And fine tall buildings, with elevators?

Laura.
Yes, it's quite a metropolis.

Eugene.
Theatres and things like that?

Laura.
A lot of good shows come to Richmond. Are you interested in shows?

Eugene.
You have a big library. Did you know it has over a hundred thousand books in it?

Laura.
No, I didn't know that.

Eugene.
Well, it does. I read that somewhere. It would take a long time to read a hundred thousand books, wouldn't it?

Laura.
Yes, it would.

Eugene.
I figure about twenty years. How many books do they let you take out at one time?

Laura.
I really don't know.

Eugene.
They only let you take out two here!

Laura.
That's too bad.

Eugene.
You have some great colleges in Virginia. Did you know that William and Mary is the second oldest college in the country?

Laura.
Is it? What's the oldest?

Eugene.
Harvard! I'd like to study there! First, Chapel Hill. That's our state university. Then Harvard. I'd like to study all over the world, learn all its languages. I love words, don't you?

Laura.
Yes, yes, I do.

Eugene.
Are you laughing at me?

Laura.
Of course not.

Eugene.
You are smiling a lot!

Laura.
I'm smiling because I'm enjoying myself. I like talking to you.

Eugene.
I like talking to you, too. I always talk better with older people.

Laura.
Oh!

Eugene.
They know so much more.

Laura.
Like me?

Eugene.
Yes. You're very interesting.

Laura.
Am I?

Eugene.
Oh yes! You're very interesting!

*   *   *

(. . . *A train whistle moans mournfully in the distance.* EUGENE *cocks an ear, listens.*)

Laura.
You *do* like trains, don't you?

Eugene.
Mama took us on one to St. Louis to the Fair, when I was only five. Have you ever touched one?

Laura.
What?

Eugene.
A locomotive. Have you put your hand on one? You have to feel things to fully understand them.

Laura.
Aren't they rather hot?

Eugene.
Even a cold one, standing in a station yard. You know what you feel? You feel the shining steel rails under it . . . and the rails send a message right into your hand——a

message of all the mountains that engine ever passed—
all the flowing rivers, the forests, the towns, all the
houses, the people, the washlines flapping in the fresh cool
breeze—the beauty of the people in the way they live
and the way they work—a farmer waving from his field,
a kid from the school yard—the faraway places it roars
through at night, places you don't even know, can hardly
imagine. Do you believe it? You feel the rhythm of a
whole life, a whole country clicking through your hand.

Laura.

(*Impressed*) I'm not sure we all would. I believe *you* do.

(*There is a moment while* LAURA *looks at* EUGENE.)

. . . . . . (EUGENE *and* LAURA *speak simultaneously.*)

Eugene.

How long do you plan to . . .

Laura.

How old are you. . . ?

Eugene.

I'm sorry—please. (*Draws a chair close to* LAURA,
straddles it, facing her)

Laura.

No, you.

Eugene.

How long do you plan to stay here, Miss James?

Laura.

My name is Laura. I wish you'd call me that.

Eugene.

Laura. It's a lovely name. Do you know what it means?

Laura.

No.

Eugene.

I read a book once on the meaning of names. Laura is the
laurel. The Greek symbol of victory.

Laura.

Victory. Maybe someday I'll live up to that! (*After a
second*) What does Eugene mean?

Eugene.

Oh, I forget.

Laura.

You, forget?

Eugene.

It means "well born."

Laura.

How old are you?

Eugene.
Why?

Laura.
I'm always curious about people's ages.

Eugene.
So am I. How old are you?

Laura.
I'm twenty-one. You?

Eugene.
Nineteen. Will you be staying here long?

Laura.
I don't know exactly.

Eugene.
You're only twenty-one?

Laura.
How old did you think I was?

Eugene.
Oh, about that. About twenty-one, I'd say. That's not old at all!

Laura.
(*Laughs*) I don't feel it is!

Eugene.
I was afraid you might think I was too young for you to waste time with like this!

Laura.
I don't think nineteen is young at all!

Eugene.
It isn't, really, is it?

Laura.
Gene, if we keep rushing together like this, we're going to have a collision. (LAURA *rises, moves away from* EUGENE. *He follows her.* . . .)

from
LOOK HOMEWARD, ANGEL
by Ketti Frings
from the novel by Thomas Wolfe

Act II, scene 1
EUGENE, LAURA

This next scene takes place at Gant's marble yard and shop
where he makes monuments. Amongst the several finished
monuments the largest and most prominent is a delicately
carved angel of Carrara marble with an especially beautiful
smiling face. Eugene, wearing one of his father's aprons, is
working when Laura enters, carrying a picnic basket. She
seems somewhat ill at ease.

There is one short omission from the original play which
include a few lines from Gant before he leaves the young
people to go into his office. (For background on the play,
see the introduction to·the previous scene.)

Eugene.
Would you like to look around, Laura?
Laura.
I'm afraid I'm bothering you at your work.

* * *

Eugene.
Why do you think you might be bothering me?
Laura.
You are supposed to be working.
Eugene.
You came here to see me. What's happened, Laura?
Something's different today.
Laura.
Oh, don't pay any attention to me. I just . . . I don't
know.
Eugene.
What's in the basket?

Laura.
I asked Helen to pack us a picnic lunch.

Eugene.
Good! Let's go!

Laura.
(*Puts basket on marble slab*) Not now.

Eugene.
(*Puts his arm around her*) What is it, Laura? What's the matter? Have I done something wrong?

Laura.
(*Shakes her head*) Gene, Helen knows about us! And your father too.

Eugene.
I don't care—I want the whole world to know. (*Picks up basket*) Here, let's go.

Laura.
No. Let's not talk about it. (*Sits on stool, near slab*) This is pretty marble. Where's it from?

Eugene.
Laura, you don't give a damn where that marble came from!

Laura.
(*Starts to cry*) Oh, Gene, I'm so ashamed, so ashamed.

Eugene.
(*Sits beside her on slab*) Laura, my darling, what is it?

Laura.
Gene, I lied to you—I'm twenty-three years old.

Eugene.
Is that all?

Laura.
You're not nineteen either. You're seventeen.

Eugene.
I'm a thousand years old, all the love I've stored up for you. (*Again puts his arms around her*)

Laura.
(*Struggling away*) I'm an older woman. . . .

Eugene.
In God's name, what does that have to do with us?

Laura.
There have to be rules!

Eugene.
Rules are made by jealous people. They make rules to love by so even those with no talent for it can at least pretend. We don't need rules. We don't have to pretend.

Oh, Laura, my sweet, what we have is so beautiful, so rare . . . how often in life can you find it?

Laura.

(*Escaping his arms, rises*) Eugene, you're a young boy, a whole world just waiting for you.

Eugene.

You are my world, Laura. You always will be. Don't let anything destroy us. Don't leave me alone. I've always been alone.

Laura.

It's what you want, dear. It's what you'll always want. You couldn't stand anything else. You'd get so tired of me. You'll forget—you'll forget.

Eugene.

I'll never forget. I won't live long enough. (*Takes her in his arms, kisses her*) Will you forget?

Laura.

(*As he holds her*) Oh my darling, every word, every touch, how could I?

Eugene.

Then nothing has changed. Has it? Has it?

from
LOOK HOMEWARD, ANGEL
by Ketti Frings from the novel by Thomas Wolfe

Act III
EUGENE, LAURA

This scene takes place in Laura's bedroom in the Gants'
Dixieland Boarding House. Eugene, 17, is the youngest
son of the Gants. Laura, a young woman in her early
twenties, has been renting a room at the house for the
summer. Their summer romance has bloomed into Eugene's
first love affair. The scene opens with Laura in bed, in her
nightgown. Eugene is at the foot of the bed by the window,
looking out. He takes his shirt from the bedpost and puts it
on. (For further background, see the introduction to the
first scene from the play on page 237.)

Laura.
   (*Stirring*) Gene? What was that?
Eugene.
   Soaks Baker with the morning papers. Plop—plop—plop
   —plop—how I used to love that sound. Every time the
   heavy bag getting lighter. I'll always feel sorry for people
   who have to carry things. (*Sighs*) It's getting light, it's
   nearly dawn.
Laura.
   Don't go yet. (*Reaches for his hand*)
Eugene.
   Do you think I want to on your last morning here?
   Mama gets up so early. Do you know that every morning
   before she cooks breakfast she visits Ben's grave? (*Sits
   on bed, takes her in his arms*)
Laura.
   Gene, Gene.

246

Eugene.

Oh, Laura, I love you so. When I'm close to you like this, it's so natural. Are all men like me? Tell me.

Laura.

I've told you I've never known anyone like you.

Eugene.

But you have known men? It would be strange if you hadn't. A woman so beautiful, so loving. You make me feel like I only used to dream of feeling. I've hardly thought to daydream in weeks—except about us.

Laura.

What did you used to dream?

Eugene.

I always wanted to be the winner, the general, the spearhead of victory! Then, following that, I wanted to be loved. Victory and love! Unbeaten and beloved. And I am that now, truly! Laura, will you marry me?

Laura.

(*Moving away*) Oh darling!

Eugene.

You knew I was going to ask you, didn't you? You knew I couldn't let you go even for a day.

Laura.

Yes, I knew.

Eugene.

You're happy with me. You know I make you happy. And I'm so complete with you. (*He draws her back into his arms.*) Do you know that three hundred dollars Ben left me? He would want me to use it for us. I'll go with you to Richmond today. I'll meet your parents, so they won't think I'm an irresponsible fool who's stolen you. That may be a little hard to prove—but there is a job I can get. Would you mind living in Altamont?

Laura.

I don't care where I live. Just keep holding me.

Eugene.

I am going to have to tell Mama first.

Laura.

Let's not worry about that now. Tell me about us.

Eugene.

All the treasures the world has in store for us? We'll see and know them all. . . . All the things and the places I've read about. There isn't a state in this country we won't know. The great names of Arizona, Texas, Colorado,

California—we'll ride the freights to get there if we have
to. And we'll go to Europe, and beyond . . . the cool,
green land of Shakespeare, the gloomy forests of Gaul,
the great Assyrian plains where Alexander feasted . . .
the crumbling walls of Babylon, the palaces of the kings
of Egypt, the towering white crags of Switzerland . . .
My God, Laura, there might not be time enough for all!

Laura.
There will be time enough, darling. (*They kiss longingly.
From a far distance, they hear the whistle of a train as it
passes.*)

Eugene.
The Richmond train leaves at noon. I'll have to get
packed.

Laura.
You do love trains, don't you?

Eugene.
I love only you. Will you have confidence in me, the unbeaten and beloved?

Laura.
Yes, darling, I will have confidence in you.

Eugene.
I'll never have to sneak out of this room again.
(EUGENE *rises, moves to the door.* LAURA, *on her
knees, reaches toward him.*)

Laura.
Eugene! (*He comes back to her.*) I will love you always.
    (*They kiss.* EUGENE *exits.* LAURA *leaps from the
bed, hurries after him.*)

Laura.
Gene!

from
THE CORN IS GREEN
by Emlyn Williams

Act II, scene 1
MORGAN, BESSIE

The play takes place in Glansarno, a small village in the
remote Welsh countryside. The Welsh language and Welsh
music permeate the play with local flavor and the dark
presence of the nearby coal mines and the brooding vil-
lagers create the mood. It is into this setting that Miss
Moffat, an educated spinster, enters when she inherits a
house in Glansarno. She is determined to start a school
to educate the illiterate village children but it is a difficult and discouraging task. She is on the point of giving
up when she reads a clumsily-written but beautiful essay
by one of her students, Morgan Evans, an impudent coal
miner of fifteen. The essay not only affects her emotionally
but also convinces her of the necessity of staying and
trying again.

In the following scene, Morgan is now seventeen and
has been studying assiduously with Miss Moffat for two
years. However, he is experiencing an emotional conflict
as he feels that he no longer belongs to the world he has
always known, and he often finds himself resenting his
domineering teacher. As the scene opens he has just had
an argument with Miss Moffat and is sitting disconsolately
drinking rum in the living room. Bessie, the daughter of
her housekeeper, enters. She is a plump, pretty girl of
about 16.

Bessie.
  Hello!

249

(He stares at her coldly, plants the bottle on the table and stares away again.)

(She clutches her leg, ostentatiously.) Caught my knee climbin' down the rainpipe, ooh . . . *(As he takes no notice.)* P'raps I'm invisible.

(She tosses her head, marches into the kitchen, singing raucously and bangs the door behind her. Far away, the sound of singing: men returning from the mine, harmonizing their familiar melody, "Yr Hufen Melyn." MORGAN brushes a tear from his cheek, but unhappy thoughts assail him; his mood is fed by the music. A pause. BESSIE returns from the kitchen. She is suddenly changed, subdued and almost timid.)

Bessie.
Morgan. Mum's gone out. *(After a pause, advancing slowly towards the foot of the stairs.)* Expect she's gone to tell Mrs. Roberts about her meetin'. Though how she manages with Mrs. Roberts knowin' no English an' deaf as well . . . *(After a pause)* Talking a lot, aren't I?

Morgan.
Yes.

Bessie.
Well, I'm not deaf.

Morgan.
(Looking up at her) Been spyin'?

Bessie.
(Pointing upstairs) If people lock me in and take the key out of the keyhole, they can't blame me for listenin' at it. *(As he turns away)* Oo, I think she's wicked.

Morgan.
(Stung) Mind your own business!

Bessie.
I won't. *(Gaining confidence)* I like to know about everything; I like doin' all the things I like, I like sweets, I don't care if it does make me fat, and I *love* earrings. I like to shake my head like a lady . . . *(She stands, hands on hips, transformed from the sullen child into something crafty, mischievous and attractive. The singing stops. A pause.)* It's funny . . . we never been by ourselves before. *(She begins to sing in Welsh.)* Didn't know I knew Welsh, did you? . . . You like that song, don't you? That's why I learnt it.

Morgan.
You are different when you sing.

Bessie.
Am I? . . . (*Picking up the bottle from the table*) What's
this, medicine? (*Taking a gulp and choking*) Tastes like
rubber. Nice, though. . . . (*As he takes it roughly from
her, rises, drains the bottle, and puts it back in his
pocket*) You know—you was quite right to put her in
her place. Clever chap like you learnin' lessons off a
woman!

Morgan.
That's right . . .

Bessie.
You don't 'ave to go to Oxford! Clever chap like you!

Morgan.
(*In a whisper*) That's right . . .

(*He turns slowly and looks at her. She crosses behind
him and sits on the back of the sofa.*)

Bessie.
What a man wants is a bit o' sympathy! (*He looks at
her, his hand on the back of the chair. It is growing
faintly darker. She laughs, and begins to sing again; she
turns, still singing, looks up at him and smiles. He pushes
away the chair, seizes her with violence and kisses her
passionately. Their arms entwine and the chair crashes to
the floor.*)

(*Blackout. The curtain falls.*)

from
A CLEARING IN THE WOODS
by Arthur Laurents

Act I
NORA, HAZELMAE, THE BOY

The setting of the play, "the clearing in the woods," has
no physical reality but is symbolic of the time and place
where all of us must come out from hiding behind the
trees and painfully face ourselves, our past, our limita-
tions, our emotions. It is in this "clearing" that the heroine
Virginia is forced to confront the parts of her past and
her character that she has been evading. The play consists
of a series of flashbacks into Virginia's past and her subse-
quent struggles with the parts of her personality that
prevent her from facing the truth.

The following scene takes place at the time of Virginia's
first affair, when she was a young girl. Nora, who is
actually Virginia, has spread a blanket on the ground. A
thermos is nearby. She lights a cigarette as Hazelmae, a
girl her own age, enters with a small picnic basket. Hazelmae has a weight problem and an exaggerated Southern
accent.

There are two short deletions of lines between Virginia
and Nora. These deletions are marked with asterisks.

Hazelmae.
I declare, Nora lamb, over hill over dale to this? It cer-
tainly isn't my idea of chic. (*Both girls settle on the
blanket during the following, and* HAZELMAE *takes a
mirror and eyebrow tweezers from the basket and sets
to work.*)
Nora.
Nature, honey lamb, is not chic. (*She opens the thermos.*)
Hazelmae.
The grass is dirty.

Nora.
Then so is the sky.

Hazelmae.
I don't know why we didn't go with the rest of the girls, in the first place.

Nora.
Because they're children. God, they're so young!

Hazelmae.
It couldn't be because Mistah Pipe-Smoker is in charge of the picnic?

Nora.
I am bored with Mistah Pipe-Smoker's love affair with himself. And his hair is too long.

Hazelmae.
You weren't bored until he laughed at your Valentine.

Nora.
I knew, I knew, I knew I shouldn't have told you about that.

Hazelmae.
You didn't. I was there.

Nora.
Then why make me feel like a fool all over again? (*Hands* HAZELMAE *the cup*) Happiness.

Hazelmae.
What's in it? (*Toasts*) Happiness. (*She drinks.*)

Nora.
Gin and pineapple juice.

Hazelmae.
Not very much gin.

Nora.
Then you steal it next time. Your father doesn't drink as much as mine, anyway. (*As the music fades away, the sound of woodchopping fades in from the trees nearest them.*) My father, all fathers! The only time they appear is when we are in danger of enjoying ourselves.

Hazelmae.
My papa calls me honey bucket.

Nora.
Is there one single, sane, logical reason why we couldn't have gone to that house party? I ask you!

Hazelmae.
I have blanked it from my mind.

Nora.
(*Mimicking*) "Young ladies don't go to house parties with young gentlemen until they're eighteen." Why? Do

they ever tell you why? (*Looking off toward chopping sound*) "Because they just don't, dear." (*Takes out a pair of glasses, the better to see the woodchopper*) I loathe when they call me dear. He's cute. (*She puts the glasses away.*)

Hazelmae.
(*Sees where* NORA *is staring*) Oh. Yeeeees.

Nora.
I saw him first.

Hazelmae.
(*Shrugs*) All we'll do anyway is talk about him. Simmer down, lamby-pie.

Nora.
Simmer yourself down, pie-face. One summer in Nashville three years ago is no excuse for that accent.

Hazelmae.
If you can arbitrarily change your name to Nora, I can certainly change my accent.

Nora.
If you just once looked into something besides a mirror—

Hazelmae.
Such as, pray?

Nora.
Such as the works of Ibsen, pray—you'd know Nora was the first emancipated woman.

Hazelmae.
Lamb, the purpose of my accent is to make certain that before I am twenty, I am definitely *un*emancipated.

Nora.
He's really very cute.

Hazelmae.
Why don't you tell it to him?

Nora.
(*Loudly*) He's really very cute!

* * *

Hazelmae.
Cursing and flirting are not qualities for a lady.

Nora.
Ladies are not only useless, they're ordinary. I'm not ordinary, nor will I be. The whole beauty of the world is that every single tiny speck in it is different from every other!

Hazelmae.
There you go; doing and saying the opposite just because it is the opposite.

Nora.
Cretin! What I do and say is Me! I am Me, I am a Person!

Hazelmae.
Hmmmmmmmmmm . . . .

Nora.
(*Snatching the mirror*) Look at you!

Hazelmae.
Smarter than you are. Outside, I save my energy and do as they want. But inside— (*Lies back on the blanket*) I know exactly what I want and I will do it and have it the day I am on my own.

Nora.
Too late by then! You'll be stuck in the rut of worrying what *they* think. (*Looking off toward the woodchopper*) That's why nobody lives. *I* worry about what *I* think, and if they don't like it— (*She breaks off. The sound of woodchopping has stopped. She stares off into the trees. HAZELMAE looks at her, then into the trees, then sets up. From the trees U.R. comes a boy of about twenty, wearing faded trousers and a soiled, sweaty singlet. His open, almost wholesome good looks are scarred by the possibility of viciousness in his eyes. He stands and looks at them for a long moment, finally focusing on NORA.*)

The Boy.
Hiyuh.

Nora.
Hi.

Hazelmae.
(*Weak, scared*) Hi.

The Boy.
(*After a moment*) You live hereabouts?

Nora.
Yes.

The Boy.
Not in the village.

Nora.
No.

Hazelmae.
Huh!

The Boy.
I do.

Nora.
Oh, but I like the village, it's charming! The atmosphere

of these little old— (*He suddenly bursts into laughter.*)
Well, I happen to think it is charming.

The Boy.
Huffy.

Nora.
When I choose to be.

Hazelmae.
(*To Nora*) I just wouldn't talk to him at all.

The Boy.
Nobody's talking to you, fatso.

Nora.
That's mean.

The Boy.
I give back good as I get. (*He wipes his brow with his forearm.*)

Nora.
What's the matter? Hot?

The Boy.
Damn. (*She hands him the thermos. He takes a short drink, frowns then takes another.*) Well! What dya know now! (*Again he laughs—but with a sexual joyousness this time.*) What dya know! . . . Got a smoke? (*Takes the cigarette she offers—and waits. She gets matches from HAZELMAE and strikes one for him. He inhales slowly and deliberately.*) Gonna be here awhile?

Nora.
Yes.

The Boy.
(*Stretching*) Got a murderous job but I'm pretty near through. (*He goes back into the trees* U.R.)

Hazelmae.
(*Forgetting her Southern accent*) We're leaving.

Nora.
(*Looking off after the boy*) We just got here.

Hazelmae.
Stop showing off.

Nora.
I'm not doing a thing.

Hazelmae.
He's filthy and he smells. (*The woodchopping sound has resumed. The light begins to darken.*)

Nora.
Hazelmae, you're a snob.

Hazelmae.
You're not even old enough to go to a house party.

Nora.
What makes you old enough? House parties? What *they* say? No, it's everything that's bothering you inside and saying; Do! You're a woman when you *have* to be!

* * *

Hazelmae.
You're not impressing me one bit. Now come on. (*The woodchopping sound stops. Frightened*) Nora . . . please come.

Nora.
Nothing is going to happen. I can take care of myself.

Hazelmae.
If your father finds out—

Nora.
Think I care?

Hazelmae.
Please! Let's hurry before— (*She stops.* THE BOY *has returned to the clearing* U.R. *He wears a shirt now; rolled sleeves, unbuttoned. The cigarette butt is behind one ear. A pause, then he kicks the thermos so that it rolls to* HAZELMAE. *Fearfully she picks it up. He grins.*)

The Boy.
(*To Nora*) Running to Momma?

Nora.
No. . . .

The Boy.
Kids scare easy.

Nora.
I'm not a kid.

The Boy.
Boo. (*Coolly, she picks up the picnic basket.*) Well?

Nora.
Well?

The Boy.
(*Takes the basket and gives it to* HAZELMAE.) Wait up at the road.

Hazelmae.
She's coming with me.

Nora.
We *are* together. . . .

The Boy.
(*To* HAZELMAE) Wait up at the road, kid.

Hazelmae.
Nora—

The Boy.
The baby's afraid of the woods.

Nora.
Don't hang on me, Hazelmae. I'll be along in a minute.
(HAZELMAE *hesitates, but* THE BOY *gestures with his
head for her to go. She looks at him, at* NORA, *then
runs quickly from the clearing* D.R. NORA *smiles.* THE
BOY *doesn't.*)

Nora.
It's very pretty here, isn't it?

The Boy.
It's pretty.

Nora.
In summer, everything is so tender. Except the colors.
I mean . . .

The Boy.
The colors're soft in the shade . . .

Nora.
Hazelmae and I always . . .

The Boy.
Like deep under the trees. . . .

Nora.
I've tried painting. . . .

The Boy.
Come on.

Nora.
Where?

The Boy.
You been here before.

Nora.
Yes, but . . .

The Boy.
You're not just all big talk?

Nora.
No.

The Boy.
Then come on.

Nora.
I . . . I should really. . . .

The Boy.
Come on. (*He takes her arm to turn her around, then
gives her a little push ahead of him. She walks slowly
into the trees* U.R. *He takes the cigarette stub from behind
his ear, puts it in his pocket and follows her . . .*)

from
ANTIGONE
by Jean Anouilh

ANTIGONE, ISMENE

This play is based on Sophocles' tragedy of the same name.
It is a modern interpretation of the struggle of an individual's own feelings of morality against repression and
tyranny. Antigone, a young girl, cannot compromise her
own principles even at the risk of her own life. After
the death of Antigone's father Oedipus, King of Thebes,
there was a struggle for power between his two sons,
Eteocles and Polynices, who eventually killed one another
in combat. Oedipus' brother-in-law Creon has become king
and has decreed that Eteocles be given noble burial while
Polynices be left to rot. He has also decreed that anyone
who attempts to give Polynices a religious burial will be
put to death.

The following scene from the early part of the play
takes place on the steps of the castle in early morning.
Antigone, a "tense, sallow, wilful girl," sits on the top
step, her hands clasped around her knees. She is barefoot,
her sandals being on the step beside her. Ismene, her
sister, enters. She is a beautiful young girl, slightly older
than Antigone.

There are a few deletions of lines with other characters,
which are marked by asterisks.

Ismene.
Aren't you well?
Antigone.
Of course I am. Just a little tired. I got up too early.
(She *relaxes, suddenly tired.*)
Ismene.
I couldn't sleep, either.

Antigone.
Ismene, you ought not to go without your beauty sleep.

Ismene.
Don't make fun of me.

Antigone.
I'm not, Ismene, truly. This particular morning, seeing how beautiful you are makes everything easier for me. Wasn't I a miserable little beast when we were small? I used to fling mud at you, and put worms down your neck. I remember tying you to a tree and cutting off your hair. Your beautiful hair! How easy it must be never to be unreasonable with all that smooth silken hair so beautifully set round your head.

Ismene.
(*Abruptly*) Why do you insist upon talking about other things?

Antigone.
(*Gently*) I'm not talking about other things.

Ismene.
Antigone, I've thought about it a lot.

Antigone.
Have you?

Ismene.
I thought about it all night long. Antigone, you're mad.

Antigone.
Am I?

Ismene.
We cannot do it.

Antigone.
Why not?

Ismene.
Creon will have us put to death.

Antigone.
Of course he will. That's what he's here for. He will do what he has to do, and we will do what we have to do. He is bound to put us to death. We are bound to go out and bury our brother. That's the way it is. What do you think we can do to change it?

Ismene.
(*Releases* ANTIGONE's *hand; draws back a step*) I don't want to die.

Antigone.
I'd prefer not to die, myself.

Ismene.
Listen to me, Antigone. I thought about it all night. I'm

older than you are. I always think things over and you
don't. You are impulsive. You get a notion in your head
and you jump up and do the thing straight off. And if
it's silly, well, so much the worse for you. Whereas, I
think things out.

Antigone.
Sometimes it is better not to think too much.

Ismene.
I don't agree with you! Oh, I know it's horrible. And I
pity Polynices just as much as you do. But all the same,
I sort of see what Uncle Creon means.

Antigone.
I don't want to "sort of see" anything.

Ismene.
Uncle Creon is the king. He has to set an example!

Antigone.
But I am not the king; and I don't have to set people
examples. Little Antigone gets a notion in her head—the
nasty brat, the wilful, wicked girl; and they put her in a
corner all day, or they lock her up in the cellar. And
she deserves it. She shouldn't have disobeyed!

Ismene.
There you go, frowning, glowering, wanting your own
stubborn way in everything. Listen to me. I'm right
oftener than you are.

Antigone.
I don't want to be right!

Ismene.
At least you can try to understand.

Antigone.
Understand! The first word I ever heard out of any of
you was that word "understand." Why didn't I "understand" that I must not play with water—cold, black,
beautiful flowing water—because I'd spill it on the palace
tiles. Or with earth, because earth dirties a little girl's
frock. Why didn't I "understand" that nice children don't
eat out of every dish at once; or give everything in their
pockets to beggars; or run in the wind so fast that they
fall down; or ask for a drink when they're perspiring;
or want to go swimming when it's either too early or
too late, merely because they happen to feel like swimming. Understand! I don't want to understand. There'll

be time enough to understand when I'm old. . . . If I
ever *am* old. But not now.

Ismene.
He is stronger than we are, Antigone. He is the king.
And the whole city is with him. Thousands and thousands
of them, swarming through all the streets of Thebes.

Antigone.
I am not listening to you.

Ismene.
His mob will come running, howling as it runs. A thousand arms will seize our arms. A thousand breaths will
breathe into our faces. Like one single pair of eyes, a
thousand eyes will stare at us. We'll be driven in a
tumbrel through their hatred, through the smell of them
and their cruel, roaring laughter. We'll be dragged to the
scaffold for torture, surrounded by guards with their idiot
faces all bloated, their animal hands clean-washed for
the sacrifice, their beefy eyes squinting as they stare at
us. And we'll know that no shrieking and no begging will
make them understand that we want to live, for they
are like slaves who do exactly as they've been told, without caring about right or wrong. And we shall suffer,
we shall feel pain rising in us until it becomes so un-
bearable that we *know* it must stop. But it won't stop,
it will go on rising and rising, like a screaming voice.
Oh, I can't, I can't, Antigone! (*A pause*)

Antigone.
How well you have thought it all out.

Ismene.
I thought of it all night long. Didn't you?

Antigone.
Oh, yes.

Ismene.
I'm an awful coward, Antigone.

Antigone.
So am I. But what has that got to do with it?

Ismene.
But, Antigone! Don't you want to go on living?

Antigone.
Go on living! Who was it that was always the first out of
bed because she loved the touch of the cold morning air
on her bare skin? Who was always the last to bed because
nothing less than infinite weariness could wean her from

the lingering night? Who wept when she was little because there were too many grasses in the meadow, too many creatures in the field, for her to know and touch them all?

Ismene.

(*Clasps* ANTIGONE's *hands, in a sudden rush of tenderness*) Darling little sister!

Antigone.

(*Repulsing her*) No! For heaven's sake! Don't paw me! And don't let us start sniveling! You say you've thought it all out. The howling mob—the torture—the fear of death . . . they've made up your mind for you. Is that it?

Ismene.

Yes.

Antigone.

All right. They're as good excuses as any.

Ismene.

Antigone, be sensible. It's all very well for men to believe in ideas and die for them. But you are a girl!

Antigone.

Don't I know I'm a girl? Haven't I spent my life cursing the fact that I was a girl?

Ismene.

(*With spirit*) Antigone! You have everything in the world to make you happy. All you have to do is reach out for it. You are going to be married; you are young; you are beautiful—

Antigone.

I am not beautiful.

Ismene.

Yes, you are! Not the way other girls are. But it's always you that the little boys turn to look back at when they pass us in the street. And when you go by, the little girls stop talking. They stare and stare at you, until we've turned a corner.

Antigone.

(*A faint smile*) "Little boys—little girls."

Ismene.

(*Challengingly*) And what about Haemon?

Antigone.

I shall see Haemon this morning. I'll take care of Haemon. You always said I was mad; and it didn't matter how little I was or what I wanted to do. Go back to bed now, Ismene. The sun is coming up, and as you see, there is

nothing I can do today. Our brother Polynices is as well
guarded as if he had won the war and were sitting on
his throne. Go along. You are pale with weariness.

Ismene.
What are you going to do?

*   *   *

Antigone.
I don't feel like going to bed. However, if you like, I'll
promise not to leave the house till you wake up. Nurse
is getting me breakfast. Go and get some sleep. The sun
is just up. Look at you: You can't keep yours eyes open.
Go.

Ismene.
And you will listen to reason, won't you? You'll let me
talk to you about this again? Promise?

Antigone.
I promise. I'll let you talk. I'll let all of you talk. Go
to bed, now. (ISMENE *goes to arch and exits.*) Poor
Ismene!

*   *   *

(ISMENE *enters again.*)

Ismene.
I can't sleep, I know. I'm terrified. I'm so afraid that
even though it is daylight, you will still try to bury
Polynices. Antigone, little sister, we all want to make
you happy—Haemon, and Nurse, and I, and Puff whom
you love. We love you, we are alive, we need you. And
you remember what Polynices was like. He was our
brother, of course. But he's dead; and he never loved
you. He was a bad brother. He was like an enemy in the
house. He never thought of you. Why should you think
of him? What if his soul does have to wander through
endless time without rest or peace? Don't try something
that is beyond your strength. You are always defying
the world, but you're only a girl, after all. Stay at home
tonight. Don't try to do it, I beg you. It's Creon's doing,
not ours.

Antigone.
You are too late, Ismene. When you first saw me this
morning, I had just come in from burying him.

(ANTIGONE *exits through arch.*)

from
ANTIGONE
by Jean Anouilh

ANTIGONE, HAEMON

The next scene from ANTIGONE is a love scene but not of the usual sort because Antigone is not an ordinary girl. That she has buried her brother against royal decree has not yet been discovered but she knows this meeting is her farewell to her lover because she will have to pay the penalty with her life. The relationship between the two young people is expressed clearly in the following tortured dialogue.

The scene takes place on the steps of the castle of Thebes. It is early morning and Antigone is sitting on the steps, barefoot, with her sandals near her. She lifts her head as she hears footsteps. Haemon enters.

Antigone.
(*Rising*) Haemon, Haemon! Forgive me for quarreling with you last night. (*She crosses quickly to* HAEMON *and they embrace.*) Forgive me for everything. It was all my fault. I beg you to forgive me.

Haemon.
You know that I've forgiven you. You had hardly slammed the door, your perfume still hung in the room, when I had already forgiven you. (*He holds her in his arms and smiles at her. Then draws slightly back*) You stole that perfume. From whom?

Antigone.
Ismene.

Haemon.
And the rouge? and the face powder? and the frock? Whom did you steal them from?

265

Antigone.
Ismene.

Haemon.
And in whose honor did you get yourself up so elegantly?

Antigone.
I'll tell you everything. (*She draws him closer.*) Oh darling, what a fool I was! To waste a whole evening! A whole, beautiful evening!

Haemon.
We'll have other evenings, my sweet.

Antigone.
Perhaps we won't.

Haemon.
And other quarrels, too. A happy love is full of quarrels, you know.

Antigone.
A happy love, yes. Haemon, listen to me.

Haemon.
Yes?

Antigone.
Don't laugh at me this morning. Be serious.

Haemon.
I am serious.

Antigone.
And hold me tight. Tighter than you have ever held me. I want all your strength to flow into me.

Haemon.
There! With all my strength. (*A pause*)

Antigone.
(*Breathless*) That's good. (*They stand for a moment, silent and motionless.*) Haemon! I wanted to tell you. You know—the little boy we were going to have when we were married?

Haemon.
Yes?

Antigone.
I'd have protected him against everything in the world.

Haemon.
Yes, dearest.

Antigone.
Oh, you don't know how I should have held him in my arms and given him my strength. He wouldn't have been afraid of anything, I swear he wouldn't. Not of the falling night, nor of the terrible noonday sun, nor of all the shadows or all the walls in the world. Our little boy,

Haemon! His mother wouldn't have been very imposing; her hair wouldn't always have been brushed; but she would have been strong where he was concerned, so much stronger than all those real mothers with their real bosoms and their aprons round their middle. You believe that, don't you, Haemon?

Haemon.
(*Soothingly*) Yes, yes, my darling.

Antigone.
And you believe me when I say that you would have had a real wife?

Haemon.
Darling, you are my real wife.

Antigone.
(*Pressing against him and crying out*) Haemon, you loved me! You did love me that night, didn't you? You're sure of it!

Haemon.
(*Rocking her gently*) What night, my sweet?

Antigone.
And you are very sure, aren't you, that that night at the dance, when you came to the corner where I was sitting, there was no mistake? It was me you were looking for? It wasn't another girl? And you're sure that never, not in your most secret heart of hearts, have you said to yourself that it was Ismene you ought to have asked to marry you?

Haemon.
(*Reproachfully*) Antigone, you are idiotic. You might give me credit for knowing my own mind. It's you I love, and no one else.

Antigone.
But you love me as a woman—as a woman wants to be loved, don't you? Your arms round me aren't lying, are they? Your hands, so warm against my back—they're not lying? This warmth that's in me; this confidence, this sense that I am safe, secure, that flows through me as I stand here with my cheek in the hollow of your shoulder: they are not lies, are they?

Haemon.
Antigone, darling. I love you exactly as you love me. With all of myself. (*They kiss.*)

Antigone.
I'm sallow, and I'm scrawny. Ismene is pink and golden. She's like a fruit.

Haemon.
Look here, Antigone—

Antigone.
Ah, dearest, I am ashamed of myself. But this morning, this special morning, I must know. Tell me the truth! I beg you to tell me the truth! When you think about me, when it strikes you suddenly that I am going to belong to you—do you have the feeling that—that a great empty space is being hollowed out inside you, that there is something inside you that is just—dying?

Haemon.
Yes, I do. I do. (*A pause*)

Antigone.
That's the way I feel. And another thing. I wanted you to know that I should have been very proud to be your wife—the woman whose shoulder you would put your hand on as you sat down to table, absentmindedly, as upon a thing that belonged to you. (*After a moment, draws away from him. Her tone changes.*) There! Now I have two things more to tell you. And when I have told them to you, you must go away instantly, without asking any questions. However strange they may seem to you. However much they hurt you. Swear that you will!

Haemon.
(*Beginning to be troubled*) What are these things that you are going to tell me?

Antigone.
Swear, first, that you will go away without one word. Without so much as looking at me. (*She looks at him, wretchedness in her face.*) You hear me, Haemon. Swear it please. This is the last mad wish that you will ever have to grant me. (*A pause*)

Haemon.
I swear it, since you insist. But I must tell you that I don't like this at all.

Antigone.
Please, Haemon. It's very serious. You must listen to me and do as I ask. First, about last night, when I came to your house. You asked me a moment ago why I wore

Ismene's dress and rouge. It was because I was stupid. I wasn't very sure that you loved me as a woman; and I did it—because I wanted you to want me. I was trying to be more like other girls.

Haemon.

Was *that* the reason? My poor—

Antigone.

Yes. And you laughed at me. And we quarreled: and my awful temper got the better of me and I flung out of the house . . . the real reason was that I wanted you to take me: I wanted to be your wife before—

Haemon.

Oh, my darling—

Antigone.

(*Shuts him off*) You swore you wouldn't ask any questions. You swore, Haemon. (*Turns her face away and goes on in a hard voice*) As a matter of fact, I'll tell you why. I wanted to be your wife last night because I love you that way very—very strongly. And also because— Oh, my darling, my darling, forgive me; I'm going to cause you quite a lot of pain. (*She draws away from him.*) I wanted it also because I shall never, never be able to marry you, never! (HAEMON *is stupefied and mute; then he moves a step toward her.*) Haemon! You took a solemn oath! You swore! Leave me quickly! To-morrow the whole thing will be clear to you. Even before tomorrow: this afternoon. If you please, Haemon, go now. It is the only thing left that you can do for me if you still love me. (*A pause as* HAEMON *stares at her. Then he turns and goes out through the arch.* ANTIGONE *stands motionless, then moves to chair at end of table and lets herself gently down on it. In a mild voice, as of calm after storm*) Well, it's over for Haemon, Antigone.

from
DARK OF THE MOON
by Howard Richardson and William Berney

Act II, scene 2
JOHN, BARBARA ALLEN, DARK WITCH, FAIR
WITCH

This is a haunting play set in the Smoky Mountains which
has a brooding folk-ballad quality. Though a simple story
of a witchboy who has fallen in love with a human, the
characterizations of these superstitious mountain people
are penetratingly real.

This scene takes place inside John and Barbara Allen's
one-room cabin. Barbara has just given birth to a baby
which, to the horror of everybody around her, has appeared
to be a witch baby. John has just chased everybody out
and is alone with Barbara.

John.
What fer they burn my baby? What fer they do a thing
like that?

Barbara.
They 'lowed hit a witch.

John.
They a-lyin'. Hit were our baby. Hit warn't no witch.

Barbara.
I wish you'd been here to tell 'em so.

John.
I were outside. I were walkin' on the mounting.

Barbara.
Why you leave me, John?

John.
I don't know! (*Pause*) His jes' that sometimes bein'
human's more'n I kin stand. I know hit what I wanta be,
but sometimes I feel I jes' got to git away.

270

Barbara.
Git away from what?

John.
I can't explain, Barbara. You wouldn't understand. But sometimes after plowin' all day in the sun, I jes' gotta go somewhar alone when hit night—somewhar far off, whar hit dark and black. So I go to Old Baldy. Up thar on the mounting. I look at them stars, all them planets a-twistin' and changin' out thar in space. Then I know that this'n I'm standin' on, hit ain't so much, hit little, hit twistin' and changin' too. And I wanta be somethin' more'n jes' this! So I pretend that things is different, that I ain't the same as I am in the day.

Barbara.
What is hit you pretend, John?

John.
I can't tell you, Barbara. You wouldn't love me if I tole you.

Barbara.
No, perhaps you'd better not. Perhaps I know already. Perhaps what all the others is sayin' is true.

John.
Sayin' 'bout what?

Barbara.
'Bout the baby. But how could hit be a witch with us both humans?

John.
(*Taking her in his arms*) We both human now.

Barbara.
What you mean, now?

John.
I mean the next time we have a baby hit'll be a human fer shore.

Barbara.
Then hit true what they been sayin'. Hit true you a witch that first night we met, that night the moon went dark.

John.
That were afore the Conjur Woman changed me. I ain't a witch no more.

Barbara.
And are you changed fer allus?

John.
I reckon, if you want me.

Barbara.
You won't never change back, will you?

John.
That depend on you.

Barbara.
On me?

John.
Conjur Woman tole me I could be a human if you'd be faithful to me fer jes' one year.

Barbara.
I ain't never been with no one, no sinst I knowed you.

John.
I love you, Barbara Allen. (*He kisses her.*)

Barbara.
I love you, John. (*He gently settles her on the pillow, and she drifts off to sleep. He watches her for a moment. Suddenly he leaps from the bedside, stops and turns back to look at* BARBARA. *Then he drops his head in his hands and goes out into the yard.*)

   (*The* DARK WITCH *appears in the tree.*)

Dark Witch.
So you had a baby, witch boy!

John.
You ain't got no business here. This here ain't no place fer witches.

Dark Witch.
I see she a red head.

John.
She got copper hair. What you doin' here?

Dark Witch.
I was flyin' by to look at yore wife.

John.
Well you seen her now. You better git goin'. (*The* FAIR WITCH *appears beside the* DARK WITCH.)

Fair Witch.
John Human!

John.
What that to you? (*By now he has backed up against the tree.*)

Fair Witch.
Lonesome, ain't you?

Dark Witch.
All humans are. The minute you're a human you want somethin' lastin'.

Fair Witch.
That's the reason they git married.

Dark Witch.
She can't ever know you.

Fair Witch.
She can't ever understand.

John.
Leave me be!

Fair Witch.
Miss the moonlight, don't you?

Dark Witch.
Moonlight's on the mounting.

Fair Witch.
Feels so soft against my shoulders. I been up thar a-layin' in hit and a-singin' to myself.

Dark Witch.
Yer eagle up thar too, boy. He gittin' lonesome.

Fair Witch.
She ain't fer you, boy.

John.
I'm *human* now!

Dark Witch.
You can't ever hold her.

Fair Witch.
She can't understand. Humans never know each other.

Dark Witch.
Never really find each other.

Fair Witch.
Kiss her, but you're alone, boy. Kiss her, but you're lost!

John.
I ast you to leave me be!

Dark Witch.
You're astin' fer all time, boy, instead of jes' tonight.

Fair Witch.
Three hundred years—don't ast fer more.

John.
What you want of me?

Dark Witch.
The earth's a-turnin', boy, to the night when Barbara leave you. Feel hit turnin'? Feel hit turnin'? (JOHN *buries his face in his hands.*) You'll be sorry, boy. (*She disappears.*)

Fair Witch.
You'll be sorry! (*She disappears.*)

John.
Barbara! Barbara Allen! (*He runs towards* BARBARA.) Barbara! Barbara Allen! (*He falls, sobbing, on the bed,*

his arms around BARBARA.) Barbara! Barbara! Barbara
Allen!

CURTAIN

from
THE ROPE DANCERS
by Morton Wishengrad
slightly revised by Lorraine Cohen

Act I
MARGARET, LIZZIE

The Rope Dancers, a sad play about human relationships,
has a devastating climax. Although it was the author's first
play, it warranted so much attention that the original cast
included Siobhan McKenna, Art Carney, Theodore Bikel
and Joan Blondell.

The Rope Dancers takes place at the turn of the century
in the New York tenement where Margaret Hyland and
her young daughter, Lizzie, has just moved. Margaret,
about 33, has a hard and care-worn demeanor. She has
left her poetic but irresponsible husband and has been
earning her living as a seamstress. Lizzie is immaculately
dressed but her dress has a large sewed-on pocket to hide
a deformed hand.

The following scene is from the opening of the play.
There are slight revisions, marked by parentheses, and
deletions to exclude a moving man and a new neighbor.

(*Early October, the turn of the century. Two-room flat
on fifth floor of a New York tenement. The Hylands are
moving in.* MARGARET, *the mother, is thirty-three and
careworn. Once she must have been a handsome woman,
but life has made her acid and too quick to defend herself
against its attack.* LIZZIE *is a pale, delicate child of
eleven dressed in white, with white shoes and a white
bow in her hair . . . as if she were going to a wedding,
and not moving into a tenement apartment. As the scene
opens* LIZZIE *is placing books in a bookcase.*)

275

Lizzie.
(*Singing to herself—by rote*)
President, President Rutherford Hayes,
Grew a beard in twenty-eight days.

(*From the hall outside MARGARET comes into the kitchen carrying a tailor's dummy. She places it in a corner of the room, rapidly removes her hat and coat and goes to a packing barrel, which shows signs of having been half-emptied.*)

Margaret.
(*Calling*) I almost forgot the dummy.

Lizzie.
What?

Margaret.
I almost forgot the dummy.

Lizzie.
(*From the bedroom*) I was wondering why you went out again.

Margaret.
I don't trust that moving man.

Lizzie.
He's a nice man. You can tell by the way he talks to his horse. He told me he never takes jobs that are too big—because of the horse.

Margaret.
(He's careless with furniture. He's supposed to be an experienced moving man and he just can't be careful.)

Lizzie.
It's heavy work and there are so many stairs.

Margaret.
You are suddenly a friend of his because he turned around and gave you the tip I gave him. You can keep the ten cents.

Lizzie.
(*She returns it to her mother, her voice tight with reproach.*) He was a nice man.

Margaret.
You mean he was a fool. Keep it.

Lizzie.
It doesn't belong to me.

Margaret.
You're another fool.

Lizzie.
(*Turning her back*) You aren't; you have the ten cents.
(MARGARET *imploringly holds the dime out to LIZ-*

ZIE, *who never turns.* MARGARET *puts the coin in her change purse, thinks better of it and puts it instead on the table. She closes the purse and fastens it with the safety pin.*)

Margaret.
You always wanted a window on the street. Well—there it is. (LIZZIE *goes to the window . . . while her mother goes through the secret operation of hiding the change purse in the pocketbook and restoring the pocketbook to the paper bag in the breadbox, etc.*) Don't lean out too far.

Lizzie.
(*From the window*) What?

Margaret.
I said, don't lean out too far.

Lizzie.
I won't. (*With more animation*) They're wading in the horse trough.

Margaret.
Who?

Lizzie.
(*Craning to see*) Some boys and girls. They're playing.

Margaret.
(*As she goes toward a packing barrel*) If they were my children I'd find something for them to do with their time.

Lizzie.
(*Dully*) I know . . . they're just silly kids. (*Turning to her*) Ma, where's my jump-rope?

Margaret.
There's more important things than jump-ropes to be unpacked.

* * *

Lizzie.
Oh, there's the same crazy rag man we had on Lispenard Street. What's he doing here?

Margaret.
(*Working all the while*) Earning his living by the sweat of his brow. He's a hard-working man. But he needn't stop for me. When I get through with clothes, there's nothing left . . . not even rags.

(*From this point and to the final curtain,* MARGARET *is constantly at work and under her skillful hands the bare flat is put in order.*)

Lizzie.
(*Leaning out*) The people on the third have got a little white poodle dog.

Margaret.
They're never clean . . . shedding all over.

Lizzie.
I'll bet it has a cute face.

Margaret:
When it rains, they have a smell. Don't lean out. Shut the window and help me unpack. (*LIZZIE tries to close the window with one hand. MARGARET, a look of sudden tenderness on her face, goes to the window and helps her. LIZZIE runs to the table, and still using only one hand, tries to remove a small stack of dishes. MARGARET nods, a nod of reassurance. LIZZIE removes the hand from the pocket—it is a mittened hand. She takes up the dishes and starts toward the cupboard.*)
What are you doing?

Lizzie.
Putting them in the cupboard.

Margaret.
You know better than that. Put them on the sink.

Lizzie.
You washed them before we moved . . . in scalding water.

Margaret.
I'm going to wash them again. And then I'm going to wash the cupboard again. I'm going to scrub this flat from top to bottom. I don't live in other people's dirt. (*LIZZIE responds with the mechanical flattery expected of her.*)

Lizzie.
You're clean, Ma. You're the cleanest thing I ever saw.

Margaret.
(*Pleased*) I'm going to make you a nice new dress, just as soon as I finish the shirtwaist for Mrs. Bernard and the velvet coat.

Lizzie.
You work too hard.

Margaret.
To work is to pray.

Lizzie.
I wish I could help you sew. Then you wouldn't have to stay up nights.

Margaret.

Tell that to James Hyland. He always said I complain ...
this is my lot in life, this is what I am, and I must be
grateful for good health and for what I have. If your
father had been a man like other men, I wouldn't have
to take in sewing. If! It's a big word. (We would argue
and we would both be upset but I knew he'd be all right.
He heals. He would walk downstairs broken-hearted but
on the corner a man would say, "Sir, can you tell me
the hour?" and he would deliver a talk on time. So full
of quotations, he would be invited to the nearest tavern
for a glass of sherry from Spain. So if I'm a devil, I
want you to know the devil is a devil because the devil
has a memory. I want to tell you all the times I sent
him downstairs to buy bread and he met a man on the
street. Or he argued a case for a lawyer, or wrote a
prescription for a medical doctor, and all the time I sat
with a baby in my arms and waited ... while he talked
... and I knew what all those people were thinking ...
how lucky I was to be married to James Hyland.) (*The
recollection of James Hyland angers her and she turns
sharply on* LIZZIE.) I don't care if I never see him again.
(*The look of misery on* LIZZIE's *face infuriates her.*)
Don't stand there like a wooden stick. If you're going to
help me, help me, if not go and sit on a chair and read
your books.

Lizzie.

I don't want to read. I want to help you.

Margaret.

I don't need anyone to help me. I'm capable of helping
myself. I earn my own piece of bread. I take no favors
from anyone. I moved by myself. I'll unpack myself. I
don't need his help. I don't need his daughter's help,
I don't need anybody's help. (*Yelling*) And I don't need
that look from you, Lizzie Hyland. I don't keep you in
white dresses for that kind of look.

Lizzie.

I'm sorry I looked.

Margaret.

But you're not sorry I'm yelling.

Lizzie.

(*Belligerently*) I love my father.

Margaret.

Of course! Because I'm the bad one, I'm the mean one, I'm the witch.

Lizzie.

I never said that.

Margaret.

That's what you think. Go on, deny it. Your mother—the witch.

Lizzie.

Please. I can't talk to you when you're like this.

Margaret.

(*Working herself up into a fury.*) You can't deny it. That's what you think of me. The mean one, the bad one. You do, say it—you do. Hate me, Lizzie, hate me, but don't lie to me or I'll take a strap and lay your back open . . . because God hates a liar. And I won't have any lies in this new house. No more lies. No more lies. I want this to be a clean house. I want this to be a good house . . . I want . . . (*Suddenly she stops.*) Oh, my God! Someday I'll take a knife and cut it out.

Lizzie.

(*Afraid*) Ma!

Margaret.

The evil tongue in my face. . . . I swear I'll bite it off with my own teeth.

Lizzie.

Don't talk like that.

Margaret.

The evil tongue in my face . . . I swear I'll bite it off with my own teeth.

Lizzie.

Don't talk like that.

Margaret.

The only thing it's good for is to tear living pieces out of people. (LIZZIE *runs to her mother and holds her fiercely* . . . MARGARET *doesn't cry, but the posture of her body, the clenching of her hands is louder than a cry.*)

Lizzie.

(*Whispering*) You're a good mother. (*She reaches up with her mittened hand and she strokes her mother's face* . . .)

Margaret.
You've been angry with me since they—those people on the fourth came in to say hello.

Lizzie.
You promised. We're in a new house and you promised.

Margaret.
I wanted to, I tried. (*LIZZIE answers by going to a rocker and sitting herself stiffly on the edge of the chair . . . to make herself as uncomfortable as possible.*) I know. You don't have to say it to me. She wanted to be a neighbor and I behaved as I always behave. But she didn't notice. I watched her. She didn't notice a thing. Only your white dress and your white shoes and your pretty bow, and she was eaten with jealousy. (*LIZZIE begins to rock herself— and seated as she is, it is a rocking without pleasure or purpose, other than to infuriate.*) Don't sit rocking like that; you'll fall. (*LIZZIE persists.*) Stop rocking like that. (*LIZZIE stops abruptly.*) It makes me nervous.

Lizzie.
I stopped.

Margaret.
You just going to sit like that?

Lizzie.
I can stand. (*She does.*)

Margaret.
(*Shrieks*) Stop punishing me.

Lizzie.
(*With injured innocence*) Standing?

Margaret.
Lizzie, please. Don't let's hate each other in the new house. We can begin all over again. Like nothing ever happened. Not like mother and daughter. Like two loving sisters. (*LIZZIE goes into the bedroom and just stands there. MARGARET looks at her, all her yearning and need in her face . . . Only at such moments when she is unobserved does she dare to exhibit her humanity. She bends now and unties the pots and pans and she holds the rope up.*) Lizzie . . . Lizzie! (*LIZZIE goes to the door to look.*) You were sure I'd leave it behind, but I didn't. (*LIZZIE runs in with a rapturous expression. She begins to skip rope, rapidly, with great skill.*) (*Anxiously*) Not too fast—(*LIZZIE abates her speed.*) And not too long. You musn't get overtired, Lizzie, it's the only thing

I ask. Stop before you get tired. It's important. (*But
LIZZIE doesn't hear. . . . All she is aware of when she
skips rope are the words and the rhymes that spring up
in her own ear. She skips now with the merest flip of her
wrist, the barest rising of her toes . . . It is the economy of
energy with which her intelligence answers her physical
frailty. Now she begins to chant what she has impro-
vised.*)

Lizzie.
President, President, Rutherford Hayes,
Grew a beard in twenty-eight days.
Shaved it off to grow another
Made a pillow for his mother.

Margaret.
(*Donning coat and hat*) Lizzie, I have to go down to the
store.

Lizzie.
(*Stops skipping*) What for?

Margaret.
Because there isn't anything in the house for supper. You
like potato soup? (*LIZZIE's look has too many questions
in it. She casts her eyes down.*) I know. I'll go down to
her in the morning, I promise. I'll knock on her door . . .
I'll say it's a nice day, isn't it? We'll talk, we'll be friends.
You'll see . . . I'll bring her a napkin for a present . . . or
the blue dish your father won that time at the seashore.
It's quite simple.

Lizzie.
Go to her now.

Margaret.
I can't. (*Concerned*) Look how tired you are.

Lizzie.
She may not be home tomorrow.

Margaret.
She's always home . . . sitting in the window. She said so.
Your lips are blue again.

Lizzie.
Why can't you do it now?

Margaret.
(*Yelling it*) Because she's a slob! (*She goes to the door
and opens it . . . Her voice is agonized again.*) Lock the
door on the chain. (*She takes a step out and returns . . .
a note of entreaty in her voice.*) Listen to me, Lizzie. . . .

There are no buttons missing on my blouse . . . and no coffee stains. Put the jump-rope away. I want you to rest. It's important for you to rest, do you hear? And. . . . (*She goes out.*) . . . lock the door on the chain. (MAR-GARET *disappears from view.*) (LIZZIE *closes the door but she neither turns the key nor fastens the chain. Then, even in her rebellion, she remembers something. She runs to the cupboard and opens it. She finds the breadbox, the paper in it, and inside the paper; her mother's pocket-book. She starts back to the door with it, opens the door, runs out.*)

Lizzie.

(*Automatically*) Ma, you forgot your money. (*She returns, allows herself a small shrug . . . and this time she does turn the key and fasten the door chain. She returns the pocketbook to its place in the breadbox, takes up her jump-rope and begins to skip as before.*)

There once was a girl,
Her name was Lizzie,
She skipped, she jumped,
Till she was dizzy,
Her dress was white,
Her blood was red,
She skipped, she jumped,
(A considerable pause.)
Till she was dead.

(*And now* LIZZIE *accelerates the pace of her jumping. She goes faster and faster . . . the rope becomes a blur . . . it is a virtuoso performance of a rope dancer.*)

from
BAD SEED
by Maxwell Anderson

Act I, scene 4
CHRISTINE, RHODA

This play is the dramatization of William March's novel, *The Bad Seed*. It is a horror story centering on the actions of an eight-year-old girl who is pretty, dainty, well-mannered yet possesses a deep, unspeakable strain of evil.

The entire play takes place in the apartment of Colonel and Mrs. Penmark in a small town in a southern state. The Colonel is away when the play opens. Rhoda, their daughter, attends an elegant private school that has recently had a picnic. Rhoda was previously disgruntled because a classmate, Claude Daigle, had won a penmanship medal that she felt she had deserved. At the picnic, Claude was accidentally drowned and the medal disappeared. Just before the opening of the following scene, Christine Penmark has found the medal hidden in the lining of a drawer in Rhoda's room.

Rhoda.
Did you want me to come in, Mother? When you waved?
Christine.
(*She slaps the medal down on the coffee table.*) So you had the medal, after all. Claude Daigle's medal.
Rhoda.
(*Warily*) Where did you find it?
Christine.
How did the penmanship medal happen to be hidden under the lining of the drawer of your table, Rhoda? Now I want you to tell me the truth. (RHODA *takes off one of her shoes and examines it. Then smiling a little in a fashion she has always found charming, she asks*)

284

Rhoda.

When we move into our new house can we have a scuppernong arbor, Mother? Can we, Mother? It's so shady, and pretty, and I love sitting in it!

Christine.

Answer my question. And remember I'm not as innocent about what went on at the picnic as you think. Miss Fern has told me a great deal. So please don't bother to make up any story for my benefit. (RHODA *is silent, her mind working.*) How did Claude Daigle's medal get in your drawer? It certainly didn't get there by itself. I'm waiting for your answer. (RHODA *is silent.*)

Rhoda.

I don't know how the medal got there, Mother. How could I?

Christine.

(*Controlling herself*) You know. You know very well how it got there. Did you go on the wharf at any time during the picnic? At any time?

Rhoda.

(*After a pause*) Yes, Mother. I—I went there once.

Christine.

Was it before or after you were bothering Claude?

Rhoda.

I wasn't bothering Claude, Mother. What makes you think that?

Christine.

Why *did* you go on the wharf?

Rhoda.

It was real early. When we first got there.

Christine.

You knew it was forbidden. Why did you do it?

Rhoda.

One of the big boys said there were little oysters that grew on the pilings. I wanted to see if they did.

Christine.

One of the guards said he saw you coming off the wharf. And he says it was just before lunch time.

Rhoda.

I don't know why he says that. He's wrong, and I told Miss Fern he was wrong. He hollered at me to come off the wharf and I did. I went back to the lawn and that's where I saw Claude. But I wasn't bothering him.

Christine.

What did you say to Claude?

Rhoda.

I said if I didn't win the medal, I was glad he did.

Christine.

(*Wearily*) Please, please Rhoda. I know you're an adroit liar. But I must have the *truth*.

Rhoda.

But it's all true, Mother. Every word.

Christine.

One of the monitors saw you try to snatch the medal off Claude's shirt. Is that all true? Every word?

Rhoda.

Oh, that big girl was Mary Beth Musgrove. She told everybody she saw me. Even Leroy knows she saw me. (*She opens her eyes wide, and smiles as though resolving on complete candor.*) You see, Claude and I were just playing a game we made up. He said if I could catch him in ten minutes and touch the medal with my hand—it was like prisoner's base—he'd let me wear the medal for an hour. How can Mary Beth say I took the medal? I didn't.

Christine.

She didn't say you took the medal. She said you grabbed at it. And that Claude ran away down the beach. Did you have the medal even then?

Rhoda.

No, Mommy. Not then. (*She runs to her mother and kisses her ardently. This time CHRISTINE is the passive one.*)

Christine.

Rhoda, how did you get the medal?

Rhoda.

Oh, I got it later on.

Christine.

How?

Rhoda.

Claude went back on his promise and I followed him up the beach. Then he stopped and said I could wear the medal all day if I gave him fifty cents.

Christine.

Is that the truth?

Rhoda.

(*With slight contempt*) Yes, Mother. I gave him fifty
cents and he let me wear the medal.

Christine.

Then why didn't you tell this to Miss Fern when she
questioned you?

Rhoda.

Oh, Mommy, Mommy! (*She whimpers a little.*) Miss
Fern doesn't like me at all! I was afraid she'd think bad
things about me if I told her I had the medal!

Christine.

You knew how much Mrs. Daigle wanted the medal,
didn't you?

Rhoda.

Yes, Mother, I guess I did.

Christine.

Then why didn't you give it to her? (RHODA *says
nothing.*) Mrs. Daigle is heart-broken over Claude's
death. It's destroyed her. I don't think she'll ever recover
from it. (*She disengages herself*) Do you know what I
mean?

Rhoda.

Yes, Mother, I guess so.

Christine.

No! You don't know what I mean.

Rhoda.

But it was silly to want to bury the medal pinned on
Claude's coat. Claude was dead. He wouldn't know
whether he had the medal pinned on him or not. (*She
senses her mother's sudden feeling of revulsion, and kisses
her cheek with hungry kisses.*) I've got the sweetest
mother. I tell everybody I've got the sweetest mother in
the world!— If she wants a little boy that bad, why
doesn't she take one out of the Orphan's Home?

Christine.

Don't touch me! Don't talk to me. We have nothing to
say to each other.

Rhoda.

Well, okay. Okay, Mother. (*She turns away and starts to
the den.*)

Christine.

Rhoda! When we lived in Baltimore, there was an old
lady, Mrs. Clara Post, who liked you very much.

Rhoda.
Yes.

Christine.
You used to go up to see her every afternoon. She was very old, and liked to show you all her treasures. The one you admired most was a crystal ball, in which opals floated. The old lady promised this treasure to you when she died. One afternoon when the daughter was shopping at the supermarket, and you were alone with Mrs. Post, she somehow managed to fall down the spiral backstairs and break her neck. You said she heard a kitten mewing outside and went to see about it and somehow missed her footing and fell five flights to the courtyard below.

Rhoda.
Yes, it's true.

Christine.
Then you asked the daughter for the crystal ball. She gave it to you, and it's still hanging at the head of your bed.

Rhoda.
Yes, Mother.

Christine.
Rhoda, did you have anything to do, anything at all, no matter how little it was, with Claude getting drowned?

Rhoda.
What makes you ask that, Mother?

Christine.
Come here, Rhoda. Look me in the eyes and tell me. I must know.

Rhoda.
No, Mother, I didn't.

Christine.
You're not going back to the Fern School next year. They don't want you any more.

Rhoda.
Okay. Okay.

Christine.
(*Crosses to telephone.*) I'll call Miss Fern and ask her to come over.

Rhoda.
She'll think I lied to her.

Christine.
You did lie to her.

Rhoda.
But not to you, Mother! Not to you!

Christine.
Hello, Fern School. (RHODA *crosses slowly to stool*.)
Miss Claudia Fern, please. No. No message. (*She hangs up*.) She's not home yet.

Rhoda.
What would you tell her, Mother?

Christine.
No! It can't be true. It can't be true. (*She turns and looks at* RHODA, *then embraces her*.)

Curtain

from
THE CORN IS GREEN
by Emlyn Williams

Act II, scene 1
MISS MOFFAT, MORGAN

This scene takes place in the living room of a house in
Glansarno, a small village in a remote Welsh countryside.
Morgan Evans is a young boy from the Welsh mines who
is being educated by Miss Moffat. She has just convinced
the local squire to recommend him for a scholarship to
Oxford, but instead of telling him immediately when he
comes for tutoring she waits until the middle of the session
and then mentions it in an over-casual manner. (For
further background on this play, see page 249.)

Miss Moffat.
Is this your essay on the *Wealth of Nations?*
Morgan.
Yes.
Miss Moffat.
(*Reading briskly*) Say so and underline it. Nothing ir-
ritates examiners more than that sort of vagueness. (*She
crosses out three lines with a flourish, reads further, then
hands him the exercise book.*) I couldn't work this sen-
tence out.
Morgan.
(*Reading*) "The eighteenth century was a cauldron. Vice
and elegance boiled to a simmer until the kitchen of so-
ciety reeked fulminously, and the smell percolated to
the marble halls above."
Miss Moffat.
(*As he hands the book back to her*) D'ye know what that
means?
Morgan.
Yes, Miss Moffat.

Miss Moffat.
Because I don't. Clarify, my boy, clarify, and leave the rest to Mrs. Henry Wood. . . . "Water" with two t's . . . that's a bad lapse. . . . The Adam Smith sentence was good. Original and clear as well. (*Writing*) Seven out of ten, not bad but not good—you *must* avoid long words until you know exactly what they mean. Otherwise domino. . . . Your reading? (*Handing the essay back to him*)

Morgan.
Yes, Miss Moffat.

Morgan.
(*Concentrating with an effort*) Burke's "Cause of the Present Discontents."

Miss Moffat.
Style?

Morgan.
His style appears to me . . . as if there was too much of it.

Miss Moffat.
(*Mechanically*) His style struck me as florid.

Morgan.
(*Repeating*) His style struck me as florid.

Miss Moffat.
Again.

Morgan.
(*Mumbling*) His style struck me as florid.

Miss Moffat.
Subject matter?

Morgan.
A sound argument, falsified by—by the high color of the sentiments.

Miss Moffat.
Mmmmm. "The high color of the sentiments" . . . odd but not too odd, good and stylish . . . For next time. (*Dictating as* MORGAN *writes*) Walpole and Sheridan as representatives of their age; and no smelly cauldrons! (*Opening another book*) By the way, next Tuesday I'm starting you on Greek.

Morgan.
(*Feigning interest*) Oh, yes? (*He writes again.*)

Miss Moffat.
I am going to put you in for a scholarship to Oxford.
　　(*A pause. He looks up at her, arrested.*)

Morgan.
Oxford? Where the lords go?

Miss Moffat.

(*Amused*) The same. (*Rising happily and crossing to desk with the two books with which she wooed the* SQUIRE) I've made a simplified alphabet to begin with. It's jolly interesting after Latin . . . (*She searches among her papers. The matter-of-factness with which she is—typically—controlling her excitement over the scholarship seems to gall him more and more; he watches her, bitterly.*)

Have a look at it by Tuesday, so we can make a good start—oh, and before we go on with the lesson, I've found the nail-file I mentioned—(*In his mood, this is the last straw. He flings his pen savagely down on the table.*) I'll show you how to use it. I had them both here somewhere— (*without noticing, rumaging briskly*)

Morgan.

(*Quietly*) I shall not need a nail-file in the coal mine.

Miss Moffat.

(*Mechanically, still intent at the desk*) In the what?

Morgan.

I am going back to the coal mine.

(*She turns and looks at him. He rises, breathing fast. They look at each other. A pause.*)

Miss Moffat.

(*Perplexed*) I don't understand you. Explain yourself.

Morgan.

I do not want to learn Greek, nor to pronounce any long English words, nor to keep my hands clean.

Miss Moffat.

(*Staggered*) What's the matter with you? Why not?

Morgan.

Because . . . (*Plunging*) because I was born in a Welsh hayfield when my mother was helpin' with the harvest—and I always lived in a little house with no stairs, only a ladder—and no water—and until my brothers was killed I never sleep except three in a bed. I know that is terrible grammar but it is true.

Miss Moffat.

What on earth has three in a bed got to do with learning Greek?

Morgan.

It has—a lot! The last two years I have not had no proper talk with English chaps in the mine because I was so busy keepin' this old grammar in its place. Tryin' to better myself . . . (*His voice rising*) tryin' to better my-self, the day and the night! . . . You cannot take a nail-file into the "Gwesmor Arms" public bar!

Miss Moffat.

My dear boy, file your nails at home! I never heard anything so ridiculous. Besides, you don't go to the Gwesmor Arms!

Morgan.

Yes, I do, I have been there every afternoon for a week, spendin' your pocket money, and I have been there now, and that is why I can speak my mind!

Miss Moffat.

I had no idea that you felt like this.

Morgan.

Because you are not interested in me.

Miss Moffat.

(*Incredulously*) Not interested in you?

Morgan.

(*Losing control*) How can you be interested in a ma-chine that you put a penny in and if nothing comes out you give it a good shake? "Evans, write me an essay; Evans, get up and bow; Evans, what is a subjunctive?" My name is Morgan Evans, and all my friends call me Morgan, and if there is anything gets on the wrong side of me it is callin' me Evans! . . . And do you know what they call me in the village? Ci bach yr ysgol! The school-mistress's little dog! What has it got to do with you if my nails are dirty? Mind you own business!

(*He burst into sobs and buries his head in his hands on the end of the sofa. She turns away from him, instinctive-ly shying from the spectacle of his grief. A pause. She is extremely upset, but tries hard not to show it. She waits for him to recover, and takes a step toward him.*)

Miss Moffat.

I never meant you to know this. I have spent money on you—(*As he winces quickly*) I don't mind that, money ought to be spent. But time is different. Your life has not yet begun, mine is half over. And when you're a middle-aged spinster, some folks say it's pretty near finished. Two years is valuable currency. I have spent two years on you. Ever since that first day, the mainspring of this school has been your career. Sometimes in the middle of the night, when I have been desperately tired, I have lain awake, making plans. Large and small. Sensible and silly. Plans for you. And you tell me I have no interest in you. If I say any more I shall start to cry; and I haven't cried since I was younger than you are, and I'd never forgive you for that. (*Walking brusquely to the front door and throwing on her cloak*) I am going for a walk. I don't like this sort of conversation, please never mention it again. If you want to go on, be at school tomorrow. (*Going*) If not, don't.

Morgan.
(*Muttering fiercely*) I don't want your money, and I don't want your time! . . . I don't want to be thankful to no strange woman—for anything!

(*A pause.*)

Miss Moffat.
(*Shaking her head helplessly*) I don't understand you. I don't understand you at all.

(She goes out by the front door.)

from
ANTIGONE
by Jean Anouilh

Act I
NURSE, ANTIGONE

This is the opening scene of the play. It is dawn and
Antigone, a young girl, is tiptoeing through the entrance of
her uncle's palace, with sandals in her hand. Her body is
taut and she is listening when the Nurse enters. (For
further background on this play, see pages 259 and 265.)

There are two deletions from the play, which involve
the entrance of Ismene, Antigone's sister. These are marked
by asterisks.

Nurse.
Where have you been?

Antigone.
Nowhere. It was beautiful. The whole world was gray
when I went out. And now—you wouldn't recognize it.
It's like a postcard: all pink, and green, and yellow.
You'll have to get up earlier, Nurse, if you want to see
a world without color.

Nurse.
It was still pitch black when I got up. I went to your
room, for I thought you might have flung off your blanket
in the night. You weren't there.

Antigone.
(*Comes down the steps*) The garden was lovely. It was
still asleep. Have you ever thought how lovely a garden
is when it is not yet thinking of men?

Nurse.
You hadn't slept in your bed. I couldn't find you. I went
to the back door. You'd left it open.

Antigone.
The fields were wet. They were waiting for something to

295

happen. The whole world was breathless, waiting. I can't
tell you what a roaring noise I seemed to make alone on
the road. It bothered me that whatever was waiting, wasn't
waiting for me. I took off my sandals and slipped into a
field. (*She moves down to the stool and sits.*)

Nurse.
(*Kneels at ANTIGONE's feet to chafe them and put on
the sandals*) You'll do well to wash your feet before you
go back to bed, Miss.

Antigone.
I'm not going back to bed.

Nurse.
Don't be a fool! You get some sleep! And me, getting up
to see if she hasn't flung off her blanket; and I find her
bed cold and nobody in it!

Antigone.
Do you think that if a person got up every morning like
this, it would be just as thrilling every morning to be the
first girl out-of-doors?

(NURSE *puts* ANTIGONE's *left foot down, lifts her
other foot and chafes it.*)

Nurse.
Morning, my grandmother! It was night. It still is. And
now, my girl, you'll stop trying to squirm out of this and
tell me what you were up to. Where've you been?

Antigone.
That's true. It was still night. There wasn't a soul out-of-
doors but me who thought that it was morning. Don't you
think it's marvelous—to be the first person who is aware
that it is morning?

Nurse.
Oh, my little flibbertigibbet! Just can't imagine what I'm
talking about, can she? Go on with you! I know that
game. Where have you been, wicked girl?

Antigone.
(*Soberly*) No. Not wicked.

Nurse.
You went out to meet someone, didn't you? Deny it if you
can.

Antigone.
Yes, I went out to meet someone.

Nurse.
A lover?

Antigone.

Yes, Nurse. Yes, the poor dear. I have a lover.

Nurse.

(*Stands up; bursting out*) Ah, that's very nice now, isn't it? Such goings-on. You, the daughter of a king, running out to meet lovers. And we work our fingers to the bone for you, we slave to bring you up like young ladies! (*She sits on chair, right of table.*) You're all alike, all of you. Even you—who never used to stop to primp in front of a looking-glass, or smear your mouth with rouge, or dindle and dandle to make the boys ogle you, and you ogle back. How many time I'd say to myself, "Not that one, now: I wish she was a little more of a coquette—always wearing the same dress, her hair tumbling round her face. One thing's sure," I'd say to myself, "none of the boys will look at her while Ismene's about, all curled and cute and tidy and trim. I'll have this one on my hands for the rest of my life." And now, you see? Just like your sister, after all. Only worse: a hypocrite. Who is the lad? Some little scamp, eh? Somebody you can't bring home and show to your family, and say "Well, this is him, and I mean to marry him and no other." That's how it is, is it? Answer me!

Antigone.

(*Smiling faintly*) That's how it is. Yes, Nurse.

Nurse.

Yes, says she! God save us! I took her when she wasn't that high. I promised her poor mother I'd make a lady of her. And look at her! But don't you go thinking this is the end of this, my young'un. I'm only your nurse and you can play deaf and dumb with me; I don't count. But your Uncle Creon will hear of this! That, I promise you.

Antigone.

(*A little weary*) Yes. Creon will hear of this.

Nurse.

And we'll hear what he has to say when he finds out that you go wandering alone o' nights. Not to mention Haemon. For the girl's engaged! Going to be married! Going to be married, and she hops out of bed at four in the morning to meet somebody else in a field. Do you

know what I ought to do to you? Take you over my knee
the way I used to do when you were little.

Antigone.

Please, Nurse. I want to be alone.

Nurse.

And if you so much as speak of it, she says she wants to
be alone!

Antigone.

Nanny, you shouldn't scold, dear. This isn't a day when
you should be losing your temper.

Nurse.

Not scold, indeed! Along with the rest of it, I'm to like
it. Didn't I promise your mother? What would she say if
she was here? "Old Stupid!" That's what she'd call me.
Old Stupid. Not to know to keep my little girl pure!
Spend your life making them behave, watching over
them like a mother hen, running after them with mufflers
and sweaters to keep them warm, and eggnogs to make
them strong; and then at four o'clock in the morning,
you who always complained you never could sleep a wink,
snoring in your bed and letting them slip out into the
bushes." That's what she'd say, your mother. And I'd
stand there, dying of shame if I wasn't dead already. And
all I could do would be not to dare look her in the face;
and "That's true," I'd say. "That's all true what you say,
Your Majesty."

Antigone.

Nanny, dear. Dear Nanny. Don't cry. You'll be able to
look Mamma in the face when it's your time to see her.
And she'll say "Good morning, Nanny. Thank you for
my little Antigone. You did look after her so well." She
knows why I went out this morning.

Nurse.

Not to meet a lover?

Antigone.

No. Not to meet a lover.

Nurse.

Well, you've a queer way of teasing me, I must say! Not
to know when she's teasing me! (*Rises to stand behind*
ANTIGONE) I must be getting awfully old, that's what
it is. But if you loved me, you'd tell me the truth. You'd
tell me why your bed was empty when I went along to
tuck you in. Wouldn't you?

Antigone.
Please, Nanny, don't cry any more. (ANTIGONE *turns partly toward* NURSE, *puts an arm up to* NURSE's *shoulder. With her other hand,* ANTIGONE *caresses* NURSE's *face*) There now, my sweet red apple. Do you remember how I used to rub your cheeks to make them shine? My dear, wrinkled red apple! I didn't do anything tonight that was worth sending tears down the little gullies of your dear face. I am pure, and I swear that I have no other lover than Haemon. If you like, I'll swear that I shall never have any other lover than Haemon. Save your tears, Nanny, save them, Nanny dear; you may still need them. When you cry like that, I become a little girl again; and I mustn't be a little girl today.

* * *

Nurse.
Come along with me, my love. I'll make you some coffee and toast and jam.

Antigone.
I'm not really hungry, Nurse.

Nurse.
(*Very tenderly*) Where is your pain?

Antigone.
Nowhere, Nanny dear. But you must keep me warm and safe, the way you used to do when I was little. Nanny! Stronger than all fever, stronger than any nightmare, stronger than the shadow of the cupboard that used to snarl at me and turn into a dragon on the bedroom wall. Stronger than the thousand insects gnawing and nibbling in the silence of the night. Stronger than the night itself, with the weird hooting of the night birds that frightened me even when I couldn't hear them. Nanny, stronger than death, give me your hand, Nanny, as if I were ill in bed, and you sitting beside me.

Nurse.
My sparrow, my lamb! What is it that's eating your heart out?

Antigone.
Oh, it's just that I'm a little young still for what I have to go through. But nobody but you must know that.

Nurse.
(*Places her other arm around* ANTIGONE's *shoulder*) A little young for what, my kitten?

Antigone.
Nothing in particular, Nanny. Just—all this. Oh, it's so good that you are here. I can hold your callused hand, your hand that is so prompt to ward off evil. You are very powerful, Nanny.

Nurse.
What is it you want me to do for you, my baby?

Antigone.
There isn't anything to do, except put your hand like this against my cheek. (*She places the* NURSE's *hand against her cheek. A pause, then, as* ANTIGONE *leans back, her eyes shut.*) There! I'm not afraid any more. Not afraid of the wicked ogre, nor of the sandman, nor of the dwarf who steals little children. (*A pause.* ANTIGONE *resumes on another note.*) Nanny? . . .

Nurse.
Yes?

Antigone.
My dog, Puff . . .

Nurse.
(*Straightens up, draws her hand away*) Well?

Antigone.
Promise me that you will never scold her again.

Nurse.
Dogs that dirty up a house with their filthy paws deserve to be scolded.

Antigone.
I know. Just the same, promise me.

Nurse.
You mean you want me to let her make a mess all over the place and not say a thing?

Antigone.
Yes, Nanny.

Nurse.
You're asking a lot. The next time she wets my living-room carpet, I'll—

Antigone.
Please, Nanny, I beg of you!

Nurse.
It isn't fair to take me on my weak side, just because you look a little peaked today. . . . Well, have it your own way. We'll mop up and keep our mouth shut. You're making a fool of me, though.

Antigone.

And promise me that you will talk to her. That you will talk to her often.

Nurse.

(*Turns and looks at* ANTIGONE) Me, talk to a dog!

Antigone.

Yes, but mind you: you are not to talk to her the way people usually talk to dogs. You're to talk to her the way I talk to her.

Nurse.

I don't see why both of us have to make fools of ourselves. So long as you're here, one ought to be enough.

Antigone.

But if there was a reason why I couldn't go on talking to her—

Nurse.

(*Interrupting*) Couldn't go on talking to her! And why couldn't you go on talking to her? What kind of poppy-cock—?

Antigone.

And if she got too unhappy, if she moaned and moaned, waiting for me with her nose under the door as she does when I'm out all day, then the best thing, Nanny, might be to have her mercifully put to sleep.

Nurse.

Now what *has* got into you this morning? Running round in the darkness, won't sleep, won't eat—(ANTIGONE *sees* HAEMON *coming.*) and now it's her dog she wants killed. I never—

Antigone.

(*Interrupting*) Nanny! Haemon is here. Go inside, please. And don't forget that you've promised me.

(*Nurse exits.* ANTIGONE *braces herself.*)

from
THE CHILDREN'S HOUR
by Lillian Hellman

Act II, scene 1
MARY, MRS. TILFORD

The following scene takes place in the living room at Mrs.
Tilford's. It is a formal room without being cold or elegant.
Mary, alone in the room when scene begins, has run away
from school to her grandmother's. She looks nervously
around the room, then rubs her shoes against her legs to
clean them, also tries to rub some of the dirt from her
face. (For further background on this play, see page 27.)

There are several short deletions of the maid's caustic
remarks as she enters and leaves the room. These are
marked by asterisks.

Mrs. Tilford enters.
Mary.
Grandma!
Mrs. Tilford.
(U.C.) Mary, what are you doing home? (MARY *rushes
to her and buries her head in* MRS. TILFORD's *dress,
crying.* MRS. TILFORD *lets her cry for a moment while
she pats her head and puts arm around her.*) Never mind,
dear; now stop crying and tell me what is the matter.
Mary.
(*Gradually stops crying, fondling* MRS. TILFORD's
hand, playing on the older woman's affection for her)
It's so good to see you, Grandma. You didn't come to
visit me all last week.
Mrs. Tilford.
I couldn't, dear. But I was coming tomorrow.
Mary.
I missed you so. (*Smiling up at* MRS. TILFORD) I was
awful homesick.

Mrs. Tilford.

(*Leads* MARY *down* C.) I'm glad that's all it was. I was
frightened when Agatha said you were not well.

* * *

Mrs. Tilford.

. . . But how did you get here? Did Miss Karen drive
you over?

Mary.

I—I walked most of the way, and then a lady gave me a
ride and—(*Looks timidly at* MRS. TILFORD)

* * *

Mrs. Tilford.

Mary! Do you mean you left without permission?

Mary.

I ran away, Grandma. (*Nervously*) They didn't know—

Mrs. Tilford.

That was a very bad thing to do, and they'll be worried.
Agatha. (*Goes to door*) Agatha, phone Miss Wright and
tell her Mary is here. John will drive her back before
dinner.

Mary.

No. Grandma, don't do that. Please don't do that. Please
let me stay.

Mrs. Tilford.

But, darling, you can't leave school any time you please.

Mary.

* * * Oh, please, Grandma, don't send me back right
away. You don't know how they'll punish me.

Mrs. Tilford.

(*Sits on* R. *end of* L. *love seat*) I don't think they'll be
that angry. Come, you're acting like a foolish little girl.

Mary.

(*Hysterically*) Grandma! Please! I can't go back! I can't!
They'll kill me! They will, Grandma! They'll kill me!
(MRS. TILFORD *stares at* MARY *in amazement. She
sits beside* MRS. TILFORD, *puts her arm through hers,
leans against her and sobs.*)

Mrs. Tilford.

(*Calling to door.*) Never mind phoning now, Agatha.

* * *

Mrs. Tilford.

Stop crying, Mary.

Mary.

It's so nice here, Grandma.

Mrs. Tilford.

I'm glad you like being home with me, but at your age you can hardly—(*More seriously*) What made you talk that way about Miss Wright and Miss Dobie? You can't say such things about people, Mary. You know very well they wouldn't hurt you for anything.

Mary.

Oh, but they would. They—I— (*Breaks off, looks around as if hunting for a clue to her next word; then dramatically*) I fainted today.

Mrs. Tilford.

(*Alarmed*) Fainted?

Mary.

Yes, I did. My heart—I had a pain in my heart. I couldn't help having a pain in my heart, and when I fainted right in class, they called Cousin Joe and he said I didn't. He said it was maybe only that I ate my breakfast too fast and Miss Wright blamed me for it.

Mrs. Tilford.

(*Relieved*) If Joseph said it wasn't serious, it wasn't.

Mary.

But I did have a pain in my heart—honest.

Mrs. Tilford.

Have you still got it?

Mary.

I guess I haven't got it much any more, but I feel a little weak, and I was scared of Miss Wright being so mean to me just because I was sick.

Mrs. Tilford.

Scared of Karen? Nonsense. It's perfectly possible that you had a pain, but if you had really been sick Joseph would certainly have known it. It's not nice to frighten people by pretending to be sick when you aren't.

Mary.

I didn't *want* to be sick, but I'm always getting punished for everything.

Mrs. Tilford.

(*Gently*) You mustn't imagine things like that, child, or you'll grow up to be a very unhappy woman. I'm not going to scold you any more for coming home this time, though I suppose I should. Run along upstairs and wash your face and change your dress, and after dinner John will drive you back. Run along.

Mary.

(*Rises. Happily*) I can stay for dinner?

Mrs. Tilford.

Yes.

Mary.

(*Slowly crosses* U.L. *of love seat*) Maybe I could stay till the first of the week. Saturday's your birthday and I could be here with you.

Mrs. Tilford.

We won't celebrate my birthday, dear. You'll go back to school after dinner.

Mary.

But— (*She hesitates, then goes to back of love seat and puts her arms around the older woman's neck. Softly*) How much do you love me?

Mrs. Tilford.

(*Smiling*) As much as all the words in all the books in all the world.

Mary.

Remember when I was little and you used to tell me that right before I went to sleep? And it was a rule nobody could say another single word after you finished? You used to say: "Wor-rr-ld," and then I had to shut my eyes tight. I miss you an awful lot, Grandma.

Mrs. Tilford.

And I miss you, but I'm afraid my Latin is rusty— you'll do better in school.

Mary.

(*Moves to above* L. *end of love seat.*) But couldn't I stay out the rest of this term? After the summer maybe I won't mind it so much. I'll study hard, honest, by myself, and—

Mrs. Tilford.

Don't be silly, Mary. Back you go tonight. Let's not have any more talk about it now, and let's have no more running away from school ever.

Mary.

(*Slowly*) Then I really have to go back there tonight?

Mrs. Tilford.

Of course you do.

Mary.

(*Comes down to below* L. *end of love seat*) You don't love me. You don't care whether they kill me or not.

Mrs. Tilford.
Mary!

Mary.
You don't! You don't. You don't care what happens to me.

Mrs. Tilford.
(*Rises. Sternly*) But I *do* care that you're talking this way.

Mary.
(*Meekly*) I'm sorry I said that, Grandma. I didn't mean to hurt your feelings. (*Crosses to* MRS. TILFORD, *puts arms around her*) Forgive me?

Mrs. Tilford.
What made you talk like that?

Mary.
(*In a whisper*) I'm scared, Grandma, I'm scared. They'll do dreadful things to me.

Mrs. Tilford.
Dreadful? Nonsense. They'll punish you for running away. You deserve to be punished.

Mary.
(*Sits* L. *end of love seat.*) It's not that. It's not anything I do. It never is. They—they just punish me, anyhow, just like they got something against me. I'm afraid of them, Grandma, and that's the truth.

Mrs. Tilford.
(*Sits beside her*) I've never heard such nonsense. What have they ever done to you that is so terrible?

Mary.
A lot of things—all the time. Miss Wright says I can't go to the boat-races and— (*Realizing the inadequacy of this reply, she breaks off, hesitates, hunting for a more telling reply, and finally stammers.*) It's—it's after what happened today.

Mrs. Tilford.
You mean something else besides your naughtiness in pretending to faint and then running away?

Mary.
I *did* faint. I didn't pretend. They just said that to make me feel bad. Anyway it wasn't anything that I did.

Mrs. Tilford.
What was it, then?

Mary.
I can't tell you.

Mrs. Tilford.
Why?

Mary.
(*Sulkily*) Because you're just going to take their part.

Mrs. Tilford.
(*A little annoyed*) Very well. Now run upstairs and get ready for dinner.

Mary.
It was—it was all about Miss Dobie and Mrs. Mortar. They were talking awful things, and Peggy and Evelyn heard them and Miss Dobie found out, and then they made us move our rooms.

Mrs. Tilford.
What has that to do with you? I don't understand what you're talking about.

Mary.
They made us move our rooms. They said we couldn't be together any more. And they have a good reason. They're afraid to have us near them, that's what it is, and they're taking it out on me. They're scared of you.

Mrs. Tilford.
You're talking like a crazy girl. Why should they be scared of me? Am I such an unpleasant old lady?

Mary.
They're afraid you'll find out.

Mrs. Tilford.
Find out what?

Mary.
(*Vaguely*) Things.

Mrs. Tilford.
You're talking gibberish. Now run along before I get angry.

Mary.
All right. But there's a lot of things. They have secrets, and they're afraid I'll find out and tell you.

Mrs. Tilford.
There's nothing wrong with people having secrets.

Mary.
But they've got funny ones. Peggy and Evelyn heard Mrs. Mortar telling Miss Dobie that she was jealous of Miss Wright marrying Cousin Joe.

Mrs. Tilford.
You shouldn't repeat things like that. It means nothing and—

Mary.
She said it was unnatural for a girl to feel that way. (*Rises, crosses up around* L. *end of love seat and* R. *to* R. *of love seat.*) That's what she said, Grandma. (MRS. TILFORD *turns her head.*) I'm just telling you what she said. She said there was something funny about it, and that Miss Dobie had always been like that, even when she was a little girl and that it was unnatural—

Mrs. Tilford.
Stop using that silly word, Mary.

Mary.
(*Vaguely realizing that she is on the right track, hurries on. She moves downstage to below* R. *love seat, sits on* L. *end.*) But that was the word *she* kept using, Grandma, and then Miss Dobie got mad and told Mrs. Mortar she'd have to get out of the house.

Mrs. Tilford.
That was probably not the reason at all.

Mary.
(*Nodding vigorously*) I bet it was, because honestly, Miss Dobie does get cranky and mean every time Cousin Joe comes, and today I heard her say to him: "Damn you," and then she said she was just a jealous fool and he was to leave her alone and—

Mrs. Tilford.
(*Rises*) You have picked up some very fine words, haven't you, Mary?

Mary.
That's just what she said, Grandma, and one time Miss Dobie was crying in Miss Wright's room, and Miss Wright was trying to stop her, and she said that all right, maybe she wouldn't get married right away if—

Mrs. Tilford.
(*Crosses* R. *to* R. *of armchair.*) How do you know all this?

Mary.
We couldn't help hearing because they—I mean Miss Dobie—was talking awful loud, and their room is right next to ours.

Mrs. Tilford.
(*Sits in armchair*) Whose room?

Mary.
Miss Wright's room, I mean, and you can just ask

Peggy and Evelyn whether we didn't hear. Almost always Miss Dobie comes in after we go to bed and stays a long time. I guess that's why they want to get rid of us— of me—because we hear things. That's why they're making us move our room, and they punish me all the time for—

Mrs. Tilford.
For eavesdropping, I should think. (*She has said this mechanically. With nothing definite in her mind, she is making an effort to conceal the fact that* MARY's *description of the life at school has shocked her.*) Well, now I think we've had enough gossip. Dinner's almost ready.

Mary.
(*Rises. Crosses below* MRS. TILFORD *to her* L. *Turns to her. Softly*) I've heard other things, too. You've always said I should tell you things that worried me. Plenty of things I've heard worry me, Grandma.

Mrs. Tilford.
What things?

Mary.
Bad things.

Mrs. Tilford.
Well, what were they?

Mary.
I can't tell you.

Mrs. Tilford.
Mary, you're annoying me very much. If you have anything to say, then say it and stop acting silly.

Mary.
I mean I can't say it out loud.

Mrs. Tilford.
There couldn't possibly be anything you couldn't say out loud. Now either tell me what's worrying you, or be still.

Mary.
Well, a lot of things I don't understand. But it's awful, and sometimes they fight and then they make up, and Miss Dobie cries and Miss Wright gets mad, and then they make up again, and there are funny noises and we get scared.

Mrs. Tilford.
Noises? I suppose you girls have a happy time imagining a murder.

Mary.
And we've seen things, too. Funny things. (*Sees the im-*

patience of MRS. TILFORD.) I'd tell you, but I got to whisper it.

Mrs. Tilford.
Why must you whisper it?

Mary.
I don't know. I just got to. (*Leans over back of* MRS. TILFORD's *chair and begins whispering. At first the whisper is slow and hesitant, but it gradually works itself up to fast, excited talking. In the middle of it,* MRS. TILFORD *stops her.*)

Mrs. Tilford.
(*Trembling*) What are you saying? (*Without answering* MARY *goes back to the whispering until the older woman takes her by the shoulders and turns her around to stare in her face.*) I don't believe you know what you're saying, Mary! *Are you telling me the truth?*

Mary.
Honest, honest. You just ask Peggy and Evelyn and— (*After a moment* MRS. TILFORD *gets up, moves away* R. *Mary whispers again briefly. She is no longer listening to* MARY, *who keeps up a running fire of conversation.*) They know, too. Just get them here and ask them. And maybe there's other kids who know, but we've always been frightened and so we didn't ask, and one night I was going to go and find out, but I got scared and we went to bed early so we wouldn't hear, but sometimes I couldn't help it, but we never talked about it much, because we thought they'd find out and— It's in a lot of books—I mean— One of the girls at camp—I mean— Oh, Grandma, don't make me go back to that awful place!

Mrs. Tilford.
(*Abstractedly*) What?

Mary.
(*Moves toward* MRS. TILFORD.) Don't make me go back to that place. I just couldn't stand it any more. Really, Grandma, I'm so unhappy there, and if only I could stay out the rest of the term, why, then—

Mrs. Tilford.
(*Makes irritated gesture.*) Be still a minute. (*After a moment, turns to* MARY.) Have you told me the truth?

Mary.

I swear on the grave of my father. Please don't send me
back—

Mrs. Tilford.

(*Looks at her.*) No, you won't have to go back.

Mary.

(*Surprised.*) Honest? Oh, Oh! you're the nicest, loveliest
grandma in all the world. You—you're not mad at me?

Mrs. Tilford.

I'm not mad at you. Now go upstairs. (MARY *walks
slowly up to arch. She pauses there for a moment, looks
back at her grandmother, then goes off* R. MRS. TIL-
FORD *stands for a long moment; then very slowly walks
up to arch, pauses, crosses to phone. Dials a number.*)
Is Miss Wright—is Miss Wright in? (*Waits a second,
hurriedly puts down receiver*) Never mind, never mind.
(*Thinks for a moment, then dials another number*) Dr.
Cardin, please. Mrs. Tilford. (*She remains absolutely
motionless while she waits. When she does speak, her
voice is low and tense.*) Joseph? Joseph? Can you come
to see me right away? Yes, I'm perfectly well. No, but
it's important, Joseph, very important. I must see you
right away. I—I can't tell you over the phone. Can't you
come sooner? It's not about Mary's fainting—I said it's
not about Mary, Joseph, in one way it's about Mary—
(*Suddenly quiet*) But will the hospital take so long?
Very well, Joseph, make it as soon as you can. (*Hangs
up the receiver, sits in chair* R. *of console table and for a
moment is undecided. Then, taking a breath, she dials
another number.*) Mrs. Munn, please. This is Mrs. Tilford. Miriam? This is Amelia Tilford. Miriam, I need to
see you immediately. No, I am sorry to interrupt, but it
must be now. Miriam! It has to do with the school—
something very shocking, I'm afraid—something that has
to do with Evelyn and Mary— Yes, immediately, please—
(*She rises, slowly exits through arch. Going off* R. *as the
Curtain Falls.*)

from
THE CHILDREN'S HOUR
by Lillian Hellman

Act I
KAREN, MARY

This scene takes place in the living room in the Wright-Dobie School for girls, a comfortable, unpretentious room used as an afternoon study-room. Several young girls have just left the room and as Mary begins to leave, Karen Wright, one of the headmistresses, stops her. (For further background on the play, see pages 27 and 302.)

There are two short deletions involving an aunt of Karen's who is present during this scene and one short line from another girl who leaves the room right at the beginning of the scene. These are marked by asterisks.

Karen.
Wait a minute, Mary.

* * *

Mary, I've had the feeling—and I don't think I'm wrong—that the girls here were happy; that they liked Miss Dobie and me, that they liked the school.
Mary.
Miss Wright, I have to get my Latin book.
Karen.
I thought it was true until you came here a year ago. But I don't think you've been happy here. I've wanted to talk with you many times before but I was hoping that you'd come to me. (*Looks at* MARY, *waits for an answer, gets none, shakes her head.*) What is the matter, Mary?
Mary.
Nothing, Miss Wright.

Karen.

(*In front of desk*) There must be something wrong or you wouldn't make up these stories so often. Why, for example, do you find it necessary to lie to us so much?

Mary.

I'm not lying. I went out walking and I saw the flowers and they looked pretty and I didn't know it was so late.

Karen.

(*Impatiently*) Stop it, Mary! I'm not interested in hearing that foolish story again. I *know* you got the flowers out of the garbage can. What I do want to know is why you feel you have to lie out of it.

Mary.

(*Beginning to whimper*) I *did* pick the flowers near Conways'. You never believe me. You believe everybody but me. It's always like that. Everything I say you fuss at me about. Everything I do is wrong.

Karen.

You know that isn't true. (*She sits in chair* L. *of desk and holds* MARY's *hand.*) Mary, let's try to understand each other. If you feel that you *have* to take a walk, or that you just *can't* come to class, or that you'd like to go to the village by yourself, come and tell me—I'll try and understand. (MARY *slowly removes her hands from* KAREN's.) I don't say that I'll always agree that you should do exactly what you want to do. But I've had feelings like that, too—everybody has—and I won't be unreasonable about yours. But this way, this kind of lying you do, makes everything wrong.

Mary.

(*Looking steadily at* KAREN) I got the flowers near Conways' cornfield.

Karen.

(*Looks at* MARY, *sighs, rises, moves* U.S. *around* R. *end of desk, stands behind desk for a moment.*) Well, there doesn't seem to be any other way with you; you'll have to be punished. Take your recreation periods alone for the next two weeks. No horseback-riding and no hockey. Don't leave the school grounds for any reason whatsoever. Is that clear?

Mary.

(*Carefully.*) Saturday, too?

Karen.
Yes.

Mary.
But you said I could go to the boat-races.

Karen.
I'm sorry, but you can't go.

Mary.
I'll tell my grandmother. I'll tell her how everybody treats me here and the way I get punished for every little thing I do. I'll tell her, I'll—

* * *

Karen.
Go upstairs, Mary.

Mary.
I don't feel well.

Karen.
(*Sits in chair* U.S. *of desk. Wearily*) Go upstairs, now.

Mary.
I've got a pain. I've had it all morning. It hurts right here. (*Pointing vaguely in the direction of her heart*) Really it does.

Karen.
Ask Miss Dobie to give you some hot water and bicarbonate of soda.

Mary.
It's a bad pain. I've never had it before.

Karen.
(*Takes papers from desk, puts them in drawer.*) Go upstairs, Mary.

Mary.
My heart! It's my heart! It's stopping or something. I can't breathe. (*She takes long breath and falls awkwardly to floor, her head upstage.*)

* * *

Karen.
(*Sighs, shakes head. Kneels beside her.*) Mary, Mary, get up. (KAREN *crosses to* L. *of* MARY, *picks her up from floor, carries her off* L.)

from
THE DARK AT THE TOP OF THE STAIRS
by William Inge

Act III
CORA, REENIE

The following mother-daughter scene takes place in the
home of Rubin Flood in a small Oklahoma town in the
early 1920's. It is late afternoon the day after a dance
that Reenie had attended with a blind date. Reenie has
not dressed all day. She sits by the fire in her robe, rubbing
her freshly shampooed hair with a towel. The mother,
Cora, enters from the dining room, wearing a comfortable
old kimono. She looks at the tray by Reenie's side. (For
further background on this play, see page 111.)

Cora.
 Reenie! Is that all you feel like eating?
Reenie.
 Yes.
Cora.
 But that's all you've had all day, Reenie. You don't eat
 enough to keep a bird alive.
Reenie.
 I . . . I'm not hungry, Mom.
Cora.
 Now quit feeling sorry for yourself, just because you
 didn't have a good time last night.
Reenie:
 Mom, is Dad coming back?
Cora.
 I don't know. I tried to call him last night but couldn't
 get him.
Reenie.
 Aren't you mad at him any more?

Cora.
No . . . I'm not mad.

Reenie.
Even though he hit you?

Cora.
Even though he hit me. I was defying him to do it . . .
and he did. I can't blame him now.

Reenie.
Do you think he *will* be back, Mom?

Cora.
This is the day he was supposed to come back. It's almost
suppertime and he still isn't here.

Reenie.
But it's been raining, Mom. I'll bet the roads are bad.

Cora.
You love your father, don't you?

Reenie.
Yes.

Cora.
Well, I'm glad. The people we love aren't always perfect,
are they? But if we love them, we have to take them as
they are. After all, I guess I'm not perfect, either.

Reenie.
You are too, Mom. You're absolutely perfect in every
way.

Cora.
No, I'm not, Reenie. I . . . I have my own score to settle
for. I've always accused your father of neglecting you
kids, but maybe I've hurt you more with pampering.
You . . . and Sonny, too.

Reenie.
What do you mean, Mom?

Cora.
Oh, nothing. I can't say anything more about it right now.
Forget it. (*For some reason we don't yet know, she tries
to change the subject.*) Are you feeling a little better now?

Reenie.
I guess so.

Cora.
Well, the world isn't going to end just because your
young man went off and left you.

Reenie.
Oh, Mom. It was the most humiliating thing that ever
happened to me.

Cora.
Where do you think Sammy went?

Reenie.
He went out to the cars at intermission time with some other girl.

Cora.
To spoon?

Reenie.
They call it *necking*.

Cora.
Are you sure of this?

Reenie.
Mom, that's what all the boys do at intermission time. They take girls and go out to the cars. Some of them don't even come back for the rest of the dance.

Cora.
But are you sure Sammy did that? Did you see him?

Reenie.
No, Mom. I just know that's what he did.

Cora.
Wouldn't *you* have gone out to one of the cars with him?

Reenie.
(*With self-disparagement*) Oh, Mom.

Cora.
What makes you say "Oh, Mom" that way?

Reenie.
He wouldn't have liked *me* that way.

Cora.
But why? Why not?

Reenie.
I'm just not *hot stuff* like the other girls.

Cora.
Reenie, what an expression! You're pretty. You're every bit as pretty as Flirt or Mary Jane. Half a woman's beauty is in her confidence.

Reenie.
Oh, Mom.

Cora.
Reenie, I've tried to raise you proper, but . . . you're sixteen now. It's perfectly natural if a boy wants to kiss you, and you let him. It's all right if you *like* the boy.

Reenie.
(*A hesitant admission*) Oh . . . Sammy kissed me.

Cora.
(*Quite surprised*) He did?

Reenie.
On the way out to the party, in Punky's car. Flirt and Punky were in the front seat, Sammy and I in the back. Punky had a flask . . .

Cora.
The little devil!

Reenie.
Mom, most of those wealthy boys who go away to school are kind of wild.

Cora.
Go on.

Reenie.
Well, Punky and Flirt started necking, very first thing. Flirt, I don't mean to be tattling, but she *is* kind of fast.

Cora.
I guessed as much. You aren't tattling.

Reenie.
Well, Sammy and I felt kind of embarrassed, with no one else to talk to, and so he took my hand. Oh, he was very nice about it, Mom. And then he put an arm around me, and said . . . "May I kiss you, Reenie?" And I was so surprised, I said yes before I knew *what* I was saying. And he kissed me. Was it all right, Mom?

Cora.
Did you like the young man? That's the important thing.

Reenie.
Yes, I . . . I liked him . . . very much. (*She sobs helplessly.*) Oh, Mom.

Cora.
There, there, Reenie dear. If he's the kind of young man who goes around kissing all the girls, you don't want to worry about him any more. You did right to leave the party!

Reenie.
Did I, Mom?

Cora.
Of course you did. I'm very disappointed in Sammy. I thought he was such a nice boy. But I guess appearances can be deceiving.

Reenie.
Oh Mom!

Cora.
There, there, dear. There are plenty of other young men

in the world. You're young. You're not going to have to worry.

Reenie.
(*Struggling to her feet*) Mom, I don't think I ever want to get married.

Cora.
Reenie!

Reenie.
I mean it, Mom.

Cora.
You're too young to make a decision like that.

Reenie.
I'm serious.

Cora.
What makes you say such a thing? Tell me.

Reenie.
I don't want to fight with anyone, like you and Daddy.

Cora.
Oh, God.

Reenie.
Every time you and Daddy fight, I just feel that the whole house is going to cave in all around me.

Cora.
Then I *am* to blame.

Reenie.
And I think I'd be lots happier, just by myself, teaching school, or working in an office building.

Cora.
No, daughter. You need someone after you grow up. You need someone.

Reenie.
But I don't want to. I don't *want* to need someone.

Cora.
(*Disturbed*) Daughter!

Reenie.
Anyway, the only times I'm really happy are when I'm alone, practicing at the piano or studying in the library.

Cora.
Weren't you happy last night when Sammy kissed you?

Reenie.
I guess you can't count on happiness like that.

Cora.
Daughter, when you start getting older, you'll find yourself getting lonely and you'll want someone; someone who'll hear you if you get sick and cry out in the night;

and someone to give you love and let you give your love back to him in return. Oh, I'd hate to see any child of mine miss that in life. (*There is a moment of quiet realization between them. Then we hear the sound of a car drawing up to the house.* CORA, *running to the window, is as excited as a girl.*) That must be your father! . . .

from
THE WINSLOW BOY
by Terrence Rattigan

Act I, scene 2
SIR ROBERT, RONNIE

This is an interesting play about a small crime that mush-
rooms into a national scandal. It centers on the problems
of pride; everyone concerned is fighting or sacrificing his
personal pride or has already lost it.

The play takes place in the drawing-room of the home
of Arthur and Grace Winslow in Courtfield Gardens,
South Kensington, England, not long before World War I.
The Winslows' son Ronnie has been expelled from the
Royal Naval College at Osborne for allegedly stealing
a five-shilling postal order from a classmate and forging
his signature in order to cash it. Arthur Winslow, in the
culmination of a long series of actions to prove his son's
innocence, hires Sir Robert Morton, a well-known lawyer
to defend Ronnie in court. In the following scene Sir
Robert interrogates Ronnie while the family looks on.

There are several short deletions of lines of other characters in the scene and Sir Robert's responses to them.
These are marked by asterisks.

Sir Robert.
(SIR ROBERT *and* RONNIE *now face each other across
the table.* SIR ROBERT *begins his examination very
quietly.*) Now, Ronald, how old are you?
Ronnie.
Fourteen and seven months.
Sir Robert.
You were, then, thirteen and ten months old when you
left Osborne; is that right?

321

Ronnie.
Yes, sir.

Sir Robert.
Now I would like you to cast your mind back to July 7th of last year. Will you tell me in your own words exactly what happened to you on that day?

Ronnie.
All right. Well, it was a half-holiday, so we didn't have any work after dinner—

Sir Robert.
Dinner?

Ronnie.
Yes. At one o'clock. Until prep at seven—

Sir Robert.
Prep at seven?

Ronnie.
Just before dinner I went to the Chief Petty Officer and asked him to let me have fifteen and six out of what I had in the school bank—

Sir Robert.
Why did you do that?

Ronnie.
I wanted to buy an air pistol.

Sir Robert.
Which cost fifteen and six?

Ronnie.
Yes, sir.

Sir Robert.
And how much money did you have in the College Bank at the time?

Ronnie.
Two pounds three shillings.

*   *   *

Sir Robert.
After you had withdrawn the fifteen and six, what did you do?

Ronnie.
I had dinner.

Sir Robert.
Then what?

Ronnie.
I went to the locker-room and put the fifteen and six in my locker.

Sir Robert.
Yes. Then?

Ronnie.
I went to get permission to go down to the post office.
Then I went to the locker-room again, got out my money,
and went down to the post office.

Sir Robert.
I see. Go on.

Ronnie.
I bought my postal order—

Sir Robert.
For fifteen and six?

Ronnie.
Yes. Then I went back to college. Then I met Elliott
minor, and he said: "I say, isn't it rot? Someone's broken
into my locker and pinched a postal order. I've reported
it to the C.O."

Sir Robert.
Those were Elliott minor's exact words?

Ronnie.
He might have used another word for rot—

Sir Robert.
I see. Continue—

Ronnie.
Well then, just before prep I was told to go along and
see Commander Flower. The woman from the post office
was there, and the Commander said: "Is this the boy?"
and she said, "It might be. I can't be sure. They all look
so much alike."

* * *

Sir Robert.
Go on.

Ronnie.
Then she said: "I only know that the boy who bought
a postal order for fifteen and six was the same boy
that cashed one for five shillings." So the Commander
said: "Did you buy a postal order for fifteen and six?"
And I said, "Yes," and then they made me write Elliott
minor's name on an envelope, compared it to the signature
on the postal order—then they sent me to the sanatorium,
and ten days later I was sacked—I mean—expelled.

Sir Robert.
I see. (*Quietly*) Did you cash a postal order belonging
to Elliott minor for five shillings?

Ronnie.
No, sir.

Sir Robert.
Did you break into his locker and steal it?

Ronnie.
No, sir.

Sir Robert.
And that is the truth, the whole truth, and nothing but the truth?

Ronnie.
Yes, sir.

Sir Robert.
Right. When the Commander asked you to write Elliott's name on an envelope, how did you write it? With Christian name or initials?

Ronnie.
I wrote: "Charles K. Elliott."

Sir Robert.
Charles K. Elliott. Did you by any chance happen to see the forged postal order in the Commander's office?

Ronnie.
Oh, yes. The Commander showed it to me.

Sir Robert.
Before or after you had written Elliott's name on the envelope?

Ronnie.
After.

Sir Robert.
After. And did you happen to see how Elliott's name was written on the postal order?

Ronnie.
Yes, sir. The same.

Sir Robert.
The same? Charles K. Elliott?

Ronnie.
Yes, sir.

Sir Robert.
When you wrote on the envelope—what made you choose that particular form?

Ronnie.
That was the way he usually signed his name.

Sir Robert.
How did you know?

Ronnie.
Well—he was a great friend of mine—

Sir Robert.
That is no answer. How did you know?

Ronnie.
I'd seen him sign things.

Sir Robert.
What things?

Ronnie.
Oh—ordinary things.

Sir Robert.
I repeat—what things?

Ronnie.
(*Reluctantly*) Bits of paper.

Sir Robert.
Bits of paper? And why did he sign his name on bits of paper?

Ronnie.
I don't know.

Sir Robert.
You do know. Why did he sign his name on bits of paper?

Ronnie.
He was practising his signature.

Sir Robert.
And you saw him?

Ronnie.
Yes.

Sir Robert.
Did he know you saw him?

Ronnie.
Well—yes—

Sir Robert.
In other words, he showed you exactly how he wrote his signature?

Ronnie.
Yes. I suppose he did.

Sir Robert.
Did you practise writing it yourself?

Ronnie.
I might have done.

Sir Robert.
What do you mean, you might have done? Did you, or did you not?

Ronnie.
Yes.

* * *

Ronnie.
It was only for a joke—

Sir Robert.
Never mind whether it was for a joke or not. The fact is, you practised forging Elliott's signature—

Ronnie.
It wasn't forging—

Sir Robert.
What do you call it, then?

Ronnie.
Writing.

Sir Robert.
Very well. Writing. Whoever stole the postal order and cashed it also *wrote* Elliott's signature, didn't he?

Ronnie.
Yes.

Sir Robert.
And, oddly enough, in the exact form in which you had earlier been practising *writing* his signature.

Ronnie.
(*Indignantly*) I say! Which side are you on?

Sir Robert.
(*Snarling*) Don't be impertinent! Are you aware that the Admiralty sent up the forged postal order to Mr. Ridgley-Pearce—the greatest handwriting expert in England?

Ronnie.
Yes.

Sir Robert.
And you know that Mr. Ridgley-Pearce affirmed that there was no doubt that the signature on the postal order and the signature you wrote on the envelope were by one and the same hand?

Ronnie.
Yes.

Sir Robert.
And you still say that you didn't forge that signature?

Ronnie.
Yes, I do.

Sir Robert.
In other words, Mr. Ridgley-Pearce doesn't know his job?

Ronnie.
Well, he's wrong, anyway.

Sir Robert.
When you went into the locker-room after lunch, were you alone?

Ronnie.
I don't remember.

Sir Robert.
I think you do. Were you alone in the locker-room?

Ronnie.
Yes.

Sir Robert.
And you knew which was Elliott's locker?

Ronnie.
Yes. Of course.

Sir Robert.
Why did you go in there at all?

Ronnie.
I've told you. To put my fifteen and six away.

Sir Robert.
Why?

Ronnie.
I thought it would be safer.

Sir Robert.
Why safer than your pocket?

Ronnie.
I don't know.

Sir Robert.
You had it in your pocket at dinner-time. Why this sudden fear for its safety?

Ronnie.
(*Plainly rattled*) I tell you I don't know—

Sir Robert.
It was rather an odd thing to do, wasn't it? The money was perfectly safe in your pocket. Why did you suddenly feel yourself impelled to put it away in your locker?

Ronnie.
(*Almost shouting*) I don't know.

Sir Robert.
Was it because you knew you would be alone in the locker-room at that time?

Ronnie.
No.

Sir Robert.
Where was Elliott's locker in relation to yours?

Ronnie.
Next to it but one.

Sir Robert.
Next but one. What time did Elliott put his postal order in his locker?

Ronnie.
I don't know. I didn't even know he had a postal order in his locker. I didn't know he had a postal order at all——

Sir Robert.
Yet you say he was a great friend of yours——

Ronnie.
He didn't tell me he had one.

Sir Robert.
How very secretive of him. What time did you go to the locker-room?

Ronnie.
I don't remember.

Sir Robert.
Was it directly after dinner?

Ronnie.
Yes, I think so.

Sir Robert.
What did you do after leaving the locker-room?

Ronnie.
I've told you. I went for permission to go to the post office.

Sir Robert.
What time was that?

Ronnie.
About a quarter past two.

Sir Robert.
Dinner is over at a quarter to two. Which means that you were alone in the locker-room for half an hour?

Ronnie.
I wasn't there all that time——

Sir Robert.
How long were you there?

Ronnie.
About five minutes.

Sir Robert.
What were you doing for the other twenty-five?

Ronnie.
I don't remember.

Sir Robert.
It's odd that your memory is so good about some things and so bad about others——

Ronnie.
Perhaps I waited outside the C.O.'s office.

Sir Robert.
(*With searing sarcasm*) Perhaps you waited outside the C.O.'s office. And perhaps no one saw you there, either?

Ronnie.
No. I don't think they did.

Sir Robert.
What were you thinking about outside the C.O.'s office for twenty-five minutes?

Ronnie.
(*Wildly*) I don't even know if I was there. I can't remember. Perhaps I wasn't there at all.

Sir Robert.
No. Perhaps you were still in the locker-room rifling Elliott's locker—

* * *

Ronnie.
I remember now. I remember. Someone did see me outside the C.O.'s office. A chap called Casey. I remember I spoke to him.

Sir Robert.
What did you say?

Ronnie.
I said: "Come down to the post office with me. I'm going to cash a postal order."

Sir Robert.
(*Triumphantly*) *Cash* a postal order!

Ronnie.
I mean get.

Sir Robert.
You said cash. Why did you say cash if you meant get?

Ronnie.
I don't know.

Sir Robert.
I suggest cash was the truth.

Ronnie.
No, no. It wasn't really. You're muddling me.

Sid Robert.
You seem easily muddled. How many other lies have you told?

Ronnie.
None. Really I haven't—

Sir Robert.
(*Bending forward malevolently*) I suggest your whole testimony is a lie.

Ronnie.
No! It's the truth.

Sir Robert.
I suggest there is barely one single word of truth in any-

thing you have said either to me, or to the judge advocate, or to the Commander. I suggest that you broke into Elliott's locker, that you stole the postal order for five shillings belonging to Elliott, and you cashed it by means of forging his name.

Ronnie.
(*Wailing*) I didn't. I didn't.

Sir Robert.
I suggest that you did it for a joke, meaning to give Elliott the five shillings back, but that when you met him and he said he had reported the matter that you got frightened and decided to keep quiet.

Ronnie.
No, no, no. It isn't true.

Sir Robert.
I suggest that by continuing to deny your guilt you are causing great hardship to your own family and considerable annoyance to high and important persons in this country—

* * *

Sir Robert.
(*Leaning forward and glaring at* RONNIE *with utmost venom.*) I suggest that the time has at last come for you to undo some of the misery you have caused by confessing to us all now that you are a forger, a liar, and a thief!

Ronnie.
(*In tears*) I'm not! I'm not! I'm not! I didn't do it—

* * *

Sir Robert.
. . . The boy is plainly innocent. I accept the brief. (*He bows and leaves.* RONNIE *continues to sob hysterically.*)

from
THE WILD DUCK
by Henrik Ibsen
revised by Lorraine Cohen

Act III
GREGERS, HEDVIG

Henrik Ibsen is known as the "father of modern drama"
but perhaps more descriptive is John Gassner's phrase
"a skeptic in a china-shop," the china being the "bric-a-
brac of conventional beliefs." Ibsen's plays, which date from
the last half of the nineteenth century, may not seem very
modern or even skeptical today but Ibsen was the first
great dramatist to use the theater for social criticism. In
play after play, his characters struggle against the pseudo-
respectability of the day as he ferrets out all their pre-
tenses and delusions. Yet although a reformer himself, in
The Wild Duck he seeks to unmask what is bad in the
reformer.

In this rather gentle, poetic play, the family of Hialmar
Ekdal is struggling to build a meaningful life in spite of
past scandal and present lies and illusion. The reformer,
Gregers Werle, determined to have Ekdal find out the
truth, destroys even his illusory happiness.

The following scene takes place in Hialmar Ekdal's
studio. There are photographic instruments and apparatus
of different kinds lying about the room. At the back of the
room wide sliding doors open to an attic where the wild
duck is kept. Hedvig, a girl of about fourteen, is at a
table retouching some photographs with a brush. She is
sitting with her eyes very close to the work. There is a
slight knock at the door which she doesn't hear. Gregers
Werle enters.

Gregers.
H'm—!

Hedvig.
(*Turns and goes towards him*) Good morning. Please come in.

Gregers.
Thank you. (*Looking towards the garret*) You seem to have workpeople in the house.

Hedvig.
No, it is only father and grandfather. I'll tell them you are here.

Gregers.
No, no, don't do that: I would rather wait a little. (*Seats himself on the sofa*)

Hedvig.
It looks so untidy here— (*Begins to clear away the photographs.*)

Gregers.
Oh, don't take them away. Are those prints that have to be finished off?

Hedvig.
Yes, they are a few I was helping Father with.

Gregers.
Please don't let me disturb you.

Hedvig.
Oh no. (*She gathers the things to her and sits down to work:* GREGERS *looks at her, meanwhile, in silence.*)

Gregers.
Your father is exceedingly lucky to have a daughter that can help him in his work. Do you do it often?

Hedvig.
When I can coax him to let me. He doesn't want me to hurt my eyes. But just now I knew he wanted to help Grandfather make a new path to the water-trough. They are both so happy in there. (*She motions to the back doors.*)

Gregers.
I hear your mother can retouch photographs too.

Hedvig.
Oh yes, she can take photographs too.

Gregers.
It seems to me it is really your mother that carries on the business then.

Hedvig.
Well, Father hasn't time himself very often—

Gregers.

He is a great deal taken up with his old father, I daresay.

Hedvig.

Yes; and then Mother says you can't expect a man like Father to do nothing but take ordinary photographs. She says he is not just a common photographer. Besides, he is working on an invention.

Gregers.

An invention? Really? Where, here in the studio?

Hedvig.

Well, there is nothing to see yet but Father thinks about it all the time.

Gregers.

What is the nature of the invention? What purpose does it serve?

Hedvig.

Father says this invention will take a great deal of time yet. He cannot give details.

Gregers.

How long does he think it will take him to finish his invention?

Hedvig.

Mr. Werle, Father says he cannot enter into particulars like that. An invention is not a thing completely under one's own control. Father says it depends largely on inspiration—on intuition—he says, and it is almost impossible to predict when the inspiration may come.

Gregers.

But it's advancing?

Hedvig.

Yes of course, it is advancing. He thinks about it every day, he is full of it. Every afternoon, when he has had his dinner, he shuts himself up in the parlor, where he can ponder and be undisturbed. But Mother and I know he can't be goaded to it; it's not a bit of good.

(*Silence for a few minutes as* HEDVIG *continues working*)

Gregers.

Did the wild duck sleep well last night?

Hedvig.

Yes, I think so, thank you.

Gregers.

Would you like to be a wild duck, Hedvig?

Hedvig.
Be a wild duck? Oh no, I love her dearly but I just would like to be Hedvig.

Gregers.
If I weren't Gregers Werle, do you know what I would like to be? (*Walking toward doors*) I should like best to be a clever dog.

Hedvig.
A dog! Oh no!

Gregers.
Yes, an amazingly clever dog; one that goes to the bottom after wild ducks when they dive and bite themselves fast in tangle and seaweed, down among the ooze.

Hedvig.
I don't understand, Mr. Werle.

Gregers.
Oh well, you would not be much the wiser if you did.

Hedvig.
I think you must mean something quite different. I think you mean something different from what you say—all the time.

Gregers.
(*Looking at* HEDVIG *for a few minutes—then changing the subject, motioning towards the garret*) It looks quite different by day from what it did last night in the moonlight.

Hedvig.
Yes, it changes ever so much. It looks different in the morning and in the afternoon; and it's different on rainy days from what it is in fine weather.

Gregers.
Have you noticed that?

Hedvig.
Yes, how could I help it?

Gregers.
Are you, too, fond of being in there with the wild duck?

Hedvig.
Yes, when I can manage it—

Gregers.
But I suppose you haven't much spare time; you go to school, no doubt.

Hedvig.
No, not now; Father is afraid of my hurting my eyes.

Gregers.
Oh; then he reads with you himself?

Hedvig.

Father has promised to read with me; but he has never had time yet.

Gregers.

Then is there nobody else to give you a little help?

Hedvig.

Yes, there is Mr. Molvik; but he is not always exactly—quite—

Gregers.

Sober?

Hedvig.

Yes, I suppose that's it!

Gregers.

Why, then you must have any amount of time on your hands. And in there I suppose it is a sort of world by itself?

Hedvig.

Oh yes, quite. And there are such lots of wonderful things.

Gregers.

Indeed?

Hedvig.

Yes, there are big cupboards full of books; and a great many of the books have pictures in them.

Gregers.

Aha!

Hedvig.

And there's an old bureau with drawers and flaps, and a big clock with figures that go out and in. But the clock isn't going now.

Gregers.

So time has come to a standstill in there—in the wild duck's domain.

Hedvig.

Yes. And then there's an old paint-box and things of that sort; and all the books.

Gregers.

And you read the books, I suppose?

Hedvig.

Oh yes, when I get the chance. Most of them are English though and I don't understand English. But then I look at the pictures. There is one great big book called "Harrison's History of London." It must be a hundred years old; and there are such heaps of pictures in it. At the beginning there is Death with an hour-glass and a woman. I think that is horrid. But then there are all the other pictures of churches, and castles, and streets, and great ships sailing on the sea.

Gregers.
But tell me, where did all those wonderful things come from?

Hedvig.
Oh, an old sea captain once lived here, and he brought them home with him. They used to call him "The Flying Dutchman." That was curious, because he wasn't a Dutchman at all.

Gregers.
Wasn't he?

Hedvig.
No. But at last he was drowned at sea; and so he left all those things behind him.

Gregers.
Tell me now—when you are sitting in there looking at the pictures, don't you wish you could travel and see the real world for yourself?

Hedvig.
Oh no! I mean always to stay at home and help Father and Mother.

Gregers.
To retouch photographs?

Hedvig.
No, not only that. I should love above everything to learn to engrave pictures like those in the English books.

Gregers.
H'm. What does your father say to that?

Hedvig.
I don't think Father likes it; Father is strange about such things. Only think, he talks of my learning basket-making, and straw-plaiting! But I don't think that would be much good.

Gregers.
Oh no, I don't think so either.

Hedvig.
But Father was right in saying that if I had learned basket-making I could have made the new basket for the wild duck.

Gregers.

So you could; and it was you that ought to have done it, wasn't it?

Hedvig.

Yes, for it's my wild duck.

Gregers.

Of course it is.

Hedvig.

Yes, it belongs to me. But I lend it to Father and Grandfather as often as they please.

Gregers.

Indeed? What do they do with it?

Hedvig.

Oh, they look after it, and build places for it, and so on.

Gregers.

I see; for no doubt the wild duck is by far the most distinguished inhabitant of the garret?

Hedvig.

Yes, indeed she is; for she is a real wild fowl, you know. And then she is so much to be pitied; she has no one to care for, poor thing.

Gregers.

She has no family, as the rabbits have—

Hedvig.

No. The hens too, many of them, were chickens together; but she has been taken right away from all her friends. And then there is so much that is strange about the wild duck. Nobody knows her, and nobody knows where she came from either. Oh, we know where she was shot.

Gregers.

We also know it was my father who shot her. But his eyesight isn't very good now and she was only wounded.

Hedvig.

The amazing thing is that she is here. Wild ducks usually dive down to the bottom and get themselves tangled in the seaweed when they are wounded and never come up again. But your father's dog dived in after her and fetched her up again.

Gregers.

An amazingly clever dog, my father had.

Hedvig.

And now she is getting fat and she is happy, even though

she cannot fly. She has lived in there so long now that she has forgotten her natural wild life, I'm certain.

Gregers.

Be sure you never let her get a glimpse of the sky and sea. She has been down in the depths of the sea.

Hedvig.

(*With a quick glance at him*) Why do you say "the depths of the sea"?

Gregers.

What else should I say?

Hedvig.

You could say "The bottom of the sea."

Gregers.

Oh, mayn't I just as well say the depths of the sea?

Hedvig.

Yes; but it sounds so strange to me when other people speak of the depths of the sea.

Gregers.

Why so? Tell me why.

Hedvig.

No, I won't; it's so stupid.

Gregers.

Oh no, I am sure it's not. Do tell me why you smiled.

Hedvig.

Well, this is the reason; whenever I come to realize suddenly—in a flash—what is in there, it always seems to me that the whole room and everything in it should be called "the depths of the sea." But that is so stupid.

Gregers.

You mustn't say that.

Hedvig.

Oh yes, for you know it is only a garret.

Gregers.

(*Looks fixedly at her*) Are you so sure of that?

Hedvig.

(*Astonished*) That it's a garret?

Gregers.

Are you quite certain of it?

Hedvig.

(*Silent, staring at him for a few minutes*) I just remembered I promised Mother to clear and set the table. (*Picks up her things, puts them on the sideboard*) Please excuse me. (*She leaves the room. GREGERS goes to garret doors and stares out.*)

from
THE CHALK GARDEN
by Enid Bagnold

Act I
MISS MADRIGAL, LAUREL

The Chalk Garden is a quiet, clever play imbued with
mystery. Miss Madrigal, an applicant for a position as
governess, comes to a manor house in Sussex. She is
hired by Mrs. St. Maugham, the capricious lady of the
house who doesn't know what to do about her grand-
child. Miss Madrigal is a reserved woman but we, as well
as her young charge, sense a "past." Laurel, a wilful girl
of 16, who has always amused herself with crime stories,
finally unearths Miss Madrigal's secret. It seems that Miss
Madrigal has recently been released from prison where
she served a murder sentence.

In the following scene from near the beginning of the
play, Miss Madrigal has just been hired. It is Laurel and
Miss Madrigal's first conversation alone. Maitland, the
butler, has just left the room rather huffily over something
that Laurel has said.

Laurel.
(*Soapily*) Poor Maitland likes the Right—even when the
Right is wrong.
Madrigal.
(*Platitudinous*) He has your interests at heart.
Laurel.
(*With interest*) Are you a hospital nurse?
Madrigal.
Why do you ask?
Laurel.
You have that unmeaning way of saying things.

Madrigal.
(*After a second's pause and with a little formal manner of adapting herself*) Now that we are alone—am I to call you Laurel?

Laurel.
It's my name.

Madrigal.
And what are you interested in—Laurel? I mean—apart from yourself?

Laurel.
What I don't like—is to be questioned.

Madrigal.
I agree with you.

Laurel.
But I don't like to be agreed with—just in case I might argue! And I don't like to be read aloud to unless I suggest it! But if read aloud to—*I don't like emphasis!* And every morning I don't like *"Good morning"* said! I can see for myself what sort of a day it is!

Madrigal.
You sound as if you had lady-companions before. How did you get rid of them?

Laurel.
I tell Pinkbell.

Madrigal.
He tells your grandmother. My mind works more slowly than yours. But it was going that way.

Laurel.
You see she loves to advertise! She loves what comes out of it. It's like dredging in the sea, she says—so much comes up in the net!

Madrigal.
I—for instance?

Laurel.
Why not?

Madrigal.
Doesn't she take a chance—that way?

Laurel.
No, she says you get more out of life by haphazard. By the way, if you want to get on with my grandmother— you must notice her eccentricity.

Madrigal.
She is fond of that?

Laurel.
She adores it! Oh, the tales I let her tell me when I am in the mood!

Madrigal.
(*Musing*) Does she love you?

Laurel.
She would like to! (*Confidentially*) She *thinks* she does!— But I am only her remorse.

Madrigal.
You try your foot upon the ice, don't you?

Laurel.
I find you wonderfully odd. Why do you come here?

Madrigal.
I have to do something with my life—

Laurel.
What life have you been used to?

Madrigal.
(*Softly*) Regularity. Punctuality. Early rising—

Laurel.
It sounds like a prison!

Madrigal.
—and what are *you* used to?

Laurel.
Doing what I like. Have you been told *why* I am peculiar?

Madrigal.
Something was said about it.

Laurel.
If you come here we'll talk for hours and hours about it! I'll tell you everything! And why I hate my mother!

Madrigal.
I too hated my mother. I should say it was my stepmother.

Laurel.
Oh, that's just an ordinary hatred. Mine is more special.

Madrigal.
The dangerous thing about hate is that it seems so reasonable.

Laurel.
Maitland won't let me say so, but my mother is Jezebel! She is so overloaded with sex that it sparkles! She is golden and striped—like something in the jungle!

Madrigal.
You sound proud of her. Does she never come here?

Laurel.
To see me? Never! She's too busy with love! Just now she's in Arabia with her paramour!

Madrigal.
With her—?

Laurel.
(*Vexed*) If you pin me down he is my stepfather! Have you read *Hamlet?* It tipped my mind and turned me against my mother.

Madrigal.
Does she know you feel discarded?

Laurel.
I don't. I left *her!* (*Pause*) The night before she married— she forgot to say goodnight to me— Do you think that sounds a very little thing?

Madrigal.
(*Passionately*) Oh no! It lights up everything.

Laurel.
(*Looking at her*) Are you talking of you? Or of me!

Madrigal.
(*Her hand on her breast*) When one feels strongly—it is always of *me!*

Laurel.
Oh, if you are not a spy sent by my mother, I shall enjoy you! Do you know about crime? Maitland and I share a crime library. Bit by bit we are collecting the Notable Trial Series.

Madrigal.
(*Looking at her—low*) Don't you like detective stories better?

Laurel.
No, we like real murder! The trials. We act the parts!

Madrigal.
(*Picking up her gloves, faintly*) Which—trials have you got?

Laurel.
So far—only Mrs. Maybrick, Lizzie Borden, Dr. Crippen. But Maitland likes the murderesses better. He's half in love with them. Oh, if you come here—

Madrigal.
Here!—

Laurel.
—couldn't we act them together? (*Gets no answer*) Maitland is so slow I make him read the prisoner. Why does the prisoner have so little to say? (*Waits*) —do you think? What a habit you have—haven't you—of not answering. (*Pause—no answer.*)

Madrigal.
(*Whose eyes have been fastened high up in the air, now lets them travel down to* LAUREL, *low, with difficulty*)
I made an answer.

Laurel.
Only to yourself, I think.

from
THE CHALK GARDEN
by Enid Bagnold

Act II
MISS MADRIGAL, LAUREL

In this next scene, Laurel continues to pursue her interest
in Miss Madrigal's past. Always curious about crime, she
senses something about her governess's demeanor that
piques her. Just before the scene opens she discovers the
initials C.D.W. on the paint box lent to her by Miss
Madrigal. (For further background on the play, see the
preceding scene.)

Laurel.
  So you've been to a trial?
Madrigal.
  I did not say I hadn't.
Laurel.
  Why did you not say—when you know what store we
  both lay by it!
Madrigal.
  It may be I think you lay too much store by it.
Laurel.
  (*Relaxing her tone and asking as though an ordinary
  light question*) How does one get in?
Madrigal.
  It's surprisingly easy.
Laurel.
  Was it a trial for murder?
Madrigal.
  It would have to be to satisfy you.
Laurel.
  Was it a trial for murder? (*Sits above her on sofa.*)
Madrigal.
  (*Without turning round to look*) Have you finished that
  flower?

344

Laurel.

(*Yawning*) As much as I can. I get tired of it. (*Wandering to the window*) In my house—at home—there were so many things to do.

Madrigal.

What was it like?

Laurel.

My home?

Madrigal.

Yes.

Laurel.

(*Doodling on a piece of paper and speaking as though caught unaware*) There was a stream. And a Chinese bridge. And yew trees cut like horses. And a bell on the weathervane, and a little wood called mine—

Madrigal.

Who called it that?

Laurel.

(*Unwillingly moved*) She did—my mother. And when it was raining we made an army of her cream pots and battlefield of her dressing table— I used to thread her rings on safety pins—

Madrigal.

Tomorrow I will light that candle in the green glass candlestick and you can try to paint that.

Laurel.

(*Looking up*) What—paint the flame!

Madrigal.

Yes.

Laurel.

(*Doodling again*) I'm tired of fire, too, Boss.

Madrigal.

(*As she notices* LAUREL *doodling*) Why do you sign your name a thousand times?

Laurel.

I am looking for which is me.

Madrigal.

Shall we read?

Laurel.

Oh, I don't want to read.

Madrigal.

Let's play a game.

Laurel.

All right. (*With meaning*) A guessing game.

Madrigal.
Very well. Do you know one?

Laurel.
Maitland and I play one called "The Sky's the Limit."

Madrigal.
How do you begin?

Laurel.
(*Sitting down opposite her*) We ask three questions each but if you pass one, I get a fourth.

Madrigal.
What do we guess about?

Laurel.
Let's guess about each other! We are both mysterious.

Madrigal.
(*Sententious*) The human heart *is* mysterious.

Laurel.
We don't know the first thing about each other, so there are so many things to ask.

Madrigal.
But we mustn't go too fast. Or there will be nothing left to discover. Has it got to be the truth?

Laurel.
One can lie. But I get better and better at spotting lies. It's so dull playing with Maitland. He's so innocent. (MISS MADRIGAL *folds her hands and waits.*) Now! First question— Are you a—*maiden* lady?

Madrigal.
(*After a moment's reflection*) I can't answer that.

Laurel.
Why?

Madrigal.
Because you throw the emphasis so oddly.

Laurel.
Right. You don't answer. So now I get an extra question. Are you living under an assumed name?

Madrigal.
No.

Laurel.
Careful! I'm getting my lie-detector working. Do you take things here at their face value?

Madrigal.
No.

Laurel.
Splendid! You're getting the idea!

Madrigal.
(*Warningly*) This is to be your fourth question.

Laurel.

Yes. Yes. I must think—I must be careful. (*Shooting her question hard at* MISS MADRIGAL.) What is the full name of your married sister?

Madrigal.

(*Staring a brief second at her*) Clarissa Dalrymple Westerham.

Laurel.

Is Dalrymple Westerham a double name?

Madrigal.

(*With ironical satisfaction*) You've *had* your questions.

Laurel.

(*Gaily accepting defeat*) Yes, I have. Now yours. You've only three unless I pass one.

Madrigal.

Was your famous affair in Hyde Park on the night of your mother's marriage?

Laurel.

(*Wary*) About that time.

Madrigal.

What was the charge by the police?

Laurel.

(*Wary*) The police didn't come into it.

Madrigal.

Did someone follow you? And try to kiss you?

Laurel.

(*Off her guard*) Kiss me! It was a case of Criminal Assault!

Madrigal.

(*Following that up*) How do you know—if there wasn't a charge by the police?

Laurel.

(*Pausing a second. Triumphant*) That's one too many questions! *Now* for the deduction!

Madrigal.

You didn't tell me there was to be a deduction.

Laurel.

I forgot. It's the whole point. Mine's ready.

Madrigal.

And what do you deduce?

Laurel.

(*Taking breath—then fast as though she might be stopped*) That you've changed so much you must have been something quite different. When you first came here you were like a rusty hinge that wanted oiling. You spoke to yourself out loud without knowing it. You had been *alone*. You may have been a missionary in Central Africa. You may have escaped from a private asylum. But as a maiden lady you are an impostor. (*Changing her tone slightly—slower and more penetrating*) About your assumed name I am not so sure— *But you have no married sister.*

Madrigal.
(*Lightly*) You take my breath away.

Laurel.
(*As lightly*) Good at it, aren't I?

Madrigal.
Yes, for a mind under a cloud.

Laurel.
Now for your deduction!

Madrigal.
Mine must keep.

Laurel.
But it's the game! Where are you going? (*Rises; steps down stage*)

Madrigal.
(*Pleasantly*) To my room. To make sure I have left no clues unlocked.

Laurel.
To your past life?

Madrigal.
Yes, you have given me so much warning. (*Exits.*)

from
SUMMER AND SMOKE
by Tennessee Williams

Part II, scene 10
ALMA, NELL

This scene takes place on an afternoon in December in
the south at a fountain in the park. It is very windy. Alma
enters and seems to move with effort against the wind
before she sinks down on a park bench. She has been ill
and continually burdened with the responsibilities of being
a minister's daughter. Also, though she has not been able
to give herself to John, the man she loves, her feelings for
him are still very intense. He has been away and just
recently returned. While she sits in the park Nellie Ewell,
a lively young girl who was once a music student of Alma's,
appears. Nellie is dressed very fashionably and is carrying
a basket of Christmas packages. (For further background
on this play and more analysis of Alma's character, see
page 17.)

Nell.
 Miss Alma!
Alma.
 Why Nellie . . . Nellie Ewell!
Nell.
 I was by the Rectory. Just popped in for a second; the
holidays are so short that every minute is precious. They
told me you'd gone to the park.
Alma.
 This is the first walk I've taken in quite a while.
Nell.
 You've been ill!
Alma.
 Not ill, just not very well. How you've grown up, Nellie.

349

Nell.
It's just my clothes. Since I went off to Sophie Newcombe I've picked out my own clothes, Miss Alma. When Mother had jurisdiction over my wardrobe, she tried to keep me looking like a child.

Alma.
Your voice is grown up, too.

Nell.
They're teaching me diction, Miss Alma. I'm learning to talk like you, long A's and everything, such as "cahnt" and "bahth" and "lahf" instead of "laugh." Yesterday I slipped. I said I "lahfed and lahfed till I nearly died laughing." Johnny was so amused at me!

Alma.
Johnny?

Nell.
Your next-door neighbor!

Alma.
Oh! I'm sure it must be a very fashionable school.

Nell.
Oh yes, they're preparing us to be young ladies in society. What a pity there's no society here to be a young lady in . . . at least not for me, with Mother's reputation!

Alma.
You'll find other fields to conquer.

Nell.
What's this I hear about you?

Alma.
I have no idea, Nellie.

Nell.
That you've quit teaching singing and gone into retirement.

Alma.
Naturally, I had to stop teaching while I was ill and as for retiring from the world . . . it's more a case of the world retiring from me.

Nell.
I know somebody whose feelings you've hurt badly.

Alma.
Why, who could that be, Nellie?

Nell.
Somebody who regards you as an angel!

Alma.
I can't think who might hold me in such esteem.

Nell.
Somebody who says that you refused to see him.

Alma.
I saw nobody. For several months. The long summer wore me out so.

Nell.
Well, anyhow, I'm going to give you your present. (*She hands her a small package from the basket.*)

Alma.
Nellie, you shouldn't have given me anything.

Nell.
I'd like to know why not!

Alma.
I didn't expect it.

Nell.
After the trouble you took with my horrible voice?

Alma.
It's very sweet of you, Nellie.

Nell.
Open it!

Alma.
Now?

Nell.
Why, sure.

Alma.
It's so prettily wrapped I hate to undo it.

Nell.
I love to wrap presents and since it was for you, I did a specially dainty job of it.

Alma.
(*Winding the ribbon about her fingers*) I'm going to save this ribbon. I'm going to keep this lovely paper too, with the silver stars on it. And the sprig of holly . . .

Nell.
Let me pin it on your jacket, Alma.

Alma.
Yes, do. I hardly realized that Christmas was coming . . . (*She unfolds the paper, revealing a lace handkerchief and a card.*) What an exquisite handkerchief.

Nell.
I hate to give people handkerchiefs, it's so unimaginative.

Alma.
I love to get them.

Nell.
It comes from Maison Blanche!

Alma.
Oh, does it really?

Nell.
Smell it!

Alma.
Sachet *Roses*! Well, I'm just more touched and pleased than I can possibly tell you!

Nell.
The card!

Alma.
Card?

Nell.
You dropped it. (*She snatches up the card and hands it to ALMA.*)

Alma.
Oh, how clumsy of me! Thank you, Nellie. "Joyeux Noël . . . to Alma . . . from Nellie and . . . (*she looks up slowly*) John"?

Nell.
He helped me wrap presents last night and when we came to yours we started talking about you. Your ears must have burned!

(*The wind blows loudly. ALMA bends stiffly forward.*)

Alma.
You mean you—spoke well of me?

Nell.
"Well of"! We raved, simply raved! Oh, he told me the influence you'd had on him!

Alma.
Influence?

Nell.
He told me about the wonderful talks he'd had with you last summer when he was so mixed up and how you inspired him and you more than anyone else was responsible for his pulling himself together, after his father was killed, and he told me about . . . (*ALMA rises stiffly from the bench.*) Where are you going, Miss Alma?

Alma.
To drink at the fountain.

Nell.
He told me about how you came in the house that night like an angel of mercy!

Alma.
(*Laughing harshly by the fountain*) This is the only

angel in Glorious Hill. (*She bends to drink.*) Her body is stone and her blood is mineral water.

(*The wind is louder.*)

Nell.
How penetrating the wind is!

Alma.
I'm going home, Nellie. You run along and deliver your presents now. . . . (*She starts away.*)

Nell.
But wait till I've told you the wonderfullest thing I . . .

Alma.
I'm going home now. Good-bye.

Nell.
Oh— Good-bye, Miss Alma. (*She snatches up her festive basket and rushes in the other direction with a shrill giggle as the wind pulls at her skirts. The lights dim out.*)

from
THE CORN IS GREEN
by Emlyn Williams

Act III
MORGAN

The following scene takes place in the same living room
in Glansarno, Wales, where Morgan has spent so much
time studying with Miss Moffat. (See pages 249 and 290
for the background of the play.) He has just returned from
taking the entrance examinations for Oxford, where he
hopes to win a scholarship, and is enthusiastically relating
his experiences to Miss Moffat who sits, happily listening.

There are a few deletions from the original play which
are comments by Miss Moffat encouraging him to continue
talking. These are marked by asterisks.

Morgan.
. . . I have *been* to Oxford, and come back, since then!
I have come back—from the world! Since the day I was
born, I have been a prisoner behind a stone wall, and
now somebody has given me a leg-up to have a look at
the other side . . . (*Vehement*) they cannot drag me
back again, they cannot, they *must* give me a push and
send me over!

* * *

. . . it would be everything I need, everything! Starling
and I spent three hours one night discussin' the law—
Starling, you know, the brilliant one . . . the words came
pouring out of me—all the words that I had learnt and
written down and never spoken—I suppose I was talking
nonsense, but I was at least holding a conversation! I
suddenly realized that I had never done it before—I had
never been *able* to do it. (*With a strong Welsh accent*)

354

"How are you, Morgan? Nice day, Mr. Jones! Not bad for the harvest!"—a vocabulary of twenty words; all the thoughts you have given to me were being stored away as if they were always going to be useless—locked up and rotting away—a lot of questions with nobody to answer them, a lot of statements with nobody to contradict them . . . and there I was with Starling, nineteen to the dozen. (*Suddenly quieter*) I came out his rooms that night, and I walked down the High. That's their High Street, you know.

* * *

I looked up, and there was a moon behind Magd-Maudlin. Not the same moon I have seen over the Nant, a different face altogether. Everybody seemed to be walking very fast, with their gowns on, in the moonlight; the bells were ringing, and I was walking faster than anybody and I felt—well, the same as on the rum in the old days!

* * *

All of a sudden, with one big rush, against that moon, and against that High Street . . . I saw this room; you and me sitting here studying, and all those books—and everything I have ever learnt from those books, and from you, was lighted up—like a magic lantern—ancient Rome, Greece, Shakespeare, Carlyle, Milton . . . everything had a meaning because I was in a new world—my world! And so it came to me why you worked like a slave to make me ready for this scholarship. . . . (*Lamely*) I've finished.

from
SAINT JOAN
by Bernard Shaw

Scene 6
JOAN

The story of Joan of Arc, the illiterate girl still in her
teens who heard voices and led soldiers in battle, is
legendary. In *Saint Joan*, Bernard Shaw has not romanti-
cized her or presented her only as a courageous visionary,
but presents her as a girl who wanted to lead a man's life,
a girl too young to understand tact, and yet old enough
to be shrewd when warranted. He also portrayed Joan's
enemies not as villains but as men who were convinced
that they were doing the right thing.

The time of the play is fifteenth-century France. The
following monologue takes place on May 30, 1431, at
Rouen in the great stone hall of the castle. The hall has
been arranged for a trial-at-law, but not a trial-by-jury.
Joan, chained by the ankles, has just been told by her
inquisitors that instead of being burned at the stake for
heresy, she will be imprisoned for life. There are slight
deletions of other characters' lines which are marked by
asterisks.

Joan.
(*Rising in consternation and terrible anger*) Perpetual
imprisonment! Am I not then to be set free?

* * *

Give me that writing. (*She rushes to the table; snatches
up the paper; and tears it into fragments*) Light your
fire: do you think I dread it as much as the life of a rat
in a hole? My voices were right.

* * *

Yes; they told me you were fools (*the word gives great offense*), and that I was not to listen to your fine words nor trust to your charity. You promised me my life; but you lied (*indignant exclamations*). You think that life is nothing but not being stone dead. It is not the bread and water I fear: I can live on bread: when have I asked for more? It is no hardship to drink water if the water be clean. Bread has no sorrow for me, and water no affliction. But to shut me from the light of the sky and the sight of the fields and flowers; to chain my feet so that I can never again ride with the soldiers nor climb the hills; to make me breathe foul damp darkness, and keep from me everything that brings me back to the love of God when your wickedness and foolishness tempt me to hate Him; all this is worse than the furnace in the Bible that was heated seven times. I could do without my warhorse; I could drag about in a skirt; I could let the banners and the trumpets and the knights and soldiers pass me and leave me behind as they leave the other women, if only I could still hear the wind in the trees, the larks in the sunshine, the young lambs crying through the healthy frost, and the blessed blessed church bells that send my angel voices floating to me on the wind. But without these things I cannot live; and by your wanting to take them away from me, or from any human creature, I know that your counsel is of the devil, and that mine is of God.

*   *   *

His ways are not your ways. He wills that I go through the fire to His bosom; for I am His child, and you are not fit that I should live among you. That is my last word to you.

from
BONTCHE SCHWEIG
by Arnold Perl

THE DEFENDING ANGEL

This monologue is taken from *Bontche Schweig*, the middle
play in the trilogy entitled *The World of Sholom Aleichem.*
Bontche Schweig is based on a story in Yiddish by Isaac
Lieb Peretz who often wrote about poor and humble Jews.
  Bontche Schweig, a beggar, appears before the court
of Heaven. A trial to determine whether he is worthy of
entrance is taking place and the Defending Angel presents
his case in the following monologue. His speech is reminis-
cent of Portia's, in that it asks for compassion and understanding, but it is also an indictment of the society that
allows the conditions that shaped Bontche to exist. The
unassuming Bontche sits cowed and awed throughout the
proceedings.
  There are several short deletions of the lines of other
angels and these are marked by asterisks.

Defending Angel.
  His name is Bontche Schweig—Bontche the Silent, and
his name fitted him like a cloak made in the hands of
a master-tailor.

* * *

His death, like his life on earth, made no impression.
If a horse had dropped dead in the street, it would have
attracted more attention. But then if there were as many
horses as there are men like him, the horse too would
have gone unnoticed.

* * *

He never complained of either God or man. Hatred never flashed into his eyes; he never lifted his voice in bitterness to Heaven.

* * *

Job was unlucky, but this one was even less fortunate. When he was a week old he was circumcised—and the Mohel who did the job, didn't know his business.

* * *

No wine was drunk at this event, and at his Bar Mitzvah no speeches were made. He lived like a grain of sand, along with millions like him, and when the wind lifted him and blew him upside down, no one noticed it.

* * *

His mother died when he was 13 and he inherited a stepmother who was a snake—

* * *

—a—beg-pardon—he didn't complain. Instead of food he got moldy bread, instead of meat he got the gristle and skin. Wintertime, he chopped the wood, barefoot in the yard, his hands and feet frozen, the black and blue marks showed through the holes in his pants. Did he complain?

* * *

He never even complained to his father. . . .

* * *

He had nobody to play with, ever; he never spent a day in a Cheder; never had a book; never had a coat that wasn't somebody else's first. He never had a minute to himself. His father, drunk one night, threw him out of the house into the street. He picked himself up and went—which ever way the wind was blowing. However hungry he got, he kept silent. He begged only with his eyes.

* * *

How many times he was arrested, vagrancy, loitering, no visible means of support—I couldn't begin to tell you. How many times he got work—the dirtiest, the heaviest, the most menial—and didn't get paid—I couldn't list them all. And worse than working, harder, was finding work—and through it all—silent.

* * *

When they splashed mud on him; when they spit on him; when they made him walk in the gutter and told him to keep off the sidewalk; when he stood in the doorway begging for the money he was owed on a job and they told him to come back later—now it's not convenient; when they paid him—as they did—only part, or cheated him, or gave him counterfeit money—he kept silent although starvation and death were constantly by his side. Once good fortune smiled. He stopped two runaway horses and saved the life of the man inside, the owner of the carriage—although the driver of the carriage was killed. He was made the coachman and inherited also a wife and more than that—a child; the wife and child of the driver killed in the accident.

* * *

When his new-found protector went bankrupt and didn't pay him what he owed, he was silent; when his new "wife" ran away and left him with the new-born baby, he was silent; and fifteen years later when the boy grew up and threw him out of the house—even then—silent.

* * *

And later when this same benefactor ran him down in the street and the carriage wheels rolled over him, he didn't even report to the police who had done it. And in the hospital, his back broken—nothing.

* * *

And when the doctor wouldn't touch his case without payment in advance, and the same for the hospital attendant who wouldn't give him a glass of water without first being paid—even then silence. Silence in his last minute on earth—in the death-struggle. Silence in death.

* * *

One minute more. He was buried in a pauper's grave. Even the gravedigger doesn't remember him. And a little stick was put up to mark the grave. The wind blew it over the next day and the grave-digger's wife found it and used it to stir a pot of potatoes. And in all—from birth to death—not a word against God, not a word against man.

from
EASTER
by August Strindberg
adapted by Lorraine Cohen

ELEONORA

The following is an adaptation from several sections of
the play, pieced together from several dialogues that
Eleonora has with Benjamin. Eleonora is 16 and has run
away from the mental institution where she has been for
a year. She has come home and sees a student of her
brother's in the living room. (For further background on
the play, see pages 133 and 142.)

Eleonora.
Do you know what this is? It's an Easter lily, of course.
My name is Eleonora and I am a daughter in this house.
If you have never heard them speak of me it is because
the dead are not spoken of. I am legally dead, for I have
committed a terrible sin. I have embezzled funds entrusted
to me and I cannot be forgiven because my father was
given the blame and is now in prison. He and I are one
and the same person. I have been very sick. For me
there is neither time nor space. I am everywhere and
whenever I will. I am with my father in prison, and
with my brother in school. . . . I am in my mother's
kitchen and in my sister's shop in America. When things
go well for my sister and she makes a sale, I feel her
joy; when business is bad, I suffer. But I suffer most, when
she does someone a wrong.

Oh, my father is suffering now. They are treating him
unkindly. (*She stops short, as if listening.*) Can you hear
the telephone wires moaning? It's the cruel words that
the soft, shiny red copper can't bear to hear. When people

362

speak ill of their neighbors over the telephone, the copper melts into tears, and moans, and cries SHAME! (*Her voice becomes hard.*) And their every word is written in the ledger. And at doomsday comes the reckoning.

Do you know that I know what the starlings are talking about? Only a moment ago, I heard two of them chattering up in the walnut tree outside. One said, "Peter!" The other one said, "Judas!" "The same to you!" said the first bird. "Fee-fee-fee" said the second bird. But have you noticed that the nightingales sing only in the garden of the deaf mutes next door? That is because people who can hear don't listen to the nightingale's song, but the deaf do. Would you like me to tell you more about birds? There is an evil bird that is called the rat buzzard; you can hear by the name that it lives on rats. This bird is a hateful bird, and so nature has made it hard for it to catch the rats. It only knows a single word and that sounds exactly like a cat's miaow. Isn't that perfectly marvelous? (*Laughing*)

You look so sad. Would you like to hear another story? Or shall I tell you about the flowers? You know—when I was sick, they made me take a drug made from henbane. It makes the eye into a magnifying glass. Belladonna, on the other hand, has the very opposite effect. And I can see farther than other people—I can see the stars in broad daylight. In fact, I was just looking at Cassiopeia. It looks like a W and is situated directly in the center of the Milky Way. Nobody else could see it but I did. You know what one human being can see, others may not be able to see. That is why you must not depend too much on your eyes. Now I must say something about the flower on the table there. It's an Easter lily; it has its home in Switzerland; its chalice has drunk of the sun's light. That's why it's golden and can alleviate suffering. I saw it in a florist's shop just a while ago, as I passed and wanted it for Elis, my brother, as a gift. As I was about to go inside, I found the door was locked—I suppose because it's Confirmation Day. I just had to have the flower, so I tried one of my own keys, and behold! One of them unlocked the door, and there

I was inside the flower shop. Do you understand the silent
language of flowers? Each and every fragrance expresses
a multitude of thoughts. These thoughts took possession
of me; and with extra-sensory vision, I could look into
their workshops, which no human eye had ever beheld.
They spoke to me of the sorrows which the gardener,
through his insensitiveness, had inflicted on them. I don't
want to say he had been cruel—merely thoughtless. I
then put the price, one crown, on the counter—together
with my card—and took the flower and left.

You are shocked! Did I do a thoughtless thing? Was it
wrong? It certainly couldn't have been a childish thing
because I never was a child. I was born old. I seemed
to know all there is to know from birth, and when I
learned something, it was just like remembering. I was
conscious of people's lack of understanding and of their
thoughtlessness when I was only four. Out of spite they
treated me cruelly.

Oh, but now I have caused trouble again. If they
find out I would be sent back—where I came from—
where the sun never shines—where the walls are white
and naked, as in a bathroom—where you never hear anything but wails and weeping—where I have wasted a
whole year of my life.

Do you know what I would find hardest to part from?
This little clock here. It saw me come into this world, and
it has measured my hours and my days. Hear how it
ticks—just like a heart. Nice little clock, go a little
faster. Tick-tock, ping-ping-ping.

Now it is the day before Easter—now the sun will soon
rise and we'll write on the Easter eggs. Do you know, this
clock always used to go faster whenever a misfortune
hovered over us. It was as though it wished to have bad
times behind, for our sake, of course. But when things
were bright, it slowed down, so that we could enjoy the
happiness longer. That was the good clock. But we had a
bad clock, too. It's been relegated to the kitchen now. It
had no ear for music. The moment Elis began playing
the piano, it started to strike. We all noticed it; not only I.
That's why we put it out in the kitchen—because it mis-
behaved. But Lina has no love for it either. It makes

a disturbance during the nights. And she says she can't boil eggs by it—they are always hard-boiled! (*Laughing*)

Think, Benjamin, of all the blossoming flowers, the blue anemones and the snowdrops that have to stand in the snow all day and all night and have to freeze in the darkness. Think how they have to suffer. The night must be hardest for them—and when it is dark and they are frightened by the shadows and can't run away. They have to stand there in stillness, waiting for dawn to come. There is suffering everywhere, everywhere—but the flowers suffer most.

Today the rod, tomorrow the Easter eggs. Today snow, tomorrow thaw! Today death, tomorrow the Resurrection— Yes, I can feel it clearing. We shall have beautiful weather. The snow is melting. I can smell the melting snow . . . and tomorrow the violets will be coming out on the south side of the house. The clouds have lifted—I can feel it when I breathe. And I know at once that the way to Heaven is open . . . Draw aside the curtains, Benjamin, I want God to see us!

from
IPHEGENIA IN AULIS
by Euripides
translated by Charles R. Walker

IPHEGENIA

Iphegenia in Aulis was the last play written by Euripides
before his death. It is less lofty in tone than earlier Greek
tragedies and is generally considered to mark the transition
between classical and post-classical drama. Although it is
based on the ancient Homeric legend of Agamemnon's
sacrifice of his daughter Iphegenia to the goddess Artemis
in order to ensure the Greek ships favorable winds on their
way to Troy, the characters are cut down to less than
legendary size. Agamemnon is shown to be an ambitious
politician and a vacillating moral coward. In turn Clytemnestra's hatred for her husband Agamemnon is more
understandable in this play than in the other plays based
on the couple. And Iphegenia is girlish, affectionate and
wants to live. However, she eventually becomes willing to
die for she believes that the war must be won. She also
begs her mother not to hate Agamemnon. The saint-like
beauty of her character transcends the play.

The following scene takes place at the tent of Agamemnon on the shore of Aulis Gulf. Agamemnon has sent for
Clytemnestra and Iphegenia on the false pretext of the
betrothal of Iphegenia to Achilles. However, Clytemnestra
discovers the truth and confronts Agamemnon with it in
front of Iphegenia and her infant brother Orestes. In the
following monologue, Iphegenia pleads for her life.

Iphegenia.
                                        O my father—
If I had the tongue of Orpheus

So that I could charm with song the stones to
Leap and follow me, or if my words could
Quite beguile anyone I wished—I'd use
My magic now. But only with tears can I
Make arguments and here I offer them.
O Father,
My body is a suppliant's tight clinging
To your knees. Do not take away this life
Of mine before its dying time. Nor make me
Go down under the earth to see the world
Of darkness, for it is sweet to look on
The days' light.
I was first to call you father,
You to call me child. And of your children
First to sit upon your knees. We kissed
Each other in our love. "O child,"
You said, "surely one day I shall see you
Happy in your husband's home. And like
A flower blooming for me and in my honor."
Then as I clung to you and wove my fingers
In your beard, I answered, "Father, you,
Old and reverent then, with love I shall
Receive into my home, and so repay you
For the years of trouble and your fostering
Care of me." I have in memory all these words
Of yours and mine. But you, forgetting,
Have willed it in your heart to kill me.

Oh no—by Pelops
And by Atreus, your father, and
By my mother who suffered travail
At my birth and now must suffer a second
Time for me! Oh, oh—the marriage
Of Paris and Helen—Why must it touch
My life? Why must Paris be my ruin?
Father, look at me, and into my eyes;
Kiss me, so that if my words fail,
And if I die, this thing of love I may
Hold in my heart and remember.

(*Turning to ORESTES*)
My brother, so little can you help us

Who love you, but weep with me and
Beg our father not to kill your sister.
Oh, the threat of evil is instinct,
Even in a child's heart. See, even
Without speech, he begs you, Father,
Pity and have mercy on my sister's life.
Yes, both of us beseech you, this little child
And I, your daughter grown. So these words
Are all my argument. Let me win life
From you. I must. To look upon the world
Of light is for all men their greatest joy—
The shadow world below is nothing.
Men are mad, I say, who pray for death;
It is better that we live ever so
Miserably than die in glory.

from
THE DARK AT THE TOP OF THE STAIRS
by William Inge

Act II
SAMMY

In this scene from the play, Reenie Flood, 16, has her
first date. The boy turns out to be different from anyone
she has ever met in her small Oklahoma town in the
early 1920's. He boards at a private military school and
is part Jewish. He has learned how to get along with
strangers because his entire life is filled with strangers. In
his shy eagerness to be accepted when he first meets
Reenie, he becomes rather effusive as the following monologue indicates. A stage direction describing his audience
has been deleted and is marked by asterisks. (For further
background on this play, see pages 111 and 315.)

Sammy.
I always worry that maybe people aren't going to like
me, when I go to a party. Isn't that crazy? Do you ever
get a kind of a sick feeling in the pit of your stomach
when you dread things? Gee, I wouldn't want to miss a
party for anything. But every time I go to one, I have
to reason with myself to keep from feeling that the whole
world's against me. See, I've spent almost my whole life in
military academies. My mother doesn't have a place for
me, where she lives. She . . . she just doesn't know what
else to do with me. But you mustn't misunderstand about
my mother. She's really a very lovely person. I guess
every boy thinks his mother is very beautiful, but my
mother really is. She tells me in every letter she writes
how sorry she is that we can't be together more, but she
has to think of her work. One time we were together,

369

though. She met me in San Francisco once, and we were together for two whole days. She let me take her to dinner and to a show and to dance. Just like we were sweethearts. It was the most wonderful time I ever had. And then I had to go back to the old military academy. Every time I walk into the barracks, I get kind of a depressed feeling. It's got hard stone walls. Pictures of generals hanging all over . . . oh, they're very fine gentlemen, but they all look so kind of hard-boiled and stern . . . you know what I mean. * * * Well, gee! I guess I've bored you enough, telling you about myself.

from
HAMLET
by William Shakespeare

Act II, scene 1
OPHELIA

The following monologue is taken from what is perhaps
the most famous play in the entire world. Hamlet, a
young prince of Denmark, has come home from England
to find his father dead and his mother remarried to his
father's brother, who is now king. To add to his grief, he
suspects that his father was murdered by the new king.
In order to ascertain whether this is true, he feigns mad-
ness. In the following scene, Ophelia, a young girl whom
Hamlet has loved, describes to her father Polonius a
meeting she has had with Hamlet. She is greatly agitated.
Deletions are marked with asterisks.

Ophelia.
  Oh, my lord, my lord, I have been so affrighted!
* * *
My lord, as I was sewing in my closet,
Lord Hamlet, with his doublet all unbrac'd,
No hat upon his head, his stockings foul'd,
Ungartered and down-gyved to his ankle,
Pale as his shirt, his knees knocking each other,
And with a look so piteous in purport
As if he had been loosed out of hell
To speak of horrors—he comes before me.
* * *
He took me by the wrist and held me hard;
Then goes he to the length of all his arm,
And with his other hand thus o'er his brow,
He falls to such perusal of my face

As he would draw it. Long stay'd he so.
At last, a little shaking of mine arm,
And thrice his head thus waving up and down,
He rais'd a sigh so piteous and profound
As it did seem to shatter all his bulk
And end his being. That done, he lets me go;
And, with his head over his shoulder turn'd,
He seem'd to find his way without his eyes,
For out o'doors he went without their help,
And to the last bended their light on me.

* * *

. . . My good lord, I have not given him any hard words
    of late,
But, as you did command, I did repel his letters
And deni'd his access to me.

from
UNCLE VANYA
by Anton Chekhov

adapted by Lorraine Cohen

SONYA

The setting for this play is the country estate of
Serebrayakov in Russia in the late nineteen hundreds where
several people have been living quietly, if not exactly,
joyfully. Vanya has been managing the estate when
Serebrayakov brings home his new wife, the exquisite
Elena. Elena's presence acts as a catalyst, bringing to sharp
focus the unhappiness and meaninglessness of all their
lives. The frustrations seethe for awhile, then build into an
explosion and when Elena leaves, everything settles back
into the outward calm of before. Nobody takes any
positive action to change their lives and this is the pathos
of the play.

In the following scene, Sonya, the plain daughter of
Serebrayakov is agonizing over her life and her unrequited
love for Astrov, a friend of the family's, who is also her
father's doctor. The monologue has been put together with
several shorter speeches of Sonya's throughout the play.

Sonya.
He has consented to have supper with us and stay the
night and he did let me serve him a bit of cheese from
the sideboard. His soul and his heart are still hidden from
me; but why do I just now feel so happy? And when I
implored him not to drink any more, he didn't. I said
to him that it was so unbecoming to him. I said, "You
are refined, noble and have such a gentle voice. More
than that," I said, "You are like nobody among the people

I know, like nobody else—you are beautiful!" Was it
the wrong moment for just that? But he did understand
when I reminded him that he always said that people
don't create but merely destroy what's given to them
from above. Then why, why, must he destroy himself?
He did understand because he began to talk about his
work and his feeling of tenderness for the peasants.
And he was so right about the intelligentsia. He said
they tire one. They have shallow thoughts, shallow feelings. And those that are clever and more important, he
said are hysterical, absorbed with analyzing themselves.
They whine, they despise everything, they slander people
cruelly and when they don't know what kind of a label to
stick on someone's forehead, they say, "He's an odd one,
odd!" And they think the Doctor's odd because he loves
the woods, and because he doesn't eat meat. He's right,
there is no longer any spontaneous, pure, free kinship
to nature or to people. . . .

Oh, he's so wise, so wise. And yet—yet he didn't understand when I told him about a younger sister. Oh how
terrible it is that I am not pretty. I know I am not pretty,
I know, I know. Last Sunday as we were leaving church,
I heard them talking about me and one woman said: "She
is kind, generous, but it's a pity she is not pretty." Not
pretty. I have such a silly face. And here he is, gone, and
I keep hearing his voice and his steps, and when I look
at a dark window I see his face there. Oh, I'm so ashamed,
I must seem so silly.

And he is clever. He can do anything, is able to do
anything. He heals the sick and he plants woodlands—
When he plants a little tree, he is already dreaming of
the happiness of mankind. Such people are rare, one must
love them. He drinks, he is sometimes rude, but what
harm is there in that? A genius in Russia can't be as
spotless as a saint. What a life he leads! Impassable
mud on the roads, frost, blinding snow, enormous dis-
tances, people crude and wild, poverty all around, dis-
eases. In such a setting it would be hard for anyone who
works and struggles day after day to keep himself steady
and sober at forty. And just now he's so sad because one
of his patients died under chloroform.

Nobody listens to him. They find his work with the trees so monotonous. I've heard Elena say so. And yet he's already received a bronze medal and a diploma for his planting of new wood plots. He petitioned not to have the old ones destroyed. If they would only hear him out they would agree with him completely. He says that forests adorn the earth, that they teach a man to understand the beautiful and inspire him to lofty moods. Forests soften a severe climate. In countries where the climate is mild, you spend less effort in the struggle with nature, and so man there is gentler and tenderer; people are beautiful there, lively, easily excited, their speech is exquisite, their movements are graceful. Their sciences and art blossom, their philosophy is not gloomy, their relation to a woman is full of exquisite nobility. . . .

Oh-h-h, how I long to be pretty, and I know I am not. When a woman is not pretty they tell her, "You have beautiful eyes" or "You have beautiful hair." Oh, I have loved him now for six years, loved him more than my own mother; every minute I hear his voice, feel the touch of his hand; and I watch the door waiting: it always seems to me he will be coming in. He is here every day now, but he doesn't look at me, doesn't see me. It's such agony! I haven't any hope. I often come to him, start talking to him, look into his eyes. He doesn't see me. I have no more pride. Everyone knows I love him, even the servants know. And he—he never notices me.

These sad autumn roses. Winter will be here soon and they will all be gone. Perhaps then, Uncle Vanya and I can get back to work. All the hay is mowed, it rains every day, everything is rotting, and Uncle Vanya and everyone here is occupying themselves with illusions. The farming has been neglected completely. I'm the only one that works and I have no strength left.

And in the long evenings, we can sit together and do our work, translating and copying papers. It's a long, long time now we haven't sat together at this table, Uncle Vanya and I. There seems to be no ink. And we must take care of all the bills too. Work will save us. We must live, we shall live. We'll live through a long, long line of days, endless evenings; we'll bear patiently the trials fate sends us; we'll work for others now and in our old age without ever knowing any rest, and when our hour comes, we'll die humbly and there beside the coffin we'll say that we suffered, that we cried, that we felt bitter, and God will take pity on us, and you and I, Uncle, darling Uncle, shall see life bright, beautiful, fine, we shall be happy and will look back tenderly with a smile on these misfortunes we have now—and we shall rest. I have faith, I believe warmly, passionately . . . (*Kneeling with Uncle Vanya's picture which she has taken off the desk*)

We shall rest! We shall hear the angels, we shall see the whole sky all diamonds, we shall see how all earthly evil, all our sufferings, are drowned in the mercy that will fill the whole world. And our life will grow peaceful, tender, sweet as a caress. I believe, I do believe. . . . Poor, dear Uncle Vanya, in your life you haven't known what joy was; but (*through her tears*) wait, Uncle Vanya, wait . . . We shall rest . . . We shall rest. . . . We shall rest. . . .

INDEXES

Scenes Classified by Number of Characters

(Letters in brackets indicate general classifications of types of plays: Drama [D], Comedy [C], Comedy-Drama [C-D], Melodrama [M].)

Scenes for One Man and One Woman—

Antigone [D]; Antigone, Haemon—265

Beautiful People, The [D]; Agnes, Owen—122

Corn is Green, The [D]; Bessie, Morgan—249
Miss Moffat, Morgan—290

Dark at the Top of the Stairs, The [D]; Reenie, Sonny—111

Diary of Anne Frank, The [D]; Anne, Peter—100, 103, 108

Easter [D]; Eleonora, Benjamin—133, 142, 147

Look Homeward Angel [D]; Laura, Eugene—237, 243, 246

Oh Dad, Poor Dad . . . [C-D]; Rosalie, Jonathan—150

Romeo and Juliet [D]; Juliet, Romeo—162

Sound of Music, The [D]; Liesl, Rolf—119

Summer and Smoke [D]; Alma, John—17

View from the Bridge, A [D]; Catherine, Rodolpho—208

West Side Story [D]; Maria, Tony—203

Wild Duck, The [D]; Hedvig, Gregers—331

Winterset [D]; Miriamne, Mio—175

Scenes for Two Women—

Alice in Wonderland; Alice, The Red Queen—65

Antigone [D]; Antigone, Ismene—259
Antigone, Nurse—295

Bad Seed [D]; Christine, Rhoda—284

Chalk Garden, The [D]; Miss Madrigal, Laurel—339, 344

Children's Hour, The [D]; Mary, Rosalie—37
Mary, Mrs. Tilford—302
Mary, Karen—312

Dark at the Top of the Stairs, The [D]; Cora, Reenie—315

Heidi [D]; Heidi, Clara—70

Jane Eyre [D]; Jane, Helen—89

Pride and Prejudice [D]; Elizabeth, Charlotte—232
Elizabeth, Jane—235

Rope Dancers, The [D]; Margaret, Lizzie—275

Summer and Smoke [D]; Alma, Nell—349

Summer Brave [D]; Madge, Millie—228

Scenes for Two Men—

Dead End [D]; Tommy, Angel—62

Member of the Wedding, The [D]; Frankie, John Henry—23

Strawberry Ice Cream Soda [D]; Eddie, Lawrence—86

Tea and Sympathy [D]; Tom, Al—126

West Side Story [D]; Tony, Riff—195

Winslow Boy, The [D]; Sir Robert, Ronnie—321

379

Scenes for More than Two Characters—

Children's Hour, The [D]; Mary, Peggy, Evelyn, Rosalie—27
Clearing in the Woods, A [D]; Nora, Hazelmae, The Boy—252
Crucible, The [D]; Abigail, Mercy, Mary Warren, Betty—96
Dark of the Moon [D]; John, Barbara Allen, Dark Witch, Fair Witch—270
Dead End [D]; Philip, Tommy, Dippy, Angel, T. B., Spit, Milton—53
Five Finger Exercise [D]; Clive, Pamela, Walter—
Little Women [D]; Meg, Jo, Amy, Beth—78
Macbeth [D]; The Three Witches—75
Rainy Afternoon, The [D]; Wilma, Billie Mae, Vic—42
West Side Story [D]; Maria, Anita, Bernardo, Chino—200

Winterset [D]; Mio, Carr, Miriamne—169, 183

Monologues for Women—

Easter [D]; Eleonora—362
Hamlet [D]; Ophelia—371
Iphegenia in Aulis [D]; Iphegenia—366
Saint Joan [D]; Joan—356
Uncle Vanya [D]; Sonya—373

Monologues for Men—

Corn is Green, The [D]; Morgan—354
Dark at the Top of the Stairs, The (D); Sammy—369
Bontche Schweig (D); The Defending Angel—358

INDEX

Alcott, Louisa May. LITTLE WOMEN (adapted by Lorraine Cohen), 78.

ALICE IN WONDERLAND, Lewis Carroll (adapted by Eva Le Gallienne and Florida Friebus), 65.

Anderson, Robert. TEA AND SYMPATHY, 126.

Anderson, Maxwell. BAD SEED, 284. WINTERSET, 169, 175, 183.

Anouilh, Jean. ANTIGONE, 259, 265, 295.

ANTIGONE, Jean Anouilh, 259, 265, 295.

Austen, Jane. PRIDE AND PREJUDICE (adapted by Helen Jerome), 232, 235.

BAD SEED, Maxwell Anderson, 284.

Bagnold, Enid. THE CHALK GARDEN, 339, 344.

BEAUTIFUL PEOPLE, THE, William Saroyan, 122.

Berney, William, and Howard Richardson. DARK OF THE MOON, 270.

BONTCHE SCHWEIG, Arnold Perl, 358.

Brontë, Charlotte. JANE EYRE (adapted by Lorraine Cohen), 89.

Carroll, Lewis. ALICE IN WONDERLAND (adapted by Era Le Gallienne and Florida Friebus), 65.

CHALK GARDEN, THE, Enid Bagnold, 339, 344.

Chekhov, Anton. UNCLE VANYA (adapted by Lorraine Cohen), 373.

CHILDREN'S HOUR, THE, Lillian Hellman, 27, 37, 302, 312.

CLEARING IN THE WOODS, A, Arthur Laurents, 252.

Cohen, Lorraine. Adapter of EASTER by August Strindberg, 362. HEIDI by Johanna Spyri, 70. JANE EYRE by Charlotte Brontë, 89. LITTLE WOMEN by Louisa May Alcott, 78. MACBETH by William Shakespeare, 75. THE ROPE DANCERS by Morton Wishengrad, 275. STRAWBERRY ICE CREAM SODA by Irwin Shaw, 85. UNCLE VANYA by Anton Chekhov, 373. THE WILD DUCK by Henrik Ibsen, 331.

CORN IS GREEN, THE, Emlyn Williams, 249, 290, 354.

Crouse, Russell, and Howard Lindsay. THE SOUND OF MUSIC, 119.

CRUCIBLE, THE, Arthur Miller, 96.

DARK AT THE TOP OF THE STAIRS, THE, William Inge, 111, 315, 369.

DARK OF THE MOON, William Berney and Howard Richardson, 270.

DEAD END, Sidney Kingsley, 53, 62.

DIARY OF ANNE FRANK, THE, Frances Goodrich and Albert Hackett, 100, 103, 108.

EASTER, August Strindberg, 133, 142, 147.

Euripides. IPHEGENIA IN AULIS (trans. by Charles R. Walker), 366.

FIVE FINGER EXERCISE, Peter Shaffer, 114.

Friebus, Florida. Adapter of ALICE IN WONDERLAND by Lewis Carroll, 65.

Frings, Ketti. Adapter of LOOK HOMEWARD ANGEL by Thomas Wolfe, 237, 243, 246.

Goodrich, Frances, and Albert Hackett. THE DIARY OF ANNE FRANK, 100, 103, 108.

GOLDEN BOY, Clifford Odets, 214.

Hackett, Albert, and Frances Goodrich. THE DIARY OF ANNE FRANK, 100, 103, 108.

HAMLET, William Shakespeare, 371.

HEIDI, Johanna Spyri (adapted by Lorraine Cohen), 70

Hellman, Lillian THE CHILDREN'S HOUR, 27, 37, 302, 312.

Ibsen, Henrik. THE WILD DUCK (revised by Lorraine Cohen), 331.

Inge, William. THE DARK AT THE TOP OF THE STAIRS, 111, 315, 369. THE RAINY AFTERNOON, 42. SUMMER BRAVE, 221, 228.

IPHEGENIA IN AULIS, Euripides (trans. by Charles R. Walker), 366.

JANE EYRE, Charlotte Brontë (adapted by Lorraine Cohen), 89.

Jerome, Helen. Adapter of PRIDE AND PREJUDICE by Jane Austen, 232, 235.

Kingsley, Sidney. DEAD END, 53, 62.

Kopit, Arthur. OH DAD, POOR DAD, MAMA'S HUNG YOU IN THE CLOSET AND I'M FEELING SO SAD, 150.

Laurents, Arthur. A CLEARING IN THE WOODS, 252.

Laurents, Arthur, and Leonard Bernstein and Stephen Sondheim. WEST SIDE STORY, 195, 200, 203.

Le Gallienne, Eva. Adapter of ALICE IN WONDERLAND by Lewis Carroll, 65.

Lindsay, Howard, and Russell Crouse. THE SOUND OF MUSIC, 119.

LITTLE WOMEN, Louisa May Alcott (adapted by Lorraine Cohen), 78.

LOOK HOMEWARD ANGEL, Thomas Wolfe (adapted by Ketti Frings), 237, 243.

MACBETH, William Shakespeare (adapted by Lorraine Cohen), 75.

McCullers, Carson. THE MEMBER OF THE WEDDING, 23.

MEMBER OF THE WEDDING, THE, Carson McCullers, 23.

Miller, Arthur. THE CRUCIBLE, 96.

Odets, Clifford. GOLDEN BOY, 214.

OH DAD, POOR DAD, MAMA'S HUNG YOU IN THE CLOSET AND I'M FEELING SO SAD, Arthur Kopit, 150.

Perl, Arnold. BONTCHE SCHWEIG, 358.

PRIDE AND PREJUDICE, Jane Austen (adapted by Helen Jerome), 232, 235.

RAINY AFTERNOON, THE, William Inge, 42.

Rattigan, Terrence. THE WINSLOW BOY, 321.

Richardson, Howard, and William Berney. DARK OF THE MOON, 270.

ROPE DANCERS, THE, Morton Wishengrad (Revised by Lorraine Cohen), 275.

ROMEO AND JULIET, William Shakespeare, 162.

SAINT JOAN, Bernard Shaw, 356.

Saroyan, William. THE BEAU-
    TIFUL PEOPLE, 122.
Shaffer, Peter. FIVE FINGER
    EXERCISE, 114.
Shakespeare, William. HAM-
    LET, 371. MACBETH (adapt-
    ed by Lorraine Cohen), 75.
    ROMEO AND JULIET, 162.
Shaw, Bernard. SAINT JOAN,
    356.
Shaw, Irwin. STRAWBERRY
    ICE CREAM SODA (adapt-
    ed by Lorraine Cohen), 85.
SOUND OF MUSIC, THE,
    Russell Crouse and Howard
    Lindsay, 119.
Spyri, Johanna. HEIDI (adapted
    by Lorraine Cohen), 70.
STRAWBERRY ICE CREAM
    SODA, Irwin Shaw (adapted
    by Lorraine Cohen), 85.
Strindberg, August. EASTER,
    133, 142, 147, 362.
SUMMER AND SMOKE, Ten-
    nessee Williams, 17, 349.
SUMMER BRAVE, William
    Inge, 221, 228.

TEA AND SYMPATHY, Rob-
    ert Anderson, 126.

UNCLE VANYA, Anton Chek-
    hov (adapted by Lorraine
    Cohen), 373.

VIEW FROM THE BRIDGE,
    A, Arthur Miller, 208.

Walker, Charles R. Translator,
    IPHEGENIA IN AULIS by
    Euripides, 366.
WEST SIDE STORY, Arthur
    Laurents, Leonard Bernstein
    and Stephen Sondheim, 195,
    200, 203.
WILD DUCK, THE, Henrik
    Ibsen (revised by Lorraine
    Cohen), 331.
Williams, Emlyn. THE CORN
    IS GREEN, 249, 290, 354.
Williams, Tennessee. SUMMER
    AND SMOKE, 17, 349.
WINSLOW BOY, THE, Ter-
    rence Rattigan, 321.
WINTERSET, Maxwell Ander-
    son, 169, 175, 183.
Wishengrad, Morton. THE
    ROPE DANCERS (revised by
    Lorraine Cohen), 275.
Wolfe, Thomas. LOOK HOME-
    WARD ANGEL (adapted by
    Ketti Frings), 237, 243, 246.